Dementia Car

The Adaptive Res

A stre eductionist approach

PAUL TM SMITH

Research Fellow, Green Templeton College,
University of Oxford

First published in 2013 by
Speechmark Publishing Ltd, Sunningdale House, Caldecotte Lake Business Park,
Milton Keynes MK7 7LF, UK
Tel: +44 (0)1908 277177 Fax: +44 (0)1908 278297
www.speechmark.net

002-5727/Printed in the United Kingdom by CMP (UK) Ltd
Typeset by Darkriver Design, Auckland, New Zealand
British Library Cataloguing in Publication Data
A catalogue record for this book is available from the British Library

ISBN 978 0 86388 812 0

Contents

Preface

The process of re-establishing homeostasis disturbed by stress is called an adaptive response. This process is so named because it allows the organism to adapt to the influence of stressors. Stress signals from the periphery as well as from various brain divisions merge and activate the stress system. An activated state of the system is what is known as stress. This can lead to exhaustion of the reserves of the systems involved in the adaptive response which in turn is manifested as various diseases.

Different people react differently to the same stressors. Short-term exposure to the same stressor results in a stress that disappears relatively quickly in strong-willed and emotionally stable individuals. However, it tends to last longer in people with less emotional stability.

This book arose out of almost 30 years of working with and living alongside people living with dementia and their families and for the last 20 years managing and coaching staff to provide better care experiences.

In particular this book arises almost 15 years after an original essay (published here as Chapter 5) which earned me my first academic qualification in dementia care. The work came about after undertaking training in psychotherapy, group psychotherapy and in particular after achieving a Masters qualification in neuro-linguistic psychotherapy (NLP) and indirect clinical hypnosis which supplemented my nursing qualifications.

After almost 15 years as a qualified nurse I suddenly realised that just like the plumber always trying to find the leak, I had spent years looking for people to 'fix'. Training in different care philosophies suddenly opened up a world of alternatives for me. I hope this book does the same for you.

When I started seeing the bigger picture and adding lots of differing perspectives I realised that what was needed to be done did not involve 'fixing' people but was more about getting 'everything else' out of the way and allowing those people to 'be' or, more accurately, 'to become'.

This book, therefore, is about getting stuff out of the way!

Dementia is a stressor. Even at its most well lived the dementia syndrome provides a source of increasing challenge to the physical and emotional resources of an individual. This constant challenge results in a condition of chronic stress punctuated frequently by a series of increasingly acute stress episodes.

At its most purely survived dementia can consist of a regular series of 24-hour catastrophic, acutely challenging and stressful experiences. Relief and respite from 'challenge' becomes elusive if the environment and the 'care' promoted do not adapt and evolve to their changing needs. Eventually, the person is overwhelmed and retreats from life.

The processes of dementing, therefore, can make the experience of day-to-day living an acute challenge. It is a challenge, I believe, that can be greatly mediated with educated and timely inputs from carers (family, professional or other) and where the caring contract is negotiated to preserve both dignity and quality of life.

This 'new contract' can begin, in the first instance, by changing our attitude as to what can and cannot be achieved by people living with dementia, and then by changing the way we subsequently plan and deliver care. You will not read the phrase 'dementia sufferer' in these pages.

The stressful experiences of living with dementia create an intolerable strain upon psychological and physical systems and, as we will demonstrate, it is through the continuing attack upon an individual's resources that these systems begin to fail.

This cycle of physical and psychological activation, coping and eventual failing leads a person into a downward spiral that is too often mistaken as the 'effects of dementia'. In reality, as this book hopes to illustrate, this is often not the case. This cycle can be something that can be prevented or at least mostly mitigated by those assisting the person, once it is understood.

This failure of the human system to be able to cope with the increasingly stress-ful challenges of day-to-day living may also be one of the major variants explaining the dramatic differences in survivability between individuals living with a demen-tia, and even if this is only a possibility it is incumbent upon us to attempt to help.

The premise of the adaptive response approach is simple: people living with dementia are often disempowered and overly 'protected', leading to dependence and loss of confidence and ability. Conversely, people living with dementia are also often left to cope and struggle with tasks, environments and social and emotional demands that they are no longer equipped to deal with successfully. This leads to stress, distress and a failure to cope and thrive.

This book contends that carers armed with a sound knowledge of dementia, person-focused processes and knowledge of the effects of stress and its cata-strophic impact when left unattended can make a real difference to the quality of life of those living with dementia. Further, I contend that when equipped with a firm understanding of whole-person-focused approaches and an awareness of our human 'built in' ability to adapt and adjust, the experiences of those living with dementia can be enhanced as 'we get things out of their way'.

By the professional carer understanding their role in enabling, adapting and adjusting, living with one of the dementias, even in the dreaded care home, can become a life to be lived and enjoyed.

The findings from many caring and social science disciplines are gathered here in these chapters and have been synthesised using a systems model to demonstrate how we can combat the life-threatening reaction to the 'stress' of the dementia experience. This can be achieved by the acceptance and integration of a few simple principles, and we show how, by applying these same principles, we can optimise the caring environment.

For example, a simple principle applies to stress: too much stress – bad; too little stress – bad; stress that allows for and fosters growth and adaptation (internally or externally controlled) – optimum. (Note: we all need some stress as without it we would stagnate and reach the only truly stress-free condition – death.)

The adaptive response approach is about simple principles such as the above and is to be viewed as a biopsychosocial approach functioning from within a 'person-focused framework'.

The approach and principles suggested here adopt the work of Lazarus, Sapolsky and other modern stress researchers and seek to show that it is an individual's ability to appraise a stressor, rather than the nature of the stressor itself, which initiates and determines the response. If a person is unable to assess when a stressor starts or ends, the subsequent state of arousal can last from minutes to hours (and perhaps longer), and what is essentially a necessary and good process can become destructive and ultimately life threatening.

The premise is that when a system remains under stress for any length of time almost all coping mechanisms eventually become overwhelmed and exhausted as hypothesised by Selye as long ago as 1936. As subsequent research has shown, however, this in itself is not the true cause of illness from stress. It is in actuality the constant adaptation of the system that depletes the coping abilities and it is this constant striving to 'adapt' that negatively affects all activities of daily living.

Try to remember a time when you yourself were in the middle of a stressful situation, a time when you could see no way out of it. You did not know when a solution and, therefore, relief were coming. Were you able to think clearly for any length of time? Were you able to look forward to brighter times? Could you even get through the day without dropping things or bumping into furniture, or biting a loved one's head off? Were you shaky, could you sleep, did you pace the floor – was there great gnashing of teeth?

This inability to successfully appraise the stressor, its magnitude and how long it may last results in the engagement of mental and physical resources and reserves sometimes totally inappropriate in magnitude to those actually required. It is this cycle, if repeated regularly, that becomes incredibly destructive to both physical and psychological function.

As you may remember from your own stress experiences, after a while it becomes 'hard to think straight'. Cognition, although initially heightened by severe stress, is impacted severely and negatively by unremitting or repeated stress and the subsequent racing of stress hormones around the body. When we add this unremitting or regularly repeated challenge for someone living with a dementia we have created a natural disaster waiting to happen.

By understanding these basic principles and devising compensative and adaptive programmes of care (the individual plan of care or 'care plan') it is suggested that this destructive downward cycle can be interrupted and even broken.

These basic ideas which make up the adaptive response approach take great optimism from the 25-year-old theory of 'rementia' which, although contentious outside of the dementia community (even inside this community for some), nevertheless has been demonstrated in practice again and again.

Rementia (Kitwood, 1987) was postulated as a theory to describe the observed 'improvement' of cognitive abilities, mood and coping mechanisms of individuals living with dementia and a related drop-off in behaviours that challenge when positive changes were made to their physical and social environments and toxic elements were reduced or removed.

The theory is contentious only because clearly the person's 'dementia' does not get better in a physical sense (with neuronal regeneration, regrowth of lost tissue and so on) but the effects of rementia are clearly observable and measurable in terms of behaviour, mood and communication.

These positive effects, in my observation, occur when there is a match between the demands on the coping ability of the person and their means to meet them, and in the subsequent removal of the challenges that can no longer be adequately met.

The central premise of this book, therefore, is that once the negative toxic stressors of living within social and built environments are removed or better externally controlled, the better the person themselves can cope with the true effects of 'dementia'. They can then in turn become more receptive and responsive to the aid available to them and live their lives productively and happily.

The message of the book is an incredibly simple and positive one; it states that people living with dementia can live better lives and that these lives are enhanced if we all work together towards this attainment. You can make a positive difference as a professional carer, a family member or friend with just a little knowledge and a lot of hope – this book hopes to provide a little of that for you.

The central aim of care, after all, is surely about providing quality to life not quantity in terms of years, although one invariably impacts upon the other.

A small note of warning: you may find some of this book challenging, even heretical to current wisdom about 'dementia caring'. It is a very complex subject we are attempting to understand, but I have tried to keep things simple. It is because I greatly respect you for purchasing this book and wanting to expand your current understanding and caring horizons that I have taken to heart what Albert Einstein instructed us: 'Everything should be made as simply as possible, but not simpler.'

Now it's up to you – go and make someone's life better! (Oh, and by the way – get everything else out of the way.)

Paul TM Smith
October 2012

This is not a scientific textbook, but it necessarily includes medical terms and descriptions, generally explained as they are introduced. The carer needs to have a basic understanding of how the brain and body work when in good order, and how they are affected by disease.

Knowing how exciting the human potential is and understanding where that potential is housed will help you move from seeing those in your care possibly as sets of problems or symptoms to be 'managed', to seeing people with many strengths and potentials and to thereafter 'working with' them rather than 'doing things to' them.

I believe you should always be looking to find and to enhance the person. Sometimes this person gets lost or hidden away behind the 'symptoms' of the 'illness', but in good dementia care we are always the detective, searching for clues and aiming to remove the subterfuge to reveal the essential human being beneath the diagnosis. Take the opportunity to think of yourself as a modern-day Sherlock or Miss Marple and 'detect' all the clues of the person desperately hoping you will 'find' them above and beyond the diagnosis.

The first chapter introduces the biological domain of dementia, what the term itself encompasses, criteria for diagnosis, possible causes, prevalence, symptoms and common forms of dementia, along with a brief discussion of the brain and its organisation. The biological basis of dementia is elucidated by examining the effects of Alzheimer's disease on the brain and its interconnected systems.

We are not just brains, however, but individual humans, distinct persons functioning and interacting in varied social settings. Chapter 2, therefore, discusses the psychological and social domains of dementia. It examines the different models of modern dementia care and introduces the theory of whole-person-focused caring – the so-called person-centred approach – along with positive and negative aspects of practice in dementia care and an overview of various therapeutic interventions. Chapter 3 continues this review of practice by looking at the progression of therapies towards modern dementia care, and the principles that underpin care today.

In Chapter 4 we look closely at the role of stress and specifically at reactions to it by those living with a dementia, as well as at adaptive nursing models.

I then present as Chapter 5 a slightly reworked version of my original essay on adaptive response ('Dementia and the effects of stress and unattended emotion upon the human system'). This covers the consequences of stress for those with dementia and how stress can be managed or alleviated by adaptive response strategies.

The final three chapters expand on the material provided in Chapter 5. Thus

Chapter 6 looks further into stress and dementia, stress reduction, systems thinking and applying an adaptive-response care programme. Armed with an understanding of the role of stress, we need to be constantly seeking ways to compensate for negative arousal through manipulation of the social and built environments. These are areas that it is within our power to control and which directly affect the well-being of those with dementia. Chapter 7 examines how we can manipulate the social environment, through programmes of care and therapeutic relationships. Chapter 8 discusses how we can design a supportive care environment that reduces stress and enhances well-being.

By adapting care and the care environment it is possible to offer unique and individual approaches for those living with a dementia even in large institutions. Quality of life is possible at all stages for all people including, importantly, the care staff.

The book, therefore, hopefully will allow you to develop a concept of care and your place in it that focuses closely upon that part of us we call our being – our essential humanness – and will seek to dispel any thoughts you may have held about dementia care being focused on symptoms and managing risk. You will read then about person-centred care and about 'personhood', which is not to be confused with personality. Personhood has been described as a conferred state, a status given to one person by another, and which implies recognition, respect and trust. (Personality, on the other hand, is the product of the brain, its 'hard' wiring and the cumulative effect your life history has had upon the organ, leading to its adaptations which has ultimately brought about 'you'.)

Ultimately, I hope to leave you with a simple caring philosophy to help shape your future practice. Care homes for too long have been associated with a type of care referred to as 'warehousing', in which people are treated and moved around like 'objects' or 'products' to be fed, toileted and put back in their rooms – a type of care aptly described as 'task orientated'.

This book challenges that assumption, and it seeks to change the popular opinion of what care homes are, what they do and how they do it. It aims to help carers in rising above these negative perceptions and to begin to view care homes and the people who work in them differently. It is a tool to help you see the beauty of those you care for and work with, and to begin to allow you to appreciate the joy and skill of what you do, unselfishly, every day of your working career.

1 What is dementia? The **biological** domain

The social model of dementia with regards to care practice in the UK is introduced in the NICE/SCIE guidelines: *Dementia: Supporting People with Dementia and their Carers in Health and Social Care*, as follows:

> For many years, people with dementia were written off as incapable, regarded as little more than 'vegetables' and often hidden from society at large.
>
> During the 1980s and 1990s, there was a move away from regarding people with dementia as incapable and excluding them from society, and towards a 'new culture of dementia care', which encouraged looking for the person behind the dementia (Gilleard, 1984; Kitwood & Benson, 1995; Kitwood, 1997).
>
> People with dementia could now be treated as individuals with a unique identity and biography and cared for with greater understanding.
>
> Building on this work, others (notably Marshall, 2004) have advocated that dementia should be regarded as a disability and framed within a social model. The social model, as developed in relation to disability, understands disability not as an intrinsic characteristic of the individual, but as an outcome produced by social processes of exclusion. Thus, disability is not something that exists purely at the level of individual psychology, but is a condition created by a combination of social and material factors including income and financial support, employment, housing, transport and the built environment (Barnes *et al*, 1999).
>
> From the perspective of the social model, people with dementia may have an impairment (perhaps of cognitive function) but their disability results from the way they are treated by, or excluded from, society.
>
> For people with dementia, this model carries important implications, for example:
> - the condition is not the 'fault' of the individual
> - the focus is on the skills and capacities the person retains rather than loses

- the individual can be fully understood (his or her history, likes/dislikes, and so on)
- the influence is recognised of an enabling or supportive environment
- the key value is endorsed of appropriate communication
- opportunities should be taken for rehabilitation or re-enablement
- the responsibility to reach out to people with dementia lies with people who do not (yet) have dementia.

The social model of care seeks to understand the emotions and behaviours of the person with dementia by placing him or her within the context of his or her social circumstances and biography. By learning about each person with dementia as an individual, with his or her own history and background, care and support can be designed to be more appropriate to individual needs.

Moreover, a variety of aspects of care may affect a person as the dementia progresses. Some extrinsic factors in the care environment can be modified, for instance noise levels can be highly irritating but are controllable. Other intrinsic factors, such as the cultural or ethnic identity of the person with dementia, may also have a bearing on how needs are assessed and care is delivered. Some aspects will be more important or relevant to one person than to another.

The social model of care asserts that dementia is more than, but inclusive of, the clinical damage to the brain.

(NICE/SCIE, 2006)

I could not have written a better introduction to the adaptive response principles than this, and if we start by broadly accepting the assertions of the social care model, as outlined above, we are ready to look at the biological basis of dementia, keeping in mind that dementia is more than, but inclusive of, the clinical damage to the brain.

It is often believed, even by some professionals, that 'nothing can be done' with regards to caring for someone with dementia other than to 'make them comfortable, safe, warm and well fed'. This kind of thinking is referred to in academic dementia studies as 'old culture' or less accurately as the consequences of the 'medical model'.

This opening chapter is designed to provide a better understanding of dementia within its neurological and physiological aspects. This book is not about the physical presentation of dementia as a disease, neither is it about population statistics and percentages, but for the lay reader or those new to the subject this chapter by necessity introduces the subject in these terms. In the context of the book the overall model we provide here, when coupled with the contents of Chapter 2 (the psychological and social domains) is referred to as 'new culture' and more specifically as the biopsychosocial model (the dynamic interaction between the biological, psychological and sociological). Read together they provide a good introduction to modern understandings of dementia which you will need to appreciate the principles of adaptive response.

This chapter is quite basic. It must also be kept in mind that, as new science emerges, we are learning that even the way we thought we understood the brain as little as five years ago is now being turned on its head by theories such as adaptive plasticity (how individual brains change and adapt to environments or insult) and the connectome (the revolutionary emerging field of research that is showing that what we 'are' may actually be contained in between the connections made by our neurons and not in the structures themselves).

So while we must never deny the presence of a degenerative neurological pathology, it is hoped that as a result of your reading you see *people* before you see *disease*, and that you see people as having many existing, preserved and possibly new capabilities, as well as possessing current needs, wants and hopes.

It is hoped by the end of the following two chapters carers appreciate the uniqueness of each person and understand dementia not just as a physical disease but as being a collection of personality, life history, neurological impairment, present circumstances, physical and psychological well-being, current environment (both the built and social) and the collective future wants, hopes and desires of the person continuing to live within their family unit but now, of course, also living within the care home.

It is rarely stated, but people living with dementia at almost all stages of the disease process have a past, a present and a future. This means they also have dreams and aspirations – just like you and me. In fact the other thing that is rarely stated is that people living with dementia are, indeed, in essence you and me.

The biological domain

Each dementia is unique

When looking at dementia and the dementias throughout this chapter it is important to understand that we generally will be looking at the commonalities of the syndrome. There are recognised signs and symptoms, which tend to be universal – common to all – but dementia is not universal; rather, it is a very personal condition. Due to the individuality of our brains (each brain is slightly different at birth to others, even in identical twins) and the unique neural connections and chemical pathways that develop within our brains as life's experiences imprint themselves on us, each dementia is unique to each individual.

This means that if there are 800,000 people living with dementia now in 2012 in the UK and that if around 62 per cent of these people are living with dementia of the Alzheimer's type (DAT), some 416,967 people are living with similar but *not* the same disease outcomes. Thus, there are almost 420,000 people living in the UK with their own variant of DAT!

Dementia is a syndrome

Dementia itself is not a specific illness or any single disease process; it is a term used to describe a collection of related diseases and pathologies. When different though potentially related disease processes lead to a similar result, this broad pattern of symptoms is grouped together for ease of reference, and this 'grouping' is referred to as a syndrome. A syndrome is a collection of signs and symptoms that can be commonly grouped together and are recognised as producing a similar outcome even if the causes may be different.

Therefore, we can state: *Dementia is a term used medically to describe a collection of various conditions or disease processes which produce similar signs and symptoms and therefore are referred to collectively as the dementias.*

There are well over 100 different types of 'dementia' currently recognised, and it is probable many more will come to light in the coming years, even though the general public commonly believe any reference to 'dementia' means someone with Alzheimer's disease.

There are a number of distinctive diseases within the 'dementia' groupings and these include some quite specific processes such as Alzheimer's disease, but we also find much more common processes resulting from common medical conditions such as vascular disease, stroke and from complications from physical illness such as diabetes, sexually transmitted disease (syphilis or AIDS) and even some types of poisoning.

Unique presentations

The spectrum of specific conditions generally grouped under the label of dementia is large and many of these individual processes have very specific presentations, particularly in their early stages. This means it is vitally important for professionals to understand how we should be responding to these various unique presentations (characteristics and associated behaviours).

We should also understand that these presentations (behaviours) in many instances are related directly to the type of or 'stage' of dementia the person is experiencing, their pre-existing personality and how they are reacting to the dementing process, its effects, where they are living and to how they are being treated. (We discuss the validity of 'stages' on p. 49.)

> **Learning Tip 1:** Individual care planning for early stages
>
> It may be largely accurate to say that as most of the major dementias progress, the outcomes will be similar in the end. However, in the early stages of most dementias that are not Alzheimer's disease, very different features will be apparent and therefore different ways of caring for people should be designed and different types of care planning should be evident.
>
> Indeed, when we take a psychological vantage point the respected author Michael Bender has suggested we do not apply the term dementia at all when we discuss this group of affected people, because their individual reactions to the dementing process can be so personal and unique. Instead, he suggests we use the term 'remedial or enduring cognitive losses' (Bender, 2003).
>
> Graham Stokes, however, urges that 'when used judiciously' dementia can be a useful concept – it can be seen as a useful 'compromise diagnosis' which acknowledges a set of characteristic signs and symptoms and excludes a range of alternative diagnoses (Stokes, 2005).
>
> (For ease of understanding we will at present refer collectively to 'dementia' and individually to specific sub-types, such as Alzheimer's disease, multi infarct, Lewy body and so on.)

Progression of dementia

Dementia is progressive, which means the characteristic symptoms will gradually get worse and the person will become more reliant on assistance and may as the process develops require full nursing care. At present there are no known cures or preventions.

There are a number of drugs currently licensed to alleviate some of the symptoms of Alzheimer's disease (rivastigmine, galantamine and donepezil for early stage, and memantine for mid to late stage), but these drugs are only appropriate in some instances and are effective only for some people and are clinically effective for only relatively short periods of time (months or years).

These drugs do not cure or stop the disease process. However, it is evident in some instances they can slow the progress of some symptoms throughout the time the drug is being taken. But these symptoms return and are sometimes exaggerated once the medication is stopped.

How fast the dementing process develops depends upon the type of dementia and on certain factors, such as the previous and current personality, circumstances and life history of the individual and particularly their ability to cope with stress (Kitwood, 1997; Smith 2011).

Each person is unique and will experience dementia in their own specific way due to these pre-morbid features. It is vital to stress that during the dementing process what goes on around the person in terms of support, living conditions and treatment plays a tremendous part in whether the experience of dementing is well lived or, tragically, merely survived.

Criteria for diagnosis

Diagnosis of exclusion

Dementia is most often diagnosed by exclusion: it is what is left after all other sources of confused behaviour have been excluded, and this means that often a diagnosis of dementia will be reached when the person doing the diagnosing runs out of explanations for the problems the person is experiencing! It is also sadly true that most people in our care will have a 'probable diagnosis'; that is, they have what can only be described as probable dementia – we don't know what else could be wrong.

Familial dementia can of course be predicted and some other predictive tests now exist. However, for many, a definitive diagnosis is most often only possible after death. This can make the process of caring very challenging.

The World Health Organization (WHO) classifies the syndrome of dementia as follows for the purpose of making a diagnosis:

> Dementia is a syndrome due to disease of the brain, usually of a chronic and progressive nature, in which there is disturbance of multiple higher cortical functions, including memory, thinking, orientation, comprehension, calculation, learning capacity, language and judgement. Consciousness is not clouded. Impairments of cognitive function are commonly accompanied and occasionally preceded by deterioration in emotional control, social behaviour or motivation.
>
> The primary requirement for diagnosis is evidence of decline in both memory and thinking which is sufficient to impair personal activities of daily living (ADL); the above symptoms and impairments should have been

evident for at least six months for a confident diagnosis of dementia to be made.

(WHO, 1992)

It is because of symptom-descriptive definitions such as the above that historically in hospitals and care homes it has long been thought that all persons with 'dementia' are 'suffering' the same 'illness'. Therefore, they have all been viewed in much the same way, which is that 'nothing can be done other than to keep someone safe, warm and fed'.

This is a very nihilistic but historically understandable approach to the care of people with dementia, and new definitions and paradigms are needed because we now know that a great deal can be done to improve the quality of lives of people living with dementia.

What causes dementia?

There are many, many theories as to what causes the various types of dementia. In some we are confident that we understand the origin, such as multi-infarct type dementia (stroke), vascular dementia (oxygen deprivation to brain structures through occlusion of blood flow), Korsakoff's dementia (alcohol abuse) and many of the various familiar and infectious causes.

There is a lot known about other dementias too, such as Alzheimer's disease, but their causes have not been definitively established. However, it can be said that, basically, Alzheimer's is a physical disease caused by changes in the structure of the brain and a shortage of vital chemicals that help with transmission of messages.

Alzheimer's and vascular dementia are the main types, and mixed dementia (the next most common) involves both Alzheimer's and vascular dementia. Dementia with Lewy bodies, a less common form of dementia, is caused by irregularities in brain cells, and there are many rarer diseases and syndromes that can lead to dementia or dementia-like symptoms. The relatively rare fronto-temporal dementia is a physical disease affecting specific areas and structures within the brain.

The main subtypes of dementia and their prevalence and possible causes are explored in more depth later in the chapter.

Risk factors for dementia

Various risk factors for dementia have become evident.

- **Age.** The risk of Alzheimer's disease, vascular dementia and several other dementias increases significantly with advancing age.

- **Genetics.** Researchers have discovered a number of genes that where present increase the risk of developing Alzheimer's disease.
- **Smoking and alcohol use.** Studies have found that smoking significantly increases the risk of mental decline and dementia: people who smoke also have a higher risk of vascular disease, which may be the underlying dementia risk. Large intakes of alcohol also appear to increase dementia risk.
- **Atherosclerosis.** This interferes with delivery of blood to the brain and can lead to stroke and to vascular dementia.
- **Cholesterol.** High levels of low density lipoprotein (LDL), the 'bad' form of cholesterol, appear to significantly increase a person's risk of developing vascular dementia.
- **Homocysteine.** Research now indicates that a higher than average blood level of homocysteine, an amino acid, is a strong risk factor for developing both Alzheimer's disease and vascular dementia.
- **Diabetes.** Diabetes is a risk factor for both Alzheimer's disease and vascular dementia.
- **Mild cognitive impairment.** While not all people who have this condition develop dementia, they do have a significantly higher risk compared to the rest of the general population.
- **Down syndrome.** Studies have shown that most people living with Down syndrome develop characteristic plaques and tangles of Alzheimer's disease before middle age. Many then go on to develop all the symptoms of dementia.

How prevalent is dementia?

Worldwide figures

Estimates of the prevalence of dementia worldwide vary greatly depending on who is conducting the research and the aims of the body using these figures. However, it is estimated that about 800,000 people are affected in the UK alone, with this number estimated to rise to almost 2 million by the year 2060. Some projections for dementia prevalence worldwide are shown in Table 1.1.

Prevalence in the UK

The conservative estimate released in 2007 by the Alzheimer's Society stated that there were 683,597 people with dementia in the United Kingdom. This represents one person in every 88 (1.1 per cent) of the entire UK population. For simplicity, the Alzheimer's Society rounded the figure to 700,000 for people with dementia in the UK for use in public messages. The society has in 2012 revised these figures

TABLE 1.1 Dementia prevalence 2001, 2020, 2040 by WHO region

	Consensus dementia prevalence (%) (80+)	New dementia cases (millions) per annum, 2001	Numbers of people (millions) with dementia, aged 80+			Proportionate increase (%) in numbers of people with dementia	
			2001	2020	2040	2001–2020	2001–2040
Western Europe – EURO A	5.4	0.79	4.8	6.9	9.9	43	102
Eastern Europe low adult mortality – EURO B	3.8	0.21	1.0	1.6	2.8	51	169
Eastern Europe high adult mortality – EURO C	3.9	0.36	1.7	2.3	3.2	31	84
North America – AMRO A	6.4	0.56	3.4	5.1	9.2	49	172
Latin America – AMRO B/D	4.6	0.37	1.8	4.1	9.1	120	393
North Africa & Middle East – EMRO B/D	3.6	0.21	1.0	1.9	4.7	95	385
Developed Western Pacific – WPRO A	4.3	0.24	1.5	2.9	4.3	99	189
China & developing Western Pacific – WPRO B	4.0	1.21	6.0	11.7	26.1	96	336
Indonesia, Thailand & Sri Lanka – SEARO B	2.7	0.14	0.6	1.3	2.7	100	325
India & S Asia – SEARO D	1.9	0.40	1.8	3.6	7.5	98	314
Africa – AFRO D/E	1.6	0.11	0.5	0.9	1.6	82	235
TOTAL	3.9	4.6	24.3	42.3	81.1	74	234

Source: Ferri *et al* (2005).

to 800,000 (Alzheimer's Society, 2012) and this rapid growth since 2007 shows more people than expected are developing a dementia and at a faster rate.

The total number of people with dementia in the UK was forecast in 2007 to increase to 940,110 by 2021 and 1,735,087 by 2051, an increase of 38 per cent over the next 15 years and 154 per cent over the next 45 years, but the revised 2012 figures may factor for even greater numbers.

Early-onset dementia (EOD)

Early-onset dementia (onset before the age of 65 years) is comparatively rare, accounting for 2.2 per cent of all people with dementia in the UK. It is estimated that there are now 15,034 people with early-onset dementia in the UK. However, given that this data was based on referrals to services, this number is likely to be an underestimation. The true figure may be up to three times higher (45,102 people).

Late-onset dementia (LOD)

The numbers of people with late-onset dementia (onset after the age of 65 years) continues to rise for each five-year age band up to the age of 80–84, and declines thereafter. Despite this, two-thirds (68 per cent) of all people with dementia are aged 80 and over, and one-sixth (17 per cent) are aged 90 or over.

The Alzheimer's Society estimated as at 2007 that 222,925 men and 445,641 women (total 668,566) in the UK have late-onset dementia; this represents approximately two women for every man affected. Both the higher mortality among men and the higher age-specific dementia prevalence in women contribute to the preponderance of women among the oldest people with dementia.

The Alzheimer's Society estimates that in 2012 some 424,378 people with late-onset dementia (63.5 per cent) live in private households (the community), whereas 244,185 (36.5 per cent) live in care homes.

Dementia types prevalence

It is estimated that 416,967 people with dementia (62 per cent) in the UK have Alzheimer's disease, the most common form of dementia. The next most common types are vascular dementia (17 per cent) and mixed dementia (10 per cent), accounting for nearly one-third (27 per cent) of all cases. Dementia with Lewy bodies represents 4 per cent of cases.

The distribution of types is different in men and women. Alzheimer's disease is more common in women, while vascular dementia and mixed dementias are more common in men (*see* Table 1.2).

TABLE 1.2 Prevalence of dementia by gender in the UK (2012)

	Male	Female	Overall
65–69	3.9%	0.5%	2.1%
70–74	4.1%	2.7%	3.3%
75–79	8.0%	7.9%	8.0%
80 plus	13.2%	20.9%	17.7%

Common symptoms of dementia

Loss of memory

In the early stages short-term memory becomes decayed and then lost, so long-term memory begins to predominate. However, later the entire processes for the storage of memory are damaged and eventually even long-term memory will be eroded and lost. The person begins to experience life with a system of memory described aptly by Dr Huub Buijssen (2005) as roll-back memory, a state where memories collide and roll back onto and over each other. This leaves the person disorientated as regards time and place and sometimes people too, as faces can appear out of place or time or appear to be in the wrong context.

As you can imagine, this is an extremely distressing and frightening experience, and on a psychological and social basis we must remember that much of who we are, our personality, our method of interpreting the world and our place within it is determined by our memories. If you forget who and what you are, how do you know what your place in society is and just how do you communicate this to others?

How stressful it must be to be living without the connections made possible by a working memory system. Dr Gemma Jones (2012) also provides a useful metaphor for memory loss in dementia which she refers to as the bookcase hypothesis. Our memory is just like an old and loved bookcase, in which we have stored all our favourite books, and as they sit neatly on shelves and are logically labelled we know which ones to retrieve and where to find them when we want them.

Jones suggests that, in the mid and late stages of a dementia, the shelving gives way and the books collapse in a jumble. Memories are still available, but we pick them up out of order and sometimes at random; sometimes the ones we are looking for just are not where we thought, or they are buried deep beneath the jumble so we have to go through lots of 'books' before we get to where we want. This takes time, time that is often denied the person by the carer pushed for some imaginary deadline. Thus, a principle of adaptive response is to work in the timeframe of the person living with dementia and to go where possible at 'their speed'.

Learning Tip 2: Outpacing

Outpacing is a sure means to produce stress – not just for someone living with a dementia but for anyone. Outpacing means doing things, saying things or expecting things to be done just that little too fast for the other person's comfort. Outpacing will most likely lead to a failure to succeed for both parties; in the above example, someone needing time to gather and sift through a failing memory system is not going to be helped by being asked to provide three or four different answers to different questions fired in quick succession. Even that last sentence induces panic! Don't walk too quickly, don't ask for too much too soon, and don't keep doing the same thing if it does not work. Slow down, find the person's preferred pace then stick with it. The results for you both will be fulfilling and you will paradoxically get to the result you both want much sooner than previously.

Mood changes

Parts of the brain responsible for controlling and regulating personality and mood are affected by the dementing process. A lot of control over the emotions is lost, and moods and reactions can become heightened or inappropriate to situations. Much of how people relate to each other is through the 'reading' of each other's moods and of their prior knowledge of our personality. This process, of course, is made possible via our memories, which inform our collective response to new stimuli and activate a system of internal interpretation. If memory systems are damaged, so is this system of interpretation.

Not only are changes in mood dictated by damage to certain areas of the brain so that responses can be erratic but it is believed that memory also contributes by distorting 'reality' further. Later, we will also demonstrate that stress further reduces cognitive capacity and raises levels of unhelpful 'fight or flight' hormones.

Communication difficulties

Areas of the brain responsible for the production of speech, reception of speech and those involved in reading and writing are all affected. These abilities decline depending on the degree and areas of progressive damage. When communication becomes affected the essential bridge between us and the world and between us and others becomes problematic. Communication is a two-way process, so when the sender or the receiver loses the shared 'code' life becomes very difficult indeed.

Movement and coordination problems

As the dementing process develops, areas of the brain responsible for basic life functions become affected, and the earliest of these occur with balance and movement. Falls are common, with loss of the ability to judge distances often a major factor in falls and accidents. Someone sees something in one place and in reality the object is elsewhere, or the contrast of objects against each other is not sufficient for the person to judge their position in relation to the objects concerned. Overbalancing, overcompensating and increasing frailty are also major factors.

The inability to coordinate limbs can also lead to an inability to dress easily or appropriately, or even to being unable to eat and drink without assistance.

Alzheimer's disease in particular is now being thought of as a visuoperceptual-cognitive disorder (Jones, van der Eerden-Rebel & Harding, 2006) due to the numerous research findings of damage and changes in the visual system of people living with the disease. This means that stress arises not just from failing physical control of limbs but from perceptual changes which mean that, even if full control was still possible, through distorted perceptions of the environment, people would remain at risk due to misinterpreting things like depth and the solidity of objects and features.

Clinical features related to the symptoms of dementia

Neuropsychological impairments

Neuropsychological impairments of dementia include the following.
- Amnesia: loss of memory.
- Aphasia: impairment of language, most common on direct questioning, ie asking a person to name an object – a nominal aphasia.
- Apraxia: the inability to carry out actions despite intact sensory and motor function (notable as in an inability to dress).
- Agnosia: inability to recognise or to associate meaning to a sensory perception (inability to recognise an object).
- Executive dysfunction: disturbances in judgement, planning and abstraction.

Other neuropsychological impairments include:
- Acalculia: inability to perform arithmetic.
- Agraphia: inability to write.
- Alexia: inability to read.

Psychiatric symptoms and behavioural disturbances

Psychiatric symptoms:

- depression
- anxiety
- hallucinations (visual, auditory etc)
- delusions
- euphoria
- misidentifications.

Behavioural disturbances:

- agitation
- aggression (physical, verbal)
- aberrant motor behaviour (pacing, wandering, restlessness)
- apathy
- irritability
- sexual disinhibition
- sleep abnormalities
- increased appetite
- change in eating habits.

Inability to perform activities of daily living

Difficulties with the following:

- handling money
- shopping
- driving
- using the telephone
- doing the laundry
- preparing meals
- managing medication.

Difficulties with the following:

- dressing
- eating
- using the toilet
- personal hygiene.

Learning Tip 3: Variation in symptoms

It is very common when working in dementia care, particularly if you are new to studying dementia, to assume that everything you read about symptoms, deficits and stages applies to everyone you meet living with dementia – it does not.

The dementias can differ markedly from each other. Even in similar syndromes, because of differing individual brain structures, the varying rate of progression and the person's individual personality and genes, not all expected symptoms are present.

Also, as you will see in the next section, depending on the type of dementia or the location of damage to the brain great variance between individuals will occur.

Chapter 3 also discusses the different psychological responses that may be produced as a result of the social and built environment which may exaggerate any physical effects of the changes to the brain.

A simple principle is: see the person before the symptoms. Sometimes if you look for the symptoms long enough and hard enough you will find them – even if they are not there!

The most common forms of dementia

Alzheimer's disease

As this is the most common form of dementia we will by necessity spend longer looking at this than other, rarer subtypes. Also, when many of the other common dementias progress in their degree of severity, symptoms can very much mimic the mid and later stages of Alzheimer's disease.

Alzheimer's is a progressive disease taking several years to run its course. It is known as a primary dementia, which is characterised by damage to or wasting away of the brain tissue itself. The chemistry of the brain changes, leading to death of cells, disruption in function and the eventual death of the person.

Although genes have been identified which may predispose someone to developing the disease, Alzheimer's generally does not have a single cause. Rather, many interacting risk factors, genetic and environmental, contribute to disease onset. Age is a strong risk factor, with dementia prevalence rising to around 25 per cent in over 85-year-olds (1 in 4).

Research suggests that Westerners are more vulnerable to Alzheimer's disease and other forms of dementia than those from developing countries, but isolating the relevant factors of environment or lifestyle has proved elusive. There is evidence, however, that in the West, people who are better educated, better off, living in the suburbs, with higher status jobs, who are married, and who keep physically and mentally active throughout life, are less likely to develop a dementia.

It has only been since the twentieth century that life expectancy has really increased to a point where scientists have found it meaningful to study old age. However, there is evidence in ancient history to indicate that age-related forgetfulness was known long before the modern era and is not a new phenomenon.

The word dementia was first used by an exceptional German scientist and hospital director Emil Kraepelin (1856–1926), famed for being one of the first people to bring scientific rigour to the study of psychiatric illness. He eventually described two major mental illnesses, which he named depressive psychosis and dementia praecox.

Among Kraepelin's other major talents was the ability to surround himself with superb colleagues, one of them being Alois Alzheimer (1864–1915) who with his study of a 51-year-old woman, 'Augusta D', discovered the characteristic brain plaques and tangles of a disease that would carry his name.

A huge research effort has gone into studying the molecular origins and development of Alzheimer's. While progress has been made in understanding the roles of brain inflammation, of oxidative stress and of vascular factors (to name just three important aspects), it is still not known exactly what triggers the onset of the disease.

Possible biological and genetic bases for Alzheimer's disease

A number of predisposing and preventative factors have been identified in the process of the development of Alzheimer's disease, although predominantly much of the research has focused on genes and hereditary factors.

Several genes have been identified that appear to affect the probability that an individual will develop Alzheimer's. These genes are inherited and are usually associated with early onset (under 65 years) or an unusually high incidence of Alzheimer's in particular families.

It is important to stress, however, that these are just susceptibility factors and that some people with these particular E4 genes remain unaffected; there are many other factors which contribute to the final outcome.

There is much disagreement as to the mechanisms of degeneration associated with the disease. A major theory suggests that there may be a malfunction in the way the brain regenerates its neural connections, and that the proteins involved in this process are E4 proteins. The resultant characteristic product is one of the two hallmarks of Alzheimer's disease: *senile plaques* (or neuritic plaques). Other theories suggest the process is due to cellular degeneration and this leads to the other characteristic of the disease – *neurofibrillary tangles* – but certainty as to how these two mechanisms work is still missing.

Alzheimer's disease is defined by brain pathology. Important aspects are senile plaques, neurofibrillary tangles, chronic inflammation, and death of neurons (nerve cells) and the loss of connections between them.

The plaques are deposits of beta-amyloid and other proteins containing damaged neurites, the processes of neurons. The tangles are clumps of tangled threads of insoluble protein inside neurons, which eventually kill the cell. These threads are largely composed of hyperphosphorylated tau protein.

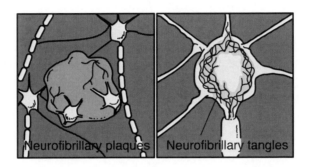

FIGURE 1.1 Neurofibrillary plaques and tangles

The most likely cause of the symptoms is the loss of connections between nerve cells, following the death of nerve cells. It is not known to what extent each of the other pathological features is the cause of the disease or the result of the disease process; although proponents of the amyloid hypothesis argue that the disease is due to the *toxic properties of beta-amyloid*. Recently, certain secretase enzymes have been discovered that are involved in beta-amyloid. One is the beta-amyloid cleaving enzyme (BACE). Another might be presenilin.

Amyloid toxicity is far from the only hypothesis of Alzheimer's causality, however, and evidence is growing to support the proposal that the pathology of Alzheimer's is partly due to aberrant functioning of the cell cycle in neurons.

Another important risk factor is high blood levels of the amino acid homocysteine. This discovery possibly links Alzheimer's to diet, since high levels of homocysteine relate to low levels of the vitamins B_{12} and folate. B_{12} deficiency has also been implicated recently as being a very high indicator of risk for Parkinson's disease.

The very latest research findings indicate what many have believed for a long time: that there may be a 'trigger' factor within the immune-suppressant system that allows stress to play a significant role, and the findings of Wozniak, Mee and Itzhaki (2009) show a very strong association with the herpes simplex virus.

What we do know is that dementia is very common and that the risk factors for developing a dementia are very specifically (but not exclusively) age related. The older you are the more likely you are to develop a dementia.

DAT is progressive, irreversible and pursues an unremitting course over a number of years.

Dysfunction usually begins with mild memory problems, poor concentration, and word-finding difficulties and impaired reasoning. These symptoms keep increasing until memories are forgotten, disorientation reigns and communication fails. Eventually, cognitive abilities are so severely impaired that the person becomes fully dependent on others (Holden & Stokes, 2002).

It is becoming clear that as the processes associated with the development of Alzheimer's disease become unravelled we may find Alzheimer's is not actually one disease but consists of many subtypes. One of these subtypes already discovered during the 1980s was dementia with Lewy bodies which until then had not been recognised. Dementia with Lewy bodies is discussed on p. 25.

Vascular dementia (VD)

Whenever damage occurs to the structure of the brain, or oxygen supply to the brain is reduced, cells die. The symptoms of vascular dementia can occur suddenly or gradually following a stroke or a series of small strokes and these eventually reach a critical mass where global performance (the whole function of the brain) is affected. Vascular dementia accounts for about 10–20 per cent of all diagnosed dementias and is usually seen in the seventh and eight decades of life.

Multi-infarct dementia (MID)

The most common form of vascular dementia is multi-infarct dementia which follows a series of strokes, or infarctions. The stroke may be 'silent' and pass almost unnoticed and these small, almost imperceptible episodes are often referred to as 'strokelets'. However, even in these instances, if enough brain tissue becomes destroyed, dementia will result.

If sufficient damage occurs, it is the disruption of the systematic communication process between different but co-dependent parts of the brain that accounts for the resultant dementia. Vascular dementia does not follow the same trajectory as a dementia such as Alzheimer's disease and whole areas of function can remain intact. Therefore, it is very important that you assess the abilities of anyone in your care with VD as yet another principle of adaptive response is to facilitate all remaining strengths while compensating fully for areas of need. To avoid creating the very conditions of stress we are attempting to eliminate we must clearly offer enough stimulation and challenge while decreasing challenge in areas where the person is no longer competent.

Stroke

A stroke or cerebrovascular accident (CVA) is what happens when the blood supply to part of the brain is disturbed or cut off. Blood carries essential nutrients and oxygen to the brain. Without a blood supply, brain cells can be damaged or destroyed and cannot function.

A stroke is sudden and the effects on the body are immediate. Because the brain controls everything the body does, damage to the brain will rapidly affect body functions. For example, if a stroke damages the part of the brain that controls how limbs move, limb movement will be affected; if a stroke occurs in the areas responsible for producing speech, speech will be affected and so on.

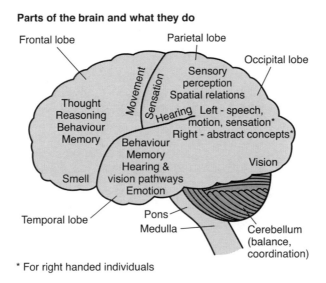

FIGURE 1.2 Parts of the brain and their function

The disturbance in the blood supply to the brain can be due to two main causes: ischaemia (lack of blood flow) caused by blockage; or a haemorrhage.

The kind of stroke that is due to a disturbance in the blood vessels supplying the brain is known as a cerebral infarction. It can result in the death of brain tissue (an infarct is an area of dead tissue) in just a small area or a much larger area. The most common cause is a blockage in blood vessels. This is called an ischaemic stroke, which happens when a clot blocks an artery that carries blood to the brain. It may be caused by:

- a cerebral thrombosis, when a blood clot (thrombus) forms in a main artery to the brain;
- a cerebral embolism, when a blockage caused by a blood clot, air bubble or fat globule (embolism) forms in a blood vessel somewhere else in the body and is carried in the bloodstream to the brain; or
- a blockage in the tiny blood vessels deep within the brain (lacunar stroke).

EARLY-ONSET DEMENTIA (EOD)

During the 1990s as diagnostics became more proficient there began to be an increasing recognition of dementia beginning in middle age, referred to either as early-onset dementia or younger onset dementia (YOD). Current estimates (which vary greatly and so demonstrate the frailty of statistics) suggest there were between 18,000 and 49,000 cases in the UK in 2007 (Alzheimer's Society 2008).

Although EOD features essentially the same pathology as later onset dementia, it does have some specific symptoms and can feature a number of uncommon cognitive responses such as hallucinations and delusions. It is also suggested that symptoms progress somewhat more quickly in this group than in their older counterparts.

TABLE 1.3 Early-onset dementia as a percentage of dementia types

EOD	Percentage of cases
Alzheimer's disease	34%
Vascular dementia	18%
Fronto-temporal dementia	12%
Alcohol-related dementias	10%
Dementia with Lewy bodies	7%
Other (Huntington's disease, Down syndrome etc)	19%

Behaviours that can be problematic to care can often present in EOD as some of the specific disease processes affect areas of the brain responsible for inhibition and the stability of personality. This is also the case with dementia with Lewy bodies, which is seen in about 12 per cent of those diagnosed before the age of 65.

The second type of stroke is a bleed, when a blood vessel bursts, causing bleeding (haemorrhage) into the brain. This is called a haemorrhagic stroke. It may be caused by:

- an intracerebral haemorrhage, when a blood vessel bursts within the brain; or
- a subarachnoid haemorrhage, when a blood vessel on the surface of the brain bleeds into the area between the brain and the skull (the subarachnoid space).

Multi-infarct dementia is a remitting dementia characterised by an abrupt onset and progressing in steps rather than a continuous decline as in Alzheimer's disease. These steps follow subsequent small strokes which may vary in their frequency, degree and location.

The damage can be local to the area of the brain affected until the degeneration becomes more widespread. After an initial episode there is usually some small recovery until the next episode. As some parts of the brain may be spared, the picture we see in vascular dementia is inconsistent levels of performance and some unique behaviour as the person struggles to make sense of a brain that works well in some aspects and not at all in others.

Eventually, however, if damage continues and becomes more global, the person may begin to take on the general characteristics of someone experiencing a form of Alzheimer's diseases.

Dementia with Lewy bodies (DLB)

In DLB tiny pink structures appear inside the nerve cells of the brain, especially within the frontal, temporal and parietal lobes, and cause their eventual destruction. Memory, language, concentration and balance are majorly affected. Although Lewy body dementia is a relatively newly discovered form of dementia, evidence

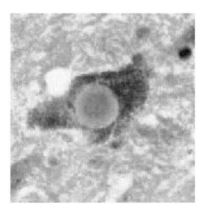

Nerve cells in cerebral cortex

Cortical Lewy body
(Haematoxylin and eosin stain)

FIGURE 1.3 Structures in the brain associated with Lewy body dementia

suggests that DLB may account for up to 15–20 per cent of diagnosed cases (Holmes *et al*, 1999).

The same degenerative lesions that are apparent in DLB have been known for many decades to be important in the neuropathological changes associated with Parkinson's disease. However, during the 1980s a team of Japanese scientists discovered that when these same bodies were found in the cerebral cortex the result was a form of dementia.

As with vascular dementia, dementia with Lewy bodies has presentations in the early stages (Byrne *et al*, 1989; McKeith *et al*, 1992) which differ from that of the typical Alzheimer's disease, and therefore it is important to list them, as follows:

- fluctuating dementia with lucid intervals
- memory impairment
- visuospatial deficits
- disordered thoughts and reasoning
- possible speech deficits
- clouding of consciousness (variable and episodic)
- hallucinations (usually visual, sometimes auditory, often scenic and worse at night)
- paranoid delusions
- depression
- movement disorders, typical of mild Parkinson's, possible falls
- neuroleptic sensitivity syndrome – neuroleptic medication (ie antipsychotics) can have adverse and at times fatal consequences. (McKeith *et al*, 1992)

Fronto-temporal dementia (FTD)

Also known as frontal lobe dementia, fronto-temporal dementia is a rarer but related form of disease of the Alzheimer's type, but it accounts for fewer than 10 per cent of diagnoses of Alzheimer's. FTD attracts much attention from clinicians due to its familial basis – almost 50 per cent of all cases are inherited.

The disease itself features cell destruction, mostly in the frontal and temporal lobes of the cerebral cortex. As damage occurs mainly to the frontal areas of the brain this affects personality and behaviour first, with memory problems coming later in the progress of the disease which is the reverse, as you will have learnt, to a dementia such as that of Alzheimer's disease.

In a minority of cases FTD also involves further cellular degeneration known as *Pick's disease*. Pick's disease is more common in persons under 65 years of age, is usually fatal within around seven years and primarily affects the frontal lobes (involving changes to personality).

While FTD is seen in both the young and old it far more common in middle age (Harvey, 1998).

There are some symptoms that differ from later onset dementia as described previously and which are therefore again worth listing:

- personality changes
- apathy, indifference or disinhibition and restlessness
- stereotyped behaviour – perseveration, rituals and food fads
- no insight or empathy for others
- loss of social awareness
- neglect of responsibilities
- sterile speech, echolalia, eventual mutism
- poor judgement and impaired reasoning
- problems of verbal fluency and production
- early onset incontinence.

As the years pass and the disease process progresses late FTD often resembles the classical picture of late Alzheimer's disease.

Rarer types of dementia

There are many rarer types of dementia resulting from (usually inherited) conditions with bizarre-sounding names that produce different early symptoms but which develop all the characteristics of the Alzheimer's syndrome as they progress. It is not within the scope of this short book to detail the rarer causes of dementia as they are clinically obscure and challenging.

What is not dementia: delirium and depression

Delirium

Delirium is a state of cognitive impairment, usually of recent onset, related to another illness. It causes confusion, disorientation and memory loss, and requires immediate medical attention. The key difference between delirium and dementia is that delirium causes a change and fluctuation in level of consciousness; those experiencing delirium are not as alert, can be drowsy, semi-comatose, or even comatose, whereas dementia is only diagnosed in alert patients.

The delirious person also can have difficulty with attention, may be agitated and be hallucinating. Symptoms occur rapidly, not over a long period of time, as is usual with dementia. There is usually a marked changed in a person relatively quickly. Symptoms may fluctuate throughout the day.

Delirium can be caused by congestive heart failure, urinary tract infection, liver failure, and drug or alcohol abuse. It is often caused by changes in the chemical transmitter between the nerves, called acetylcholine. Some medications or inter-actions of multiple medications can also cause this to happen.

The risk of delirium increases for people who are living with a dementia, are dehydrated, or are taking drugs that affect the nervous system. Sometimes there are no disruptive features, just a withdrawal which makes it easy to miss, especially in those who may be considered withdrawn as a result of the dementia process.

Dementia may have a rapid onset, as with stroke. However, dementia is a sus-tained state whereas delirium is typically an acute and fluctuating state.

A number of other medical conditions can resemble Alzheimer's disease. Many of these conditions can be treated in a way that can decrease or even cure these so-called pseudo-dementias. One such condition is depression.

Depression

Depression is the number one mental health problem among older adults and one of the most treatable. It affects nearly twice as many women as men (NIMH, 1999). The prevalence of depression is particularly high among older adults in nursing homes and in those hospitalised for a physical illness.

Depressive illness frequently occurs with heart attack, stroke, diabetes and cancer. In addition, individuals with a history of major depression are four times as likely to suffer a heart attack compared to people without a history of depres-sion. Minor depression in older men and major depression in both older men and women increase the risk of death (Penninx *et al*, 1999).

Depression in older adults differs from that of younger adults. It often develops very gradually and because it may occur simultaneously with other events (eg death of a spouse, physical illness) it often goes unrecognised and untreated. It is easy to see life changes like the loss of a spouse or even admission into a care home as just part of the way of the world and not realise the profound impacts these events have.

The most common types of depression in older adults are major depression, chronic low-grade depression (dysthymia), and subsyndromal depression. They can range from mild to severe in their symptoms. Although older adults often see their GP, they are seldom assessed, diagnosed or treated for depression due to our belief that as old age brings about loss most will simply cope. Depression is not a normal part of ageing and it can be life-threatening when it goes unrecognised and untreated. Older adults account for 20 per cent of all suicide deaths, even though they comprise only 13 per cent of the total population.

There are a number of tools such as the Geriatric Depression Scale, which can be easily administered by a carer, that can alert us to changes or fixed mood states that are below normal. It should not be assumed that someone living with a dementia should be depressed or that every symptom arises simply because of the dementing process. Low mood, lack of appetite, withdrawal, and crying should all be signs to refer to the GP.

Treatments are available and where they may help a person to live life rather than endure these should always be considered.

The brain and the effects of dementia

To better understand the effects of dementia within and upon a person we need to take a brief (though not very technical) look at the brain.

> **Learning Tip 4:** Looking at the brain is important
>
> Don't worry if the brain seems complicated – it is. However, by studying actions and behaviours in healthy brains scientists have been able to work out a lot of what the brain does and also which parts of the brain are doing it. Therefore, we have also been able to see what happens when these areas are damaged in some way – as occurs in dementia – so we can offer some guidance on what the person will do, or will not do, when certain areas suffer trauma.

The brain is an organ that uses *electricity and fluid* to communicate through vast neural networks and is the most sophisticated organism known.

The brain has been described as a plastic organ, in that when it sustains damage (sometimes substantial damage), other areas within its two connected hemispheres can compensate for this damage either fully or partially, often with amazing success.

However, if damage occurs in certain regions compensation is not possible, and when damage is constant and progressive as in the progress of Alzheimer's disease a state of catastrophic collapse occurs. At this stage the damage will appear as *'global'* because the brain at this point can no longer operate as an interconnected 'whole' system.

> **Learning Tip 5:** They are still people
>
> Just because a disease such as Alzheimer's in its advanced stages is referred to as global does not mean that every area and all abilities are affected. Parts of the brain do remain intact and functional and the detective in you must seek out each unique person's way of still communicating. Just because a person may not look or act like you or me does not mean they are no longer a person, so take time to really see the person struggling through the changes to be heard, to be recognised and to be involved.

The brain's three main sections: hindbrain, midbrain and forebrain

The brain consists of three main sections: the *hindbrain* often referred to as the reptilian brain, the *midbrain*, and the *forebrain*; and these sections contain various structures which are discussed below.

The hindbrain and midbrain are basically involved in the functions of life support, such as blood flow, blood pressure and respiration. They tell the rest of the body what to do and to keep going. The midbrain controls breathing, reflexes and swallowing reflexes. It includes the thalamus, hippocampus, and amygdala. The forebrain is the part responsible for the majority of the higher functions such as memory, language and personality (although other sections of the brain play a role in memory too: the midbrain is now being indicated as the seat of memory, and many areas of the brain are involved in both the storage and retrieval of memories).

The forebrain

The forebrain is composed of the cerebrum (or telencephalon), together with the diencephalon (comprising the thalamus, subthalamus, hypothalamus and epithalamus). The cerebrum is composed of the cerebral cortex, basal ganglia and limbic system.

The cerebral cortex

One of the most important parts of the forebrain, and the part that distinguishes us from other animals, is the cerebral cortex – the tightly crumpled thin (2–4 mm diameter) layer of grey mass which covers the surface of the brain and gives the characteristic cauliflower appearance. This mass contains ten thousand million brain cells in densely packed bundles of fibres, which transfer information around the cortex and to other brain regions. The cerebral cortex plays a vital role in attention, perceptual awareness, thought, language, memory and consciousness.

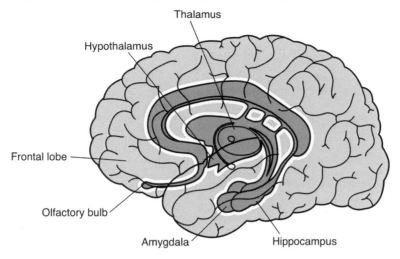

FIGURE 1.4 The cerebral cortex and other structures

Lobes of the forebrain

There are four lobes making up the cerebrum and these lie in conjunction with each other and work across the two connected hemispheres of the brain.

- **Occipital lobe.** Located at the back and deals primarily with vision and the recognition of objects.

- **Parietal lobe.** Lies in the upper rear and deals primarily with spatial relationship and structure. It is involved with processing of nerve impulses related to the senses, such as touch, pain, taste, pressure and temperature. It also has language functions.

- **Temporal lobe.** Lies just beneath the parietal lobe and deals primarily with hearing, memory, meaning and language. It also plays a role in emotion and learning. It is involved with interpreting and processing auditory stimuli.

- **Frontal lobe**. This lobe primarily manages information from the rest of the lobes. It is concerned with emotions, reasoning, planning, movement and parts of speech. It is also involved in purposeful acts such as creativity, judgement, problem solving and planning.

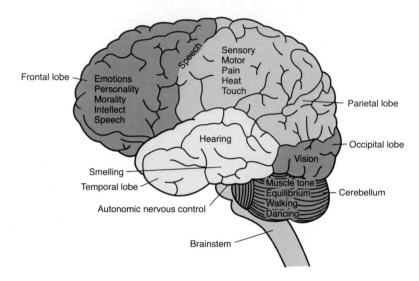

FIGURE 1.5 Lobes of the forebrain

Other important brain structures and their functions

- **Cerebellum.** A cauliflower-shaped structure located in the lower part of the brain next to the occipital area and the brain stem. It controls movement, balance, posture and coordination. New research has also linked it to thinking, novelty and emotions.
- **Thalamus.** Part of the limbic system, so it is located in the centre of the brain. The thalamus controls sensory integration and motor integration. It receives sensory information and relays it to the cerebral cortex. The cerebral cortex also sends information to the thalamus which then transmits this information to other parts of the brain and the brain stem.
- **Hypothalamus.** Part of the limbic system, it is composed of several different areas and is located at the base of the brain under the thalamus. The hypothalamus controls body temperature, emotions, hunger, thirst, appetite, digestion and sleep. It is only the size of a pea, but is responsible for some very important behaviours.
- **Pituitary gland.** Part of the limbic system, although it hangs below the rest of

the limbic system. It controls hormones and it helps to turn food into energy. Without the pituitary gland, you could eat but you wouldn't get any energy.

- **Pineal gland.** Part of the limbic system so it is located in the internal portion of the brain. It controls growth and maturity. It is activated by light.
- **Amygdala.** The almond-shaped amygdala is part of the limbic system so it is located in the internal portion of the brain. The amygdalae (there are two of them) control emotions.
- **Hippocampus.** The crescent-shaped hippocampus is found deep in the temporal lobe, in the front of the limbic system. It forms and stores memories (and possibly other functions yet unknown) and is involved in learning. It is one of the most important parts of the brain when studying Alzheimer's disease. People living with Alzheimer's disease lose the functioning of their hippocampus gradually but significantly first and then this progresses to almost total destruction over the course of the disease.

Hemispheres

The brain can be described as being divided into left and right cerebral hemispheres. The main principle of the brain seems to be lateralisation – literally some functions appear to be performed predominantly by one hemisphere of the brain and others by the opposite connected hemisphere. Strangely, the left hemisphere of the brain controls the right side of the body and vice versa. Not all functions, however, are shared equally and some areas like language are predominantly handled in the left hemisphere.

Interestingly, people living with brain trauma have demonstrated that in certain instances and with regularity the plasticity of the brain even allows opposite hemisphere function to be incorporated by the opposite lobe and sometimes to equal or almost indistinguishable degrees where damage has been sustained.

The brain really is a remarkable organ and it seems the more we know the less we understand the amazing potential we humans possess – housed in this mass in our skulls.

The tragic progression through the brain structures of Alzheimer's disease

To help us understand the course of a dementia we can track the changes that occur due to the progression of Alzheimer's disease. This is very unpleasant reading and will shock you; however, the full story must be told so that you become aware of the internal changes that can go unnoticed.

Remember we are detailing here a generic progression, and individuals may act in unique ways or experience different feelings and exhibit different behaviours due to individual resilience, personality and of course, importantly for us, their reaction to stress and the individuality of their unique social and built environments.

This section has been adapted from 'Gentlecare' by Moyra Jones (2000).

First signs: damage to the limbic system

In Alzheimer's disease the first nerve cells to die are those in the limbic system deep within the brain. The limbic system has a role in memory and emotional control. When you are scared or aroused hormones are released to help you fight, freeze or run; there is no waiting to analyse the situation – the reaction occurs before the areas of the brain that analyse information are involved.

It is probable that memory creation occurs throughout the whole brain but certain areas within and bordering the limbic system, particularly the hippocampus, appear to be vital for memory. As this area first begins to fill with plaques and tangles (dying cells) so memories of the recent past begin to fade and memory processing starts to fail. Over time long-term memories too will fade and the whole memory system will become jumbled (experience roll-back).

As the limbic system cells begin to die, affected persons report that they experience emotional instability, rapid changes in mood and uncontrollable anxiety, which switches between fearfulness, restlessness, irritability and aggressiveness. Eventually, those affected may lapse into a feeling of helplessness and at this point in the disease process the following behaviours may arise.

- People may act tearful and anxious.
- They may act suspicious or begin to feel depressed.
- They are certainly terrified and frustrated.
- They may have distressed verbal outbursts.
- They are agitated.
- They may begin to engage in seemingly purposeless activity, wandering to and fro, trying to make sense of what is happening.
- They begin to have difficulty with retaining the meaning of written words but can read.
- They begin to forget where they have placed objects, and then become suspicious that others may be taking them, or hiding them.
- They may become overtly sexually active.

Damage begins to spread to the parietal lobes

Damage begins to spread upwards to the parietal lobes, which are the centres for spatial perception, sensory integration and concentration. As these areas become more and more affected the person begins to lose the ability to recognise places, objects and people (faces), as follows.

- The person will easily become disorientated and lost even in familiar places.
- They may begin to lose the ability to recognise ordinary sensory stimuli – a condition called agnosia.
- They may begin to have problems in identifying objects in terms of their function.
- They may begin to have problems identifying people – especially those of a different generation or those they don't see often (called visual agnosia).
- They may begin to experience imaginary visual images (hallucination), but this is not a defining feature of Alzheimer's disease.
- One in ten people living with a dementia suffer seizures: grand mal (a generalised convulsion, which usually involves loss of consciousness, body stiffening and jerking) or petit mal (a brief loss of consciousness with few or no symptoms other than staring absently).
- They will begin to lose the ability to concentrate and to focus.
- They will be easily distracted and can become very distressed by noises or activity in the environment – these stressors can severely lessen the person's ability to listen effectively, process information or perform given activities, often leading to a perception in observers that the dementia is more advanced.
- They may find themselves increasingly unable to control stress or their response to it.

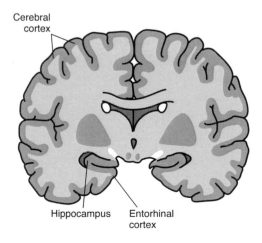

FIGURE 1.6 Brain functions – a broad representation

- The person may at this stage begin to lose the ability to locate certain parts of the body, making dressing or eating difficult.
- Deterioration of hand skills makes daily activities of living further complex and causes a condition known as constructional apraxia (a form of apraxia – inability to perform tasks or movement – characterised by the inability to copy drawings or to manipulate objects to form patterns or designs).
- Speech ability deteriorates.
- Sign recognition deteriorates.
- They may begin to experience problems putting words correctly in sentences (auditory agnosia).
- They also now may start to have problems with touch identification – objects cannot be recognised unless seen (tactile agnosia).

Damage continues: involvement of the temporal lobe

The disease next attacks the temporal lobe, which is the area responsible for speech, language and time awareness.

- The person forgets names, even those of close family members.
- They have problems finding the right words to express themselves (anomia).
- They ask questions repeatedly, seeking information they cannot retain.
- They cannot string ideas together and may lose their train of thought mid-sentence (abulia).
- They may speak haltingly (Boca's aphasia) or substitute wrong words.
- They may repeat seemingly meaningless words, sounds or numbers over and over again or repeat words or sounds (echopraxia) or speak in 'word salad' – a mix of wrong words (Wernicke's aphasia).
- They may later develop a complete loss of the sense of any words (expressive/receptive aphasia).
- Time slips away and becomes almost meaningless with the past leaving, the present confused and no ability to look forward into the future – at this stage people constantly ask for assistance with time orientation.
- They have decreased knowledge of current events.
- They cannot remember their own recent history well.
- They exhibit severe problems with activities where sequencing is required.

All the damage described so far happens as Alzheimer's destroys the limbic system, the parietal lobe and the temporal lobe through stages 1–4 of the disease. This is usually when carers become involved as the person enters a care home setting.

As the disease process begins to move to the back of the brain where the occipital and the parietal lobes meet, the challenge to daily living and quality of life is now severe. As well as other functions of these areas, as already mentioned these areas govern visual processing and visual significance. There is evidence mounting, however, that visuospatial ability is affected much earlier in the disease, which signifies damage to these brain areas occurs much sooner than previously thought.

Cell death and tissue shrinkage progresses

The loss of tissue adds to the previous difficulties, creating many more problems:

- The person begins to lose their peripheral vision; they can see only straight ahead and as there is a significant loss of peripheral vision as we age anyway this further loss can be significant.

Learning Tip 6: Loss of peripheral vision

It is important to understand the loss of peripheral vision, because if people now moving into care are seated in chairs placed around walls, or sat at dining tables with people sitting directly beside them, the people next to them can become invisible. This not only increases the person's sense of abandonment but also accounts for much reactive aggression as someone unexpectedly and suddenly appears in the line of vision (this of course also immediately activates the stress response).

- They begin to lose the ability to look up and their gaze becomes directed downward. This has implications for the height of any way-finding signage in care homes.
- They now lose their ability to focus on or to track moving objects, such as people, so it becomes very frightening and increasingly stressful when a person just looms up at them.
- Some people can become very obsessive and some now begin to repeat movements over and over again.
- Many may develop delusions.
- Agitation increases and stress systems become increasingly activated, especially as the person's ability is diminished to appraise when stressful situations and stimuli will be resolved or removed. Thus the stress now becomes chronic but is still punctuated by critical peaks. This pattern of chronic and critical stress is the most damaging and destructive, and it begins to affect the physical organs of the body by the flood of anabolic and then catabolic hormones.

- Catastrophic reactions occur whenever stress is unavoidable or not controlled by others.
- Rummaging becomes an engaging activity.
- Walking and wandering (walking without purpose or as a psychomotor response) increases, often accompanied by sudden defensive aggression as objects and people suddenly just seem to appear out of nowhere.
- Disorientation now covers three spheres: time, place and person.
- Personality may have appeared to have changed and there is often a marked loss of willpower, often accompanied by aggression and non-participation. In reality this may be more the result of a series of psychological and social losses and is not always condition specific.
- Ideas are not able to be held long enough now for voluntary actions to be completed without assistance (cognitive abulia).
- Nausea is often present, accompanied by a loss of energy.
- Ability to read is now sadly lost; if a person has now moved into care, the signage used to assist way finding must have both words and pictograms. This assists the person in retaining their sense of worth and respect by allowing them to remain independent for longer (and often continent and less susceptible to accidents).

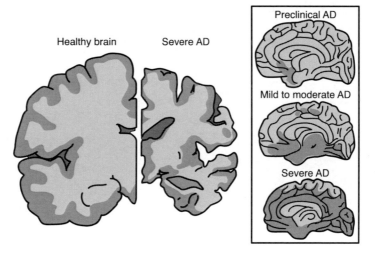

FIGURE 1.7 Tissue shrinkage in the Alzheimer's brain

Concluding stages

As the illness progresses towards the concluding stages the motor areas become affected and these produce many further distressing symptoms. Damage in this area leads to the following difficulties.

- The person experiences problems following through on intended movements such as eating where the body fails to respond correctly to instructions from the brain (apraxia).
- Swallowing problems develop (dysphagia).
- Gait, posture and balance are all affected.
- The person has trouble getting up from sitting; the design of chairs in care environments needs special consideration so as to preserve this ability for as long as possible.
- Rigidity (pseudo Parkinsonism) can occur due to many of the drugs used to treat (inappropriately) some of the previously described symptoms.
- The person tends to lean forward or to the side and tends to pull backwards while being assisted. Knees are often bent and a shuffling occurs during walking as the person has problems lifting and placing their feet appropriately, and there may be signs of muscle weakness (hypotonia).
- The person becomes restless (hyperkinesis).
- There may be acute muscle cramping.
- The person may exhibit fascination with small things or focus on a small single spot (hypermetamorphosis).
- As the disease progresses and now affects physical function, the person may often roll into the foetal position.

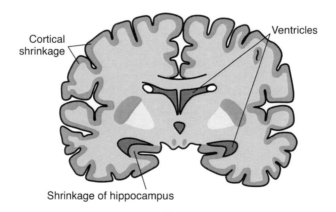

FIGURE 1.8 Further shrinkage of tissue and enlargement of ventricles

Note: As Alzheimer's disease progresses, the ventricles, chambers within the brain that contain cushioning cerebrospinal fluid, are noticeably enlarged.

Final ravages

Damage still continues to both the limbic system and the occipital region at the same time as the disease process begins its final ravages of the pre-frontal lobe, the frontal lobe and the cerebellum.

Occipital region

While the damage becomes acute in the occipital region, the following occurs.

- The person cannot distinguish anything other than bold contrast – if caregivers wear plain colours these will disappear into the environment, especially at night.
- Toilets, hand basins and other white facilities vanish as white on grey becomes indistinguishable; therefore in these places objects that stand out often become the recipient of urine and faeces. It is very important that care homes understand the need to provide deep contrast in environments where a functional response is desired – a black toilet seat against a white background is much more likely to encourage active and accurate use.
- Day and night also can become indistinguishable as mind-blindness occurs and the person will often be wakeful at night and wishing to sleep or nap during the day.

Limbic system

As the limbic system, including the hypothalamus, is destroyed control over temperature, thirst and appetite almost completely disappears. In addition the following problems may occur.

- The person feels cold to their bones or uncomfortably hot.
- Thirst can be extreme or be non-existent.
- The person may stop eating or conversely develop an enormous appetite – partly due to memory loss but mainly due to the mechanism governing hunger and thirst becoming redundant.
- Memory of recent events even in their own environment becomes lost and the person begins to exist in an increasingly contracting 'bubble'. Anyone entering into this bubble must be aware that as the person is now functioning with very little cognitive control over basic brain function, a startle response and adrenal activation occur with almost all physical interventions.
- Behaviours wrongly referred to as challenging are evident whenever a stress is encountered. For those people who remain mobile or who retain some limb control reflexive grabbing, pushing, nipping or hitting may be the result of defence against misperceived physical interventions. Understanding that this

response is a reflexive series of actions precipitated by extreme damage to the physical structure and function of the brain will hopefully allow you to see these reactions in a different, more accepting and understanding way.

Pre-frontal area

Motor changes associated with further damage to the pre-frontal area now become dangerous for those still mobile.

- The person cannot get their body to cooperate fully.
- They develop visual field neglect – usually for the left side – and so don't see obstacles (or food on the left side of the plate) and can injure themselves.
- The person cannot now follow caregivers' instructions and may react defensively to care interventions.

Frontal lobe

Frontal lobe damage now means that the person also:

- cannot think clearly or strategically
- struggles with thought formation
- loses reasoning
- has lost judgement (capacity)
- cannot think abstractly and has lost social awareness
- becomes disinhibited
- does not anticipate consequences of behaviour.

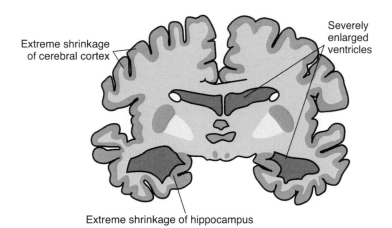

FIGURE 1.9 Extreme shrinkage of tissue and severe enlargement of ventricles

Subcortical damage

Finally, subcortical damage occurs. The subcortex (hindbrain or cerebellum) controls the vital autonomic (involuntary) body systems, such as the heart, lungs, diaphragm, digestive systems and some final coordination and balance systems. At this stage the body begins to shut down and death approaches.

● The body fails to thrive, no matter what interventions are tried.
● The person experiences irreversible weight loss as the body metabolism speeds up and burns fat.
● The autonomic system begins to fail.
● The person still processes hot or cold, positive or negative, sweet or sour, pleasant or frightening, albeit via a very damaged system.
● It is not unusual for the person to die at this stage from some secondary infection such as in the lung or bladder.
● It is at this point that the remarkable human system stops.

2 What is dementia? The **psychological** and **social** domains

Bestowing personhood

The late Professor Tom Kitwood wrote about a 'conferred condition' and in his widely influential book *Dementia Reconsidered* (Kitwood, 1997) he describes this condition as 'personhood', which is: 'A standing or status that is bestowed upon one human being, by others, in the context of relationship and social being. It implies recognition, respect and trust.'

This challenging concept sets the tone for what this chapter will cover — it is not about creating the ubiquitous 'person-centred care plan' or about providing a 'room with a view'; rather, it concerns how to think about dementia and dementia caring. If you are new to the 'new culture' it will challenge you; if you are familiar with the subject let this chapter act as a refresher as it brings some key ideas together.

Kitwood and other writers on the subject of dementia both past and present have attempted to share their understanding of what it means first and foremost to be a person and of the subtlety and complexity that this brings to the caregiving process. They and I ask that before you see any form of disease or symptom that you first see the person. This is not always easy in dementia care and often these writers will refer to the far-reaching work of Carl Rogers and his client-centred approaches to psychotherapy as a way of conceptualising this primary objective.

It is essential we understand that dementia caring is not and cannot be reduced to a set of tools or models — although elements of these are encompassed within any care approach — but that dementia caring is a really a 'state of mind'. What is this state of mind? It is as Buddhist colleagues and Suzuki (1992) would say, 'beginner's mind': developing the humility and maintaining the inquisitiveness to constantly learn from your teacher. Let's be clear: spending an hour with someone living with dementia will teach you more than this whole book, no matter how deeply you read into it. It is about understanding enough of what is necessary to bestow personhood.

Before we begin let us understand that dementia caring must by its very nature be essentially outcome-based, meaning it can only be judged as effective by the results it produces for the individual experiencing both the dementia and the care. However, in a business context these results are also held up to scrutiny by the business owners and the operational managers. One question we have to ask – which is often the elephant in the room – is can an approach emerging from a one-on-one philosophy and demanding a unique and individual approach really be transferred into a setting where staff ratios dictate anything but one-on-one caring?

This is not an easy question and this book cannot give a definitive answer, but this chapter looks at the elements required from a care regime to begin providing care that is more personalised, that is more than custodial and that moves beyond caring for a diseased brain in an inconvenient body. Care for those living with dementia has a number of coexisting elements that must be present if it is to succeed, and these elements therefore are essential to its overall successes.

Dementia – not just a pathology

Dementia is a collective term given to a number of conditions that have similar signs and symptoms. These conditions vary and a significant opportunity for further individualised care is often lost by reliance upon vague diagnostic criteria. One way of never falling into the trap of delivering poor-quality dementia care and missing the opportunities for individualising is to never use the excuse of the poorly informed, the ignorant and the arrogant: 'It's because of the dementia' or 'They wander because they have dementia'. These excuses of the ill-informed and the unthinking should never be heard (or written) in a dementia care establishment.

Unfortunately, as long as we continue to group the various conditions under one banner or continue to care for persons with dementia collectively as a 'homogeneous group' we will never develop real understanding of the complexities of caring for vulnerable people. Neither will we be providing sufficient skilful care devised around each variant within the syndrome, and in particular we will never understand how to provide specific person-focused care interventions within group settings.

As we have seen in the first chapter a number of distinct conditions exist under the misleading 'dementia' banner, but the most common, and referred to as the primary dementias, are Alzheimer's disease, dementia with Lewy bodies, and multi-infarct dementia. Other sub-categories exist and these are often dependent on the location or spread of most of the physical damage occurring within the brain structures. This biological domain alone, however, does not create the individual variances of 'dementia' but a person's experience of dementia is also greatly influenced by and is reflective of their unique individual circumstances. The dementia 'experience' is also further influenced by the person's personality and their significant life history, current location, relationships and regimens.

The impact of environment and experience

It is important to consider that brains change shape and function based on the environment and experience of their user. We are born with incredible 'basic equipment', but it is nevertheless in its raw basic state. However, it is pre-programmed to grow, change and develop.

FIGURE 2.1 Our basic 'wiring' as shown by the Connectome Project

We are born into this world, unlike some other mammals, helpless. However, if you take two helpless babies (studies of twins are most useful), raise them with differing variants of love, safety, abuse, wealth and poverty, you will produce different brain structures, each fostering a different person. Many similarities remain of course to the basic structures, but even in shape, size, weight and density there can be marked differences. If we were then to reverse the inputs for a few years again, we would find further physical brain changes. Chemistry and neural connections would have changed and, importantly, it now turns out not all changes are about new growth and new connections but also there is a natural pruning – some cells and connections will have withered and died as a natural process.

In fact, almost shockingly, as we grow from children into teenagers we shed millions of cells and neurons that made up earlier connections in the brain and our teenage hormonal burst seems designed to create a new human being. This process it seems, to a lesser extent, is a normal feature of the life of the brain all the way through to death. So while cells are dying and connections are being destroyed by the dementing disease our own biological processes are attempting to compensate. Some more physically and psychologically robust people may survive massive damage and seem relatively unaffected while others are less protected.

Studies show people who have coped well with life's ups and downs and are less prone to stress and depressive and anxious internal reactions to external events are again somewhat protected. In fact it has long been known that some personality types (Type A as opposed to type B) suffer more physical ailments and psychological wear and tear than their more easy-going counterparts (Jones & Bright, 2001).

So while it cannot be argued that dementia lacks a major physical component, as have some extreme proponents of the social construction theory, it should always be understood that the condition of dementia also has psychological, biographical, social, environmental, political and even financial contexts.

A discussion of social construction theory is beyond the scope of this book, but it is an essential piece of the jigsaw in understanding the experience of dementia, so please do give it some serious study if you have the time and inclination. Harding and Palfrey (1997) provide an extraordinary discussion in their book *The Social Construction of Dementia: Confused Professionals?*

Briefly, social construction theory is concerned with the ways we think about and use categories to structure our experience and analysis of the world; and it is useful when considering nature versus nurture ideas. We will discuss some aspects of this as applied to the experience of dementia later in this chapter and in particular the views of Richard Cheston and Mike Bender which I consider profoundly helpful in understanding the experience of dementia.

Kitwood's equation: seeing beyond disease

Kitwood (1997) used an equation to express many of these elements coming together when he revolutionised dementia thinking in the late 1980s. Using his lead we can understand that an individual's dementia (**D**) is not just pathology but is a result of complex interactions between:

P = Personality

B = Biography

H = Physical health

NI = Neurological impairment and

SP = Social psychology

Thus:

$$D = P + B + H + NI + SP$$

This equation, which we will examine within this and coming chapters, with its roots in the humanistic psychology of Carl Rogers, should form the baseline from which all your thoughts, actions, and care programmes and interventions should be formulated.

For an excellent critique of Kitwood, his ideas, work and influence it is worth digesting the scholarly book *Tom Kitwood on Dementia: A Reader and Critical Commentary* by Baldwin and Capstick (2007). For now, though, let's proceed by accepting that Kitwood's ideas changed dementia care in the UK and beyond and that this equation is central to that new understanding.

Stokes: holistic model

Stokes (2000) also put forward a way of understanding the person living with dementia which he named the holistic model of dementia. This holistic model, like Kitwood's, challenged the status quo and attempted to place the person with dementia in the context of their experienced life – here and now – by understanding and accounting for their history and then placing them within the current social (interpersonal relationships, attitudes and care practices) and built (architecture, interior design and living arrangements) environments.

Stokes demonstrates the interaction in this situation of existing neuropathology, morbidity and disability (and any medication factors), which he sees as barriers to successful interactions for the person living with dementia, 'arising due to the distorted communication and perceptual capabilities brought about by the psychogenic factors'.

Stokes's model is important for us as he places the individual within a specific geographical context and seeks to account for the impacts of that context.

Dependence determining care?

We have stated that dementia affects memory, cognition, orientation, judgement and problem solving. It also disengages the person's ability to successfully and independently perform activities of daily living (ADL) and the instrumental activities of daily living (IADL) which are very adult traits. Is this return to dependence one of the reasons why people living with dementia begin to view themselves differently within their world and is it one reason that the world begins to do the same?

Without these functional losses would we view the person with dementia in quite the same way – as someone somehow regressed, childlike? Does this colour our use of language and why we seem to coo over people in the latter stages of dementia as we do over the newborn, despite the facts that this is usually an older person with a lifetime of experience and adventures inside them?

> *Mrs 'AL', a retired professor who helped usher in women academics at one of the country's leading male-dominated universities, sits gazing out the window over a misty morning scene. Who knows what historical and political events are being replayed as she sits and contemplates the coming day?*
>
> *'Hello Auntie, who put you there?' coos a carer. 'You should have been in for the breakfast. Let's go and get you breakfast now, shall we? Yes, that's right, something to eat. To fill you up, make you big and strong – oh look Juanita,' she says to another passing carer, 'she's smiling ...'*

I am not smiling – are you?

The remainder of this chapter asks us to work at changing our own 'construct' of those living with dementia and our role in their subsequent care. Please read with 'beginner's mind'.

People living in care homes don't live alone

Although dementia presents uniquely and individually, ultimately the losses suffered by all those who experience the final stages of the syndrome are tremendous and lead to a state of high dependence on others and eventually to death – either through the effects of the disease process itself as in Alzheimer's disease or the effects of interconnected pathology.

Many arguments exist as to the 'best' approaches or care regimes and programmes to be implemented to provide dignified and skilful care to groups of persons living in care homes, hospitals and other institutions. Most miss an essential fact – people living with dementia in care don't live alone; they live in groups. Often these groupings are indiscriminate and have only one common denominator: the people in 'control' generally do not live with a dementia and those without control generally do.

The problems with stage theory of care

One such approach to group living has been to provide care using theories of stages within the progression of the dementia pathology to help individualise the programmes, regimes and environments of caring.

Many theoretical and philosophical arguments persist over the use of a stage theory approach to the syndrome, especially when it is applied as a generalist method. Essentially, the argument is that stage theory has a nihilistic view of individuals and proposes ultimately negative endings and, further, while it is true that people vary within their conditions and can and do become very dependent at the end of their life, this is not always the case. Many persons with dementia die ultimately of other physical ailments long before reaching an 'end stage' and live with a high quality of life.

To apply a developmental stage generalisation, therefore, which seems based upon the length of time the person has been experiencing symptoms, seems too simplistic.

Would it make sense to explore an approach assimilating some of the features of a 'strengths' stage argument as one model for 'group' living or would that imply generic care of individuals within a group?

The pertinent issue in my mind is not to argue over theoretical positions but to discuss how we can create group caring in a way that allows for variation and individuality but also meets the needs of the system. The answer relates to constant use of assessment and review both of the individual and the care system within which the person is living.

Systems theory shows us that it is often the system that produces 'emergent properties' and it is the system that maintains these properties. This should interest us as it means that in caring *and* uncaring establishments it may be the 'system' that produces the end product not the care of the individuals performing their respective functions.

The stage theory approach in its basic concept is clearly flawed, however, because, as we have shown, even within a single disease like Alzheimer's disease, which anyway may turn out to be multiple disease processes, stage theory does not adequately allow for the human individualisations within this disease process.

Care profiling

As an alternative, we may adopt as a general principle for individualised caring within groups the use of the term 'care profiling'. This is an approach which allows individualised care programmes to be organised most efficiently around the person's existing or remaining abilities instead of as a preparation for an 'inevitable' declining stage. Can I suggest (perhaps heretically) that we may substitute the term 'care profiling theory' where we read literature that applies stage-dependent theory in error mostly on time of survivability within the care model?

This rather clumsy approach still allows us to make use of many of the ideas the original theory contains, including that for most individuals dementia is progressive and that most will experience at some time or other many or all the symptoms associated with this progression, and so we should be prepared and equipped to provide care for these eventualities.

Effectively, with good ongoing and regular assessment of both physiological and psychological processes we can determine the person's current ability level – physically, cognitively and emotionally – and work together with the person, their family, friends or advocates to design care packages and programmes appropriately.

Pool (2007) has used this approach as has Perrin (Perrin & May, 2000), albeit termed occupational profiling, when looking at the provision of activities and occupational programmes for people living with a dementia. Indeed the movement to introduce the 'no fail' methodology of Montessori for the provision of activities seems to use similar thought and assessment processes. Within this approach we can also allow for group dynamics and population profiles instead of trying to ignore (or deny) the current care system limitations. If we cannot as yet change the system, we can at least change the way we choose to work within that system – and the more of us who choose to work this way the better.

Individual care profiling allows us to design prosthetic living environments where people are supported to live together individually but collectively within groups of like individuals and by terms of ability rather than being warehoused homogeneously as a result of their disability.

This approach allows for those with very similar levels of function to share common enhanced and enriched environments (built and social), whereas in the one-stop-shop approach prevalent in most care homes the individual's abilities and needs may be under- or overestimated. For instance, those approaching palliative care (in the last six months of life) could have an appropriate environment free from the intrusions of those needing a lot of stimulation or those exhibiting some behaviour that may impact upon others negatively. Conversely, an area may be staffed and enhanced to meet the needs of those individuals who are using behaviour that challenges, in order to prevent their condition needing to become overly problematic to themselves or others.

We are encouraging you to challenge the terminology and methodology of control, depersonalisation and labelling highly prevalent within dementia care, personified by trying to fit everyone into one approach or model, and to take control of your actions and change your practices.

Poor care often arises in care homes not by the collective will of 'bad' people but by a failure on behalf of the management system to account for the constraints of group living within a semi-organised structure, usually with indiscriminate group-ings, and by a systematic acceptance of the model that supports this.

I fully understand that managers in care homes are in a very difficult position because I have been one – they are expected to make profits for their organisa-tions while at the same time delivering expert care with a small, often inadequately trained but mostly willing workforce. They are also expected to conform to the prevailing wishes of their mid and senior management structures and are often harshly judged by a misinformed and negatively biased general public who are led in this direction by a media eager for scandal. Added to this pressure, many of the care environments they have at their disposal are just not 'fit for purpose'.

To make the current situation more challenging still, managers are pressured to keep occupancy high. With current funding structures, people are too often indiscriminately placed into a care home simply because an establishment has a vacancy, provides 'dementia care' and does so within an affordable budget.

This is a picture of the current reality of a care home and within this pressured situation we still expect excellence of care, value for money and – what's more

---

Learning Tip 7: The person is present

As you read through this chapter please adjust your perception to understand that the person living with dementia is still and always 'present' but that they are now living within their day-to-day context with all the barriers of an advancing disease process and often inadequate care systems.

This perception on your part accurately allows you to see the person as still being 'here' and that their essential 'humanness' never leaves. It becomes incumbent upon you, therefore, to attempt within your caring role to peel away the barriers of 'dementia' to once again reveal the living person beneath the symptoms and to offer respect, compassion and understanding at all times.

– for the last 10 years we have also wanted the elusive 'person-centred care' and person-centred care regimes to emerge.

Understanding modern dementia care

As professionals we rely upon frameworks and models – and we hope at least that these models are both sufficient and ethical. As a framework it would appear that adaptive response approaches supported with care profiling can be conducive to good person-focused practice. Does it, however, sit comfortably with models in the UK as we know them?

Three main schools of thought have developed within the field of dementia over the last 25 years in the UK, and these three models when applied systematically often dictate the quality of care provided and often the quality of life of those receiving care.

The medical model

Although much maligned, the medical model still has something to offer, although its basic tenets can and should be challenged.

The medical model sees dementia as a purely physical degenerative disorder and tends to treat the underlying problems accordingly. Behaviour is seen as caused by the degenerative process and not as a consequence of the person's care regime, environment or past history. The philosophy of this model is not to be applied within care homes as it is illustrative of nihilism in care.

The person-centred approach

Much hailed as being the saviour of dementia care, the person-centred model is facing tough times trying to bind theory with real day-to-day practice. In essence, the person-centred movement hinges on the tenet of personhood, and it is believed that the underlying pathology and the person's complete history along with present care regime create the dementia reaction. Behaviour is seen as a consequence of the losses experienced by the person coupled with the day-to-day problem of coping with society and the environment.

Person-centred care claims to have fostered a new culture in dementia. While we accept fully that person-centred approaches to dementia care (probably beginning with Kitwood's criticism of the medical models) have certainly changed the intellectualisation of dementia, as Stokes (2000) has pointed out starkly, 'person-centred care is easier to articulate than it is to deliver'.

The disability model

This is not a completely new approach, but one that is making positive inroads into dementia literature if not yet practice. The disability model seeks to offer a set of principles and ideals that enhance remaining abilities while trying to compensate for disability. The disability model has broad appeal and could be one possible future of dementia care provision. The model grew from the writings around 'the new culture of dementia care' and seeks to remove the obstacles to performance in such a way as to minimise disability and maximise ability, in much the same way as would be expected for someone suffering from a physical disability. The progressive nature of many of the dementias, however, offers challenges to this approach but coupled with a resolution-type model (*see* p. 78 it could become a significant movement. Its other more powerful benefit is that use of the model allows services and practitioners to tap into the political and legal successes of the disability movement.

For example, if we employ someone with no legs we are required by law to provide prosthetics, to ensure all areas of the environment are disability-friendly with ramps and the like. By contrast, where we care for someone with damage to short-term memory who is disabled by not being able to find their way around an unfamiliar environment we are not required to provide signage and other way-finding aspects. Should we not be similarly required to enable and not disable that individual? I would argue that the Disability and Equality Act 2010 could be cited in such cases where organisations fail to provide such prosthetics.

In addition to the three key models above, there is the relationship-centred approach.

The person-focused or relationship-centred approach

A relatively new model, again growing from the UK model of person-centeredness but morphing with other European and international approaches, is to espouse a triadic approach that sees the person with dementia, their family and interpersonal relationships and the care giver(s) in an equal partnership: the central tenets of the model have been termed 'relational'.

In relationship approaches the family is viewed as both an equal partner in the caregiving process and as the main support system for the person with dementia. This model places the care organisation in its correct place – not the giver or with-holder of the 'power' but as only one aspect of the person's current situation with lesser or greater impact governed by circumstance.

The adoption of relationship-based practices would inevitably force systems to change by fundamentally destabilising them. Perhaps this is one reason the care

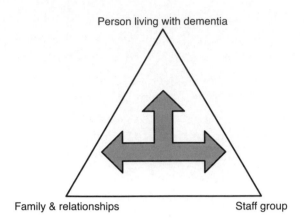

Person living with dementia

Family & relationships

Staff group

FIGURE 2.2 The relationship-centred approach

systems tend to resist change, as the will is not there, the money is not there and the 'risks' for business in unstable financial times may be too great. Nonetheless, in this book we ask you to at least consider alternatives.

We will now look at the model of person-centred care in greater detail, beginning by looking at its context.

What is a person-centred framework?

While the 'new' language of social policy across the UK promotes active person-centred care, the elements that ensure person-centred care delivery is successful remain elusive and in many cases undefined. However, two current authors are helping us to understand the coexisting elements that can lead to the ideal conditions within which person-centred approaches can flourish in caring.

Brooker (2004) proposes that 'in person-centred care the relationships between all the people in the care environment should be nurtured', and similarly McCormack (2004) proposes that relationships, environmental conditions and individual values epitomise person-centred nursing. Would relationship-based care models meet these 'core conditions'?

The elements of person-centred care

Brooker (2007) has striven to use a formula base that would be familiar to those who have been influenced by the work of the late Tom Kitwood. Just as Kitwood used equations to express complex associations so Brooker has chosen to represent the elements she describes as essential to the provision of the person-centred care approach in the following manner:

V = a **value base** that asserts the absolute value of all human lives regardless of age or cognitive ability

I = an **individualised** approach that recognises uniqueness

P = an empathic approach to try to understand the world from the **perspective** of the service user

S = encompasses the provision of a social environment that supports psychological need; that is, a **supportive social psychology**

Thus:

PCC (Person-centred care) = V + I + P + S

When this is coupled with Kitwood's assertions of what dementia means (D = P + B + H + NI + SP) you can perhaps now begin to appreciate why we need a much broader means of delivering care and measuring care perimeters than the limits of just an individualisation of our basic care model or models.

McCormack (2004) states further that person-centred care has four aspects:
- being in relation (social relationships)
- being in a social world (biography and relationships)
- being in place (environmental conditions)
- being with self (individual values).

McCormack summarises what he believes are the necessary elements for person-centred care to be successful as the 'nurse' being 'the facilitator of an individual's personhood' and states there is a need for 'nurses' to move beyond a focus on technical competence and engage in authentic humanistic caring practices that 'embrace all forms of knowing and acting, in order to promote choice and partnership in care decision making' (McCormack, 2004, p36). If you further consider the writing of Stokes (2000) you begin to see a synergy emerging between individual needs and system requirements that would be necessary for person-centred care properties to begin to emerge.

Other important definitions of what constitutes the elements of person-centred care are: good communication (Bryan *et al*, 2002), treating people as individuals (Moniz-Cook *et al*, 2000; Cobban, 2004) and that for person-centred care to occur, staff need person-centred management (Jacques and Innes, 1998; Ryan *et al*, 2004).

Kharicha *et al* (2004) suggest that collaborative working and putting the needs of the 'patient' at the centre of the care process is essential, while Moniz-Cook *et al* (2000) argue that staff should receive training about person-centred care but, unfortunately, they offer no guidance on what this is or how it should be delivered.

While the notion of person-centred care itself has received much recent attention, the conditions for achieving person-centred care practices are much less researched. Of those working in the field who are providing accounts, Brooker's (2007) work on improving dementia care in care homes seems to offer the best chance we in the industry have had up to now with a means to measure the presence of these elements. Her VIPS model of assessment and audit is taking a strong foothold in both the state and private sectors of UK care in 2012 (Brooker, 2010).

Understanding the experiences of the person with dementia

As well as understanding how we should care for and help resolve difficulties for people, we need a framework for understanding the experiences of the person with dementia.

Dementia needs to be understood as an interaction between psychosocial and neurobiological influences and it is preferable to understand it using the Kitwood (1998) equation: $D = P + B + H + NI + SP$. The main focus of dementia care therefore must be on the person living with the illness. Alongside this there needs to be a strong awareness of the needs of any relatives or friends, and a further understanding of our own relationships as carers within and not outside this dynamic. The approach to caring we generate should be designed to accommodate this triad and to further the fulfilment of needs for all.

Dementia is a terrifying ordeal that creates an enormous sense of insecurity within individuals and generates an intense emotional reaction. The impact of the process of psychological unravelling within dementia is also experienced in terms of a threat to the person's view of themselves as a coherent entity and as part of an experienced (or lived) social situation. The threat to the person's identity that is posed by dementia precipitates a range of behaviours whose function, according to Michael Bender (2003), is to assert the individual's identity. Without an understanding of the emotional and the identity needs of the person living with dementia we are liable to misinterpret the behaviour that arises when these needs are not met as resulting from neurological damage ('It's because they have dementia', which in many cases it is absolutely not), and design our systems to 'manage' the condition.

We also need to understand how a person with dementia is valued in their society, both inside and outside the care home, and the psychological, economic and social effects of that valuing.

Cheston and Bender (1999) state that 'only once we have begun to understand

the emotional, identity and social frameworks' within which a person with dementia lives can we begin to develop effective, life-enhancing forms of help' that are
not limited and distorted by the imposition of an organic or medical model of care
or framed within an overprotective custodial and institutional care home model.

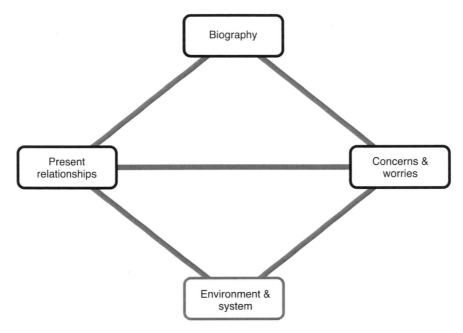

FIGURE 2.3 A framework for understanding psychological 'positions' for persons with
dementia in care homes, with environmental and system impacts added by the author
(*Source*: adapted from Cheston & Bender, 1999)

Cheston and Bender in their excellent book, *Understanding Dementia: the Man
with the Worried Eyes* (1999), depict the experiences of living with dementia as
being made up of:

- the person's life history, its major events, its crises and how it has formed the
  person
- their present concerns and worries
- their present network of relationships.

But based upon further research and inclusive of the work of McCormack (2004)
and Stokes (2000) I have added a further element:

- the person's environment and the system within which they are living.

Social roles

It is important to understand the role of society within the dementia context. First, the wider the range of social roles the person maintains or is engaged in, the more alternative means there are of maintaining self-esteem. Second, the wider the range of roles the larger the person's social network is likely to be. We know that effective social support can act as a buffer against the stressful effects of life events, which we discuss further in later chapters. Finally, it is important to understand that it is through our social roles that we gain a sense of 'who' we are – our social identity.

Therefore, with loss of role comes identity crisis. If social roles shrink too far, the person is likely to withdraw from the social world and their engagement with it can become so limited that they are at risk of becoming disorientated. With this disorientation comes increased stress and distress, and, as will be discussed, this stress exacerbates any existing effects of the underlying pathology. Shrinking of our social standing and our loss of role and esteem may allow the person to be seen and for them to see themselves as more 'disabled' than needs be in reality. Sadly, for many once this 'position' is adopted it will be maintained.

This perspective can be seen as interactive with organic changes. Social and organic changes do not occur in isolation from each other; each acts a stressor to the body system and its functions and each may precipitate a lessening of 'status'.

Information processing: safety system and mind system

The physical progression of dementia must also be considered as, in part, involving damage to the information-processing system of the person. In Chester and Bender's (1999) simple diagrammatic model of mind, as opposed to brain, two forces of processing are expressed: *the system of safety and the system of meaning*.

In the system of meaning the 'mind' interprets stimuli by processing its meaning in regard to past learned knowledge and intellectual responses. In the system of safety, automatic responses occur, with the primary objective of protecting the integrity of the system. The safety system is a simple one that perceives threat and reacts before any intellectual processes are applied; in brain terms, this is the process of allowing free rein to the limbic system without frontal lobe constraints. Because of its rapid response and importance to survival, if activated, the safety system's response takes precedence over the possible responses that might be generated by the meaning system.

In simple evolutionary contexts this is where reptiles still lie, and why the oldest parts of the brain are labelled in Paul MacLean's triune (three in one) model as developing in evolutionary order.

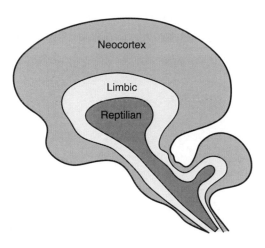

FIGURE 2.4 MacLean's triune model of the brain (*Source*: adapted from MacLean, 1990)

Although the triune system is only a conceptual model, it does allow us to consider some overriding principles. In Chester and Bender's hypothesis the early stages of dementia are characterised by damage to the person's information-processing ability, but the two systems, meaning and safety, are still intact. Later, as dementia progresses, the meaning system suffers damage to the point where it is barely functioning. This results in increased insecurity due to the person having severely diminished skills with which to make sense of their environment. Therefore, there

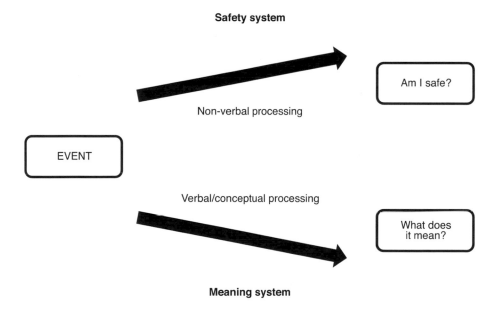

FIGURE 2.5 Safety system and mind system (*Source*: Cheston & Bender, 1999)

is a high level of activity in the safety system, while the damaged meaning system is powerless to prevent the triggering of the safety system or its switching off. Please remember this simple explanation as it is a central theoretical thread for understanding and applying adaptive response principles.

Such frequent activity in the safety system is highly stressful to the organism and, as we will see in coming chapters, causes psychological, social and physical ill effects.

The simple diagram (Figure 2.5) is a way of distinguishing between a meaning system and a safety system.

Seeking safety: attachment theory

Attachment theory has been widely used to explain the highly distressed behaviour of young children when they are separated from their parents. Consistent with our position with regard to the effects of stressors, Miesen (1999) has used attachment theory to argue that dementia is essentially a strange and frightening situation that activates very deep-rooted fears and that consequently a range of behaviours aimed at making the world less frightening, including what he has termed as 'parent fixation', may arise in persons living with dementia.

If the attachment needs of young babies are not met, this can result in a failure to thrive and, in extreme cases, even death. If the attachment needs of people with dementia are not met, there is evidence that this too can have similar consequences (Smith, 2000). (See further discussion of attachment on p. 172)

The experience of loss and the threat of further losses

From the above, it would seem that the most appropriate starting point for any psychological consideration of people with dementia and the services they need (and we should deliver) should be the subjective experience of people with dementia. This subjective experience is characterised by both the experience of loss (of social roles and relationships as well as of neurological functioning) and the threat of further losses to come.

This results in a range of emotions including grief, depression, anxiety, despair and terror. The experience of dementia, therefore, can be said to represent a profound threat to the individual's identity, to their very sense of who they are, and, when coupled with the physical destruction of the processes of memory, to their very humanness.

The adaptive responses of people with dementia – the ways in which they attempt to cope with dementia – are often misinterpreted as further evidence of cognitive impairment. Consequently, these behavioural strategies and emotional reactions are often not seen as the responses of people to a terrible predica-ment but as proof of a degenerative process occurring within the brain (medical nihilism).

> **Learning Tip 8:** Struggling to cope with threats to identity
>
> People with dementia need to be seen as active agents. They are engaged in both an active struggle to cope with the threat to their identity posed by the direct and indirect effects of dementia, and in an attempt to work through the emotional challenges posed by the built and social environments.

Care services: assisting the hold on identity and processing of the experience

The social context within which people who live with dementia are cared for needs intrinsically to be one that encourages people with dementia to cope and to manage their lives in as useful a way as they possibly can. In particular, people with dementia need to be seen as capable of both emotional growth and change, and also of maintaining a coherent identity into the later stages of the illness. Our role is not only to support these processes but to provide the conditions in which people can work through these challenges.

This does not sound like the underlying principle governing modern care homes, does it?

Services for people with dementia and their relatives therefore need to be set up to assist this process. These services need to enable the person to hold on to their sense of self, while also appreciating the deep emotional trauma that is involved. Good programmes of dementia care will allow people with dementia to work their way through or emotionally process their experiences. For many this will take the form of anger or in grieving for their losses, and we must move far beyond seeing such attempts at resolution as being 'challenging'; in fact, we need to move to a place where we embrace the struggle not attempt to snuff it out at the first opportunity.

Coping with the process of dementing: avoidance strategies

Some of the methods people with dementia use to cope with the process of dementing can be seen as avoidance or deflection strategies. Through their use the threat that dementia represents can be pushed away, avoided or deflected, with the result that the person's view of themselves alters little. These processes may be either consciously employed or arise as unconscious systems of defence Although these strategies can be effective, if the person with dementia persists with them over an extended period of time, their ability to act effectively within their world as it has become will be greatly reduced and conscious or unconscious processes of denial, deflection and avoidance produce their own stressors (often arising as converted symptoms).

Acts of omission (withdrawal and passivity) can become a person's preferred response and often these go unnoticed or are seen as being somehow preferable to acts of commission (often mistakenly referred to as challenging behaviours).

Acts of omission (*dependency*) are historically and typically well tolerated – with the probable exception of disengagement (an absence of behaviour). Acts of commission (*assertion of will*), on the other hand, are typically experienced as being challenging and are generally seen as something that must be 'managed'.

Bender (2003) proposes that 'It is often thought that people with dementia use denial as a way of dealing with loss, and that they consequently lack insight'. However, denial, like all coping strategies, needs to be seen as both functional and variable. Other coping strategies often include fantasy and the blaming of others (relatives and friends, but in care homes staff authority figures and even other residents are often substituted).

Assisting self-expression and sense of identity: reminiscing

Good dementia care, therefore, should enable people with dementia to display their emotional reactions in whichever way they choose (as long as they are not damaging or hurtful to themselves or others) and the care provided should be able to contain and support this emotion. Where expression is damaging to self or others, approaches such as the resolution approaches of Stokes and Goudie are preferable as they seek to find the meaning behind the behaviours and remove the need for the behaviours by meeting the unmet need (Stokes & Goudie, 1990, 2002; Stokes, 2000).

When staff are trained to provide 'person-centred' and 'resolution'-based caring many people with dementia will be able to hold on to a positive identity for themselves either by maintaining the appearance of being 'normal' in context or by accentuating a part of their lives that fits with an existing way of viewing themselves and their current situations positively.

Cheston and Bender (1999) explain that an important part of this process of adjustment and assimilation is provided by reminiscing and storytelling: 'The telling of stories to an appreciative audience allows people with dementia to make sense of what is happening to them, creates a sense of continuity with the past and creates a shared sense of social being.' Good caring also adapts this process as a part of the imbuing of 'personhood', and life history and life story work should be a universal feature of all modern dementia caring supporting these very processes.

Erikson (1965) also proposed that the process of life review is an essential element of moving into healthy old age. One aspect, therefore, of good dementia care is the provision of time, space and opportunity for people to reminisce, to recall and to recount and at times just plainly to tell their life story. McCormack (2004) states that it does not matter if these stories are truisms or fantasy – it is the process that provides the therapeutic benefits. I would add that as a buffer against stress, the sharing of emotional contact has been shown time and again to provide respite, safety and 'healing'. In later 'stages' of the dementing process it is the provision of this emotional contact that becomes the therapeutic goal. Garry Prouty's pre-therapy approach can be one such means of continuing to provide this feature even when language is lost and many cognitive functions are severely affected (Prouty *et al*, 2002).

McCormack (2004) has provided a direction of travel when he illustrates that the carer needs to be an active agent in the preservation of 'personhood' and the active facilitation of reminiscence (life history, life story work or the participation in therapies such as cognitive stimulation therapy) and holding onto a sense of self through storytelling is one integral method of therapeutic caregiving.

When there is no opportunity for self-expression the person with dementia may begin to act in a way in which they think others want them or expect them to. (For an entertaining and enlightening lesson on how prevalent and how quickly 'positioning' occurs in hospitals and other institutions read *Asylums* by Erving Goffman (1961). It will change the way you deliver care.) This can include withdrawing from the world as described above. Often it can be impossible to distinguish between behaviour that arises from neurological deterioration and behaviour which is part of the person's attempt to cope with their illness or the impacts of the social environment (Smith, 2006). It is the system that produces the outcome, or more accurately the impacts of dementia pathology, and the system that produces the person's positioning. The way we deliver our care may exacerbate rather than lessen the impact of dementia pathology.

It is not difficult to find evidence of 'learned helplessness' in most care homes – a process whereby after many attempts at expression and assertion (acts of commission) the person realises that nothing they can do or say affects the outcome, so simply decides to give up trying. It is now time to acknowledge that it is acceptable to view these decisions to give up, as part of the person's attempts to cope, as behaviour that challenges and to see these reactions as a direct response to the threat of future losses and betrayals and to the 'loss of self'. We can accept, therefore, that we have a duty of care to provide positive interventions – this is the premise of adaptive response.

Services for people with dementia should be structured around the need to help them feel more secure and of more worth and to restore or impart personhood, not to maintain the regime. The personal cost for people living with dementia is already too high and too great a price is being paid.

This assistance would involve at least three elements:

- increasing emotional security
- helping to maintain a clear sense of personal and social identity
- removing or minimising noxious, stressful impacts.

Increasing emotional security and helping maintain identity

A sense of security can possibly be achieved through regular individual counselling which encourages a move from global devaluation to focused problem solving. Work should also be done which encourages the use of attachment figures, both old and new (family, friends and staff), and to develop other forms of attachments within the new environment.

It is essential to encourage the maintenance of existing social relationships and to encourage new ones, and these will include relationships with carers and care staff. This allows us to see our model of 'triadic partnerships' as being directly relevant to preserving the person's sense of self and to maintaining their person-hood. The relationship model is required to frame this approach.

As dementia progresses we should strive to create an environment that is free from stress and random, unexplained events. As the person's skills decrease so the importance of the environment in determining the quality of the person's life increases.

Identity work needs to move away from exclusively verbal working such as reality orientation and some forms of validation to methods that incorporate using other means of communication such as sound and music, and to the use of resolution and pre-therapy as a means of facilitating the person continuing to be an active agent in the care relationship and not just a reactive physical care receiver. (Pre-therapy is introduced below and these therapies are discussed in detail in the next chapter.)

The need to reach out to others through attempted words and conversation remains a part of the human condition until end of life. Although identity work is easier as a procedure if the person can use words and symbols, the need for such 'contact' work remains just as great – if not greater – when they cannot. It is as we move to the realm of the emotion and the senses that the use of pre-therapy methods devised by the American Garry Prouty become so essential, and we see the work of John Killick in the UK as mirroring many of the pre-therapy ideals (Killick and Allen, 2001; Smith 2011).

While Prouty was a trained psychologist John Killick has an arts background and is a renowned poet – that they uncovered such similar methods decades and continents apart demonstrates perhaps two things: when language is removed or distorted then care requires an artist's touch, and that when 'self' is severely threatened highly developed psychological *and* emotional understandings are required to continue to reach in behind the mask of dementia.

Both of these approaches guide us to continue identity affirmation work till the very end of life is reached. Prouty focused his approaches initially on the six 'necessary and sufficient conditions for constructive personality change' as proposed by Rogers (1957). In the context of dementia, 'constructive personality change' refers to resolving inner conflicts and distress.

Prouty recognised that with diminished capacity the first condition, of 'psychological contact', can be problematic. Pre-therapy, therefore, was initially conceived as a method of facilitating this early and difficult psychological contact, as a precondition of therapy for those with severely reduced capacity or psychological function. Prouty's work showed that however diminished a person's capacity appeared to be, human contact remained possible – and often at a profound level.

While Prouty called the work required to reach someone profoundly challenged 'contact functions and reflections', Killick has suggested a much simpler term: 'making contact'. Both of these approaches share phenomena with validation therapy, the work of Naomi Feil, the American social worker, who has suggested we call this contact work 'tuning in' (Feil, 1993). Goldsmith (1996) also suggests we work with persons living in later stages of profound cognitive challenge where there is an emphasis on listening to the cadence of attempted words, and the damaged structures of attempted sentences, to tune into the metaphorical and musical language often used by people with dementia as attempts to continue social contact and in order to enter into their subjective world.

The understanding this leaves us is that where good practice in dementia care had previously been seen to move from the person-centred at some juncture to a more palliative-type approach (again a nihilistic view) it now seems possible that meaningful person-centred work can continue to the very last stages where indeed end-of-life pathways would be initiated. There is not an arbitrary cut-off point as so often referred to in medical jargon where the physical needs outweigh the dementia needs. In reality terminology such as this is simply a means of justifying 'giving up' or for placing someone inappropriately into 'cheaper' care.

These suggested approaches state a need for an empathic presence on the part of the carer, focusing on promoting emotional security for the person with dementia. Cheston and Bender (1999) draw attention to the importance of empathic listening, and Dodds (2008) relates the importance of bearing witness to the uncertainty and fear that the dementia process may provoke. These types of approach can also help to bring deep appreciation on the part of the carer for the person in their care living and now dying with dementia. A word of warning, however: this is not work to be taken lightly and all care homes should have processes in place for staff to be supported and offered ongoing supervision when they engage in these deep and prolonged periods of emotional contact.

Engaging in person-centred care approaches from first meeting to end of life can be traumatic, demanding but ultimately life-affirming for carers. Watching and participating are fundamentally different things and good dementia care giving means active participation not passive observation.

Psychological needs of the person with dementia (the petal model)

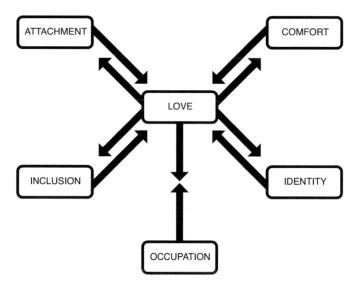

FIGURE 2.6 The psychological needs of persons living with dementia

Attachment

Attachment is the first real need we have as children. It provides a kind of safety net when the world is full of uncertainty. Without the reassurance and certainty that attachments provide it is hard for anyone to thrive. Although the need for attachments may lessen in full adulthood, there is every reason to believe that the need for attachment in those with dementia can be as strong as that of a very young child. Perrin and May have devised a model where the higher and later developed psychological processes are lost in a reverse developmental sequence. This they have demonstrated is the reverse of the psychologically developing and maturing brain as described in children by Piaget and others. Therefore, early fears of separation, anxiety and the need for strong attachments which are key features of early childhood may well be the resultant prevailing psychological condition (Perrin & May, 2000) as the brain's higher functions unravel, much as an onion sheds its outer layers to reveal its core elements, as dementia develops.

Life becomes overshadowed by confusion, fear and uncertainty. Ties, relationships and environments may also have been lost especially if admission to a care home has occurred and grounding and reassuring memories become further lost. Bere Miesen (Jones & Miesen, 1992–2006) suggests that because people with dementia are continuously finding themselves in new and distressing situations the need for attachment is powerfully activated.

Inclusion

In some cultures banishment is used as punishment and in our culture the need for inclusion is very strong. Many displays of what can be mistakenly referred to as 'attention-seeking behaviour' can be understood clearly in the context of needing both attachment and inclusion.

Being in a room full of strangers is not inclusion and all efforts must be made to ensure that the psychological needs of persons with dementia are not treated in a secondary way but are seen as integral to their quality of living. If these two needs in particular are not met much evidence exists that the person will decline and retreat until life is lived almost entirely in a behaviour 'bubble' as described by Tessa Perrin (1996).

Occupation

Being involved in the processes of life that are highly personally significant and which draw on a person's inner ability and powers is an essential quality we all seek. When people are deprived of occupation their abilities atrophy and their self-esteem and willpower dwindle away. The more that is known and understood about the person's past and particularly about their inner sources of satisfaction the better this need can be met. The provision of meaningful occupation as opposed to the provision of distracting activities is one of the least understood and least delivered of all care needs.

Identity

Identity means having a past, a story to tell about oneself. To some extent also the person moulds themselves to what is needed to allow relationships and therefore attachments and inclusion to become possible. We all need to fit in, to have our place.

Negative reactions and particularly banishment can erode and distort personality. It is so very important that the individual uniqueness of the person be maintained and respected through interactions and involvement and the constant reaffirming of identity through family involvement and life history work.

The primary task of dementia care should be the maintenance of personhood; identity stands at the centre of the person.

Comfort

Comfort symbolises so much more than just the physical realm. It carries meanings of tenderness, closeness, the soothing of pain and sorrow, the calming of anxiety and to instil the feeling of security which comes from being close to another. To comfort another person is to provide warmth and strength when they are in danger of falling apart.

Love

While all the above can be seen as important features of a good care regime, the need for love is central to the experience of a human being and it is pivotal to well-lived dementia. Throughout life we strive for love and warm contact; with the losses faced with the onset of dementia there can be no greater need than that of love.

Central to all our caring should be the theme of genuine giving and receiving of love. While all of the other components are necessary for genuine dementia care to be effective, without this central provision all will be for nothing as the spark that ignites our being will have been lost. Love is the basic ingredient of all our needs.

Good and bad practice in dementia caring

Professor Tom Kitwood coined a term that has entered the annals of dementia care history – malignant social psychology. This term when understood fully expresses dramatically the toxic effect of poor care provision. Kitwood does not just claim that poor care is bad for people, he states that it has at its core a malignancy – a cancer among the psychology of those providing and maintaining the care and its regime.

In the remit of a normal working day spent caring you may come across the use of one or probably more of the behaviours listed below. These types of behaviour are indicative of an abusive social culture that may be intentional or non-intentional but nevertheless exists. Its existence prohibits the provision of any of the care factors we have discussed as being so necessary for good dementia care. (Conversely, Kitwood writes that certain psychological imperatives are required for a health social culture and these are also listed below.)

Malignant social psychology

- **Treachery**: using forms of deception in order to distract or manipulate a person, or force them into compliance.
- **Disempowerment**: not allowing a person to use the abilities they do have, failing to help them complete actions they have initiated.
- **Infantilisation**: treating a person very patronisingly, as an insensitive parent might treat a very young child.
- **Intimidation**: inducing fear in a person through the use of threats or physical power.
- **Labelling**: using a category such as dementia, or 'organic mental disorder' or 'elderly mentally infirm' as the main basis for interacting with a person or as an excuse for their behaviour.
- **Stigmatisation**: treating a person as if they were a diseased object, an alien or an outcast.
- **Outpacing**: providing information, presenting choices and the like at a rate too fast for the person to understand; putting the person under pressure by expecting them to do things at a rate far exceeding their current capability.
- **Invalidation**: failing to acknowledge the subjective reality of a person's experience and especially their feelings attached to it.
- **Banishment**: sending a person away, or excluding them – physically or psychologically.
- **Objectification**: treating a person as if they were a piece of dead matter or an item of furniture rather than as the real person they are.
- **Ignoring**: carrying on in the presence of someone as if they were not there.
- **Imposition**: forcing a person to do something, overriding a desire or denying any possibility of choice.
- **Withholding**: refusing to give asked for attention or to meet an evident need.
- **Accusation**: blaming a person for actions or failures of action that arise from their inabilities or their misunderstanding of the situation.
- **Disruption**: intruding suddenly or disturbing upon a person's action or reflection – crudely breaking the frame of reference.

- **Mockery**: making fun of a person's 'strange' behaviour, action or remarks, teasing or humiliating or making jokes at the person's expense.
- **Disparagement**: telling a person that they are incompetent, useless, worthless etc. Giving them messages, verbally or psychologically, that are damaging to their self-esteem.

Requirements for healthy caring

- **Recognition**. The caregiver brings an open and unprejudiced attitude, free from tendencies to stereotype or pathologies and meets the person with dementia in their uniqueness.
- **Negotiation**. The caregiver sets aside any ready-made assumptions about what is to be done and dares to ask, consult and listen.
- **Collaboration**. There is a deliberate abstinence from the use of power and hence from all form of imposition or coercion; 'space' is created for the person with dementia to contribute as fully as possible to the action.
- **Play**. The caregiver is able to access a free, childlike and creative way of being.
- **Stimulation**. The person with dementia receives stimulation through the direct avenue of the senses; and this means that the caregiver is at ease with their own sensuality – untroubled by guilt or anxious inhibition.
- **Celebration**. Beyond the burdens of the immediate demands of work, the caregiver is open to joy.
- **Relaxation**. The caregiver is free to stop active work, for a while; the caregiver identifies with the need people with dementia have to slow down and allow both body and mind respite.
- **Validation**. The caregiver goes beyond their frame of reference in order to have an empathetic understanding of the other; cognition is tuned down and sensitivity to feeling and emotion is heightened.
- **Holding**. Whatever the distress the person is undergoing, the caregiver remains fully present, steady, assured and responsive, able to tolerate the resonance of all disturbing emotions.
- **Facilitation**. The carer shows a readiness to respond to the gesture made, not forcing meaning upon it, but sharing in the making of gesture and enabling it to occur.
- **Creation**. The creative action made by the person with dementia is seen as such and the caregiver responds without taking control.
- **Giving**. The caregiver is humble enough to accept whatever gift of kindness or support the person with dementia bestows, and honest enough to regard this in the context of their own needs.

Therapeutic interventions

Interventions aimed at helping to establish emotional security

You can help establish emotional security in the person with dementia by keeping the following in mind.

- See emotional needs as of prime importance.
- Recognise attachment need.
- Minimise catastrophising.
- Maximise stability of environment.
- Maximise interpersonal security.
- Minimise stress in the person's system.
- Minimise random events and extraneous noise.
- Create conditions to increase the likelihood of all the above.
- Offer long-term support from the beginning of interventions.
- Never leave a resident distressed.
- Facilitate maintenance of loving relationships between relatives and people with dementia, and people with dementia and staff.
- Explore the possibility of simulated presence therapy.
- Explain reasons and methods of all assessments and practical procedures, etc.
- Set up regular individual counselling.
- Initiate care only in familiar surroundings (regular environments).
- Where possible take a procedure to the person.
- Person to be helped by a small team of staff with high skill quotient and low staff turnover.
- Optimise communication between person and important others.
- Monitor and minimise stress levels in the environment and in actions between self and important others through carer support and family input and support.
- Control noxious aspects of the environment and provide care in small units that provide maximum orientation, continuity and interpersonal security.
- The most important aspects of your job remain respect and dignity at all times. You must never knowingly place yourself or any other person in a risk situation physically or psychologically.
- You should work in twos wherever this is required and you should allow plenty of time for one-to-one personal interventions.
- Speed is not of the essence, quality is.

Interventions aimed at creating a consistent sense of identity

You can help create a consistent sense of identity by keeping the following in mind.

- Allow grieving for losses.
- Teach problem solving.
- Encourage new relationships.
- Encourage the development of emotional support by re-expanding the social network.
- Reverse internalisation and feeling of unemployment leading to fears of uselessness.
- Maximise esteem-creating activities.
- Reverse dependency.
- Increase ease of memorising.
- Encourage new learning and relearning.
- Minimise disability.
- Initiate individual counselling/person work with staff skilled in handling losses and grief.
- Use a problem-solving approach, maximising person agency and environmental controls.
- Look at ways of providing care which encourages people to interact.
- Look at establishing group work, drawing on common experiences to encourage group cohesion and networking outside the group.
- Attempt to establish contact with old friends, for example through the church or the British Legion, etc.
- Encourage expansion and enjoyment of the retired position.
- Help with the use of long-term memory and abilities to be useful and creative here and now.
- Encourage the person to make and give gifts, perform own tasks, enjoy and use social activities groups.
- Structure daily living so as to include personally memorable and meaningful events, outings, visits, groups, etc.
- Establish failure-free teaching for staff.
- Provide structured outings to previously familiar localities.
- Substitute activities to maintain interest.
- Use aids to compensate for failing or lost abilities.
- Creativity on your part will help to enable these ideas and more to be put into practice.
- The only limit on the way we can help people with dementia to maintain their identity lies within us.
- Anything that you think would reinforce the person of those we help should

be tried. If we accept that people with dementia are in a constant struggle to maintain their self-identity, our duty is to assist in this process.

ARE YOU GIVING PERSON-CENTRED, RELATIONSHIP-BASED CARE?

- A flexible routine of care which is concerned with meeting the psychological, physical, emotional and social needs of the individual person living with dementia.
- Time allocated to caring procedures, so that people are not rushed.
- Time for staff to stand back and encourage people to become engaged in self-care activities.
- An appropriate level of help when a difficulty in self-help caring is reached, with staff giving appropriate physical, verbal and gesture prompts.
- Persons are grouped depending on skills and dependencies – where abilities are recognised and promoted.
- A homely environment, which promotes the person's psychological, social and emotional well-being where dignity and unique human value as an older person is recognised.
- Restraints of any form are banished – problematic behaviours are managed by recognised therapeutic approaches.
- A high level of interaction between those cared for and the carer exists at every opportunity and dialogue is used that is relevant to each individual person.
- A high level of organised therapeutic activity with all staff engaged in reality orientation, reminiscence, validation, resolution, social activity programmes and so on. (See next chapter.)
- A low level of apathy, withdrawal or disturbed behaviour is exhibited by people with dementia and there is a minimal reliance on sedative medication.
- Optimistic and positive attitudes exist among staff to the continued caring for those with dementia.
- High morale and job satisfaction among staff.

Source: Adapted from O'Donovan, 1997.

3 Modern contexts of dementia care

(The introductory section of this chapter is an adapted, updated and expanded work by the author based originally on work by Andrew Morton, 2000.)

The pure application of techniques from any one school of counselling or psychotherapy is uncommon in dementia care. A purist approach has often produced limited results due to the fact that most schools of psychotherapy apply models and frameworks of 'normal' neurological and physiological functions.

However, combination or integrative techniques have been used in dementia caring since the early 1960s in an attempt to aid the distress and disorientation experienced by those living with a dementia. Some of these integrative approaches have fallen prey to fashion and others have been somewhat discredited, but each has shown a level of invention by their founders equal to any of the more traditional schools. Moreover, some have recently experienced a rebirth – sometimes using new names but essentially holding true to much of the original thought.

This chapter gives a brief background and a sense of the application of various models of care. I am indebted to Morton's work *Person-centred Approaches to Dementia Care* (1999) for much original source material for early sections on reality orientation, validation, resolution and pre-therapy approaches.

Models of dementia care

Reality orientation (RO)

Begun by Dr James Folsom in Alabama, USA, in the late 1950s, the RO movement was strongly influenced by the behavioural school of psychotherapy, which came to dominate many avenues of psychotherapy for the next 30 years.

The aim of RO was to modify behaviour by providing highly structured groups, which made use of objective topics of conversation and visual aids. Accurate statements regarding the appropriate stimuli or conversation topic were rewarded explicitly while incorrect answers or inappropriate use of the visual material was discouraged or corrected, also often explicitly.

The objective of the approach was to 'reorientate' people living with dementia to a time and place familiar to 'us'; that is, our understanding of the here and now as being the only 'truth', and therefore in the mind of the therapist the 'correct' time frame. The contention was that this approach assisted in providing improved interest and greater awareness of the here and now and that this would somehow aid current levels of cognitive function and 'correct' certain forms of behaviour in those to whom the therapy was applied.

RO was most often performed in a classroom-type atmosphere with the therapist offering pre-chosen topics from within which the group was expected to respond positively and 'normally'. Failure to respond positively over a number of sessions could mean exclusion from the group or, possibly more damaging still, isolation within the group. While it is still felt that RO can have therapeutic benefits in the early stages of disorientation accompanying dementia, when the person has the ability and the desire to reorientate at will, it has become common thought that the process of RO in itself can be damaging to those individuals who have passed beyond this stage.

It has also become accepted that at certain levels of function the attempts to reorientate will be resisted and any insistence upon the continuation of the process will be detrimental to the ego functioning of the individual. Progressive thinking around RO has, however, begun to understand that non-explicit use of orientation through the use of cueing and redundant cueing and through non-classroom-type individual therapeutic integration has a place, and this has led to resurgence in a modified approach. It is accepted that life history and life story work can prove highly beneficial long after a classroom-type approach may have become harmful and to this extent reminiscence becomes protective.

While a good degree of cognitive ability remains, use of non-explicit RO will likely aid the person to find a degree of competence in an often confusing environment. For instance, a person wakes up but does not know if the clock reading four is four in the morning or four at night. By adding a clock that changes its graphic display to show day or night and non-explicit RO – although very different from the original behaviourist dogma – now helps with self-esteem and well-being. When the ability to orientate at will has diminished, guided reminiscence may still prove effective but would be dependent on its opportunistic use and not in a prescribed manner which could prove distressing.

Validation therapy

Validation therapy was begun by Naomi Feil in the late 1960s as an attempt to offer an alternative to the reality orientation revolution that was at that time beginning to sweep through America (and later swept through the British NHS and across Europe).

It was also an attempt based on the work of Rogers and that of Laing to bring a certain person-centeredness to the plight of what Feil described as the old, old person (a rather unfortunate euphemism for a person living with dementia, although it was not clear Feil was actually implying her 'old, old' were living with the dementia condition).

Although much of Feil's work is now seen as contradictory and not necessarily applicable to people with dementia, the validation approach has provided interesting concepts and techniques to the field. Indeed it can be claimed that Feil was the first to accept that the subjective world of the confused person was the area for working and that only by entering into this world could we possibly provide the empathy necessary for a person-centred approach.

'Through entering the inner world and bringing the inner reality outward residents can experience each other and feel like somebody. In verbalising the fantasy or inner reality individuals gained a feeling of gratification, of being understood, and a sense of self in the knowledge that their world was meaningful and acceptable' (Feil, 1972).

Feil's validation therapy ideas were about something more than 'control and command' and provided insights into the human condition and the need to 'walk a mile in my shoes' to appreciate the great worth of older persons and specifically older persons with mental health needs. (I acknowledge a debt to Naomi Feil because without stumbling across validation therapy in my early development I am not sure I would have followed the specialist path I have. Feil allowed me to gain the perspective of not judging someone without having 'walked a mile in their shoes'.)

Feil's original work was called 'tuning in therapy' and the essential attribute of the therapist was considered their ability to empathise and to be congruent with the inner feelings of the person with whom they were working. It is perhaps regrettable that such a term has now been largely forgotten as dementia work is surely all about being able to 'tune into' another's reality and to empathise and engage with it as people like Garry Prouty, John Killick and Kate Allen have demonstrated so well.

In 1982 Feil entered the mainstream with her first book, *Validation: the Feil Method*, and this one book unfortunately is where much of the criticism of Feil's work stems. In this book Feil developed theories that were more in line (as Morton points out) with psychoanalysis than person centeredness – it included a four-stage model of disorientation, a modified version of Erikson's life-stage theory and an integration of Freudian interpretation and language with further attempts at the assimilation of the Jungian theory of symbols.

According to Morton, Feil saw a need to understand and interpret confused speech and behaviour; in this way she rejected the medical reductionist view of dementia as being simply the result of failing neurological systems. Feil 'described people with dementia as having lost ego contact with reality and to have regressed because of this' (Morton, 1999).

Feil has never in her writings provided conclusive evidence that people with dementia make up the client group for which she sees validation as being effective, although training programmes bearing the fruit of Feil's thoughts and innovations certainly now do. It is this sense of psychotherapeutic and analytic confusion and integration that has allowed Feil's work to be attacked consistently by those who are experts in the field of person-centred dementia care. Stokes and Goudie (1990) consider that validation is not appropriate for those suffering from Alzheimer's or multi-infarct dementia, perhaps with the exception of when the dementia is in the earliest and mildest stages. I agree with much of Graham Stokes's work but I am afraid here we differ as I believe the essence of what Feil was attempting to say was profound and ahead of her time. In fact, resolution therapy, which is about seeing the problem from the perspective of the person living with dementia rather than our own, owes much to the ideas within validation therapy – whether acknowledged or not – and approaches that encourage us to view positions other than our own are to my thinking essential for modern approaches to dementia caring .

Resolution therapy

It was not until the latter half of the 1980s that any serious interest was shown in the internal world of the person living with dementia in the UK – 20 years after this occurred in the United States and owing much to the work of Feil and her contemporaries, who it must be said at that time were still few in number.

At this time reality orientation was the major approach used with those living with a dementia in care in the UK as it had been in America, and practitioners everywhere were beginning to question, as had Feil, the validity of the approach. The first British attempt to help caregivers treat the emotional needs of people with dementia was resolution therapy. The therapy gained an enormous amount of interest based on just one article and one chapter in a broader book on dementia care, such was the lack of available literature on this type of approach (Goudie &

Stokes, 1989, Stokes & Goudie, 1990). It is likely this scarcity of material, and very little expansion since, has led to recent approaches to challenging behaviour that almost completely fail to acknowledge the influence of resolution therapy.

In fact, the recent emergence of the Colombo Approach (or the Newcastle model as it is more commonly known) (James, 2006) as a predominant approach to working with behaviour that challenges makes only a cursory acknowledgement of Stokes's work in the field, merely referencing fleetingly his psychogenic model.

Stokes and Goudie are clinical psychologists who undertook one of the first programmes of evaluation of both RO and validation therapy. After dissecting both they announced that RO had aims other than meeting the needs of people with dementia and that validation in itself did not go far enough.

They argued that if someone was suffering from depression or anxiety as well as dementia it was not enough to simply validate that position; an attempt needed to be made to deal with the source of distress, in essence to 'resolve' the issue. This urge to action sits comfortably with the missives of the adaptive response philosophy which states that when someone can support and facilitate they should do so but where someone cannot they should compensate and initiate.

They cautioned against the reliance on psychodynamic interpretation of confused speech and behaviours as they felt this may distract the worker from seeing the situation in terms of the here and now.

The position adopted by Stokes and Goudie is summarised by Morton as follows.

- People with an organic mental health problem can, and often do, also have a degree of affective (mood) disorder.
- There is no fundamental reason why such disorders in people with a dementia should not respond to the same types of psychological intervention that are used with people who do not have a dementia.

Like its predecessor validation, resolution therapy involves paying close attention to all attempts at communication by people living with a dementia. While Feil throughout her work has striven to show that confused speech and behaviour is probably understandable in psychodynamic terms, Goudie and Stokes argued that it is more likely to be an attempt at communicating expressions of current need or an effort to make sense of the environment. This thought likely led to Stokes's later creation of his psychogenic model of challenging behaviour and the rise of the unmet needs hypothesis.

The task of resolution therapy, therefore, is to overcome the barrier of unmet needs by using counselling skills of reflective listening, exploration, warmth and acceptance in the Rogerian 'reflection of feeling' tradition where we can empathise with the hidden meaning behind confused verbal and behavioural expressions and seek, once an interpretation of unmet need is achieved, to resolve the need for the behaviour by meeting the identified needs.

Criticism of resolution as shown by Morton is that it is offers too little and has not been developed further, although Stokes in his book *Challenging Behaviour in Dementia: A Person-centred Approach* (2000) developed aspects of the original work. Fiona Goudie too has developed her work and now sees value in non-verbal communication and in approaches other than counselling.

Although criticism of both validation and resolution has been made and some of it refreshed here, we should not underestimate their importance in influencing the Bradford Dementia Group and Tom Kitwood and his colleagues, such as Dawn Brooker, who have gone on to develop their own theories and tools which I refer to throughout this book.

The new culture

The late Tom Kitwood during his lifetime and since has been one of the most influential figures in dementia care.

Kitwood introduced a deeper and broader approach, which combined classical training with social thought, and he called for a psychoanalytic approach to the care of those with dementia rather than a reliance on the medical model.

Kitwood began his work by dissecting the prevailing model of care, the medical reductionist position and in his later work constructed a theory of care based on positive social psychology (Morton, 1999). For a fuller understanding of Kitwood's work, its importance, influence and for a coherent and intelligent criticism of its sometimes contradictory nature read *Tom Kitwood on Dementia: A Reader and Critical Commentary* by Clive Baldwin and Andrea Capstick (2007).

One of Kitwood's strengths was his acceptance of the pathology of dementia and Alzheimer's disease as opposed to the social construction theorists who almost, it seemed at times, denied or seriously underplayed the existence of structural damage and change to the brain. Kitwood perceived these changes as being an additional problem of mind as opposed to an inclusive problem of brain. This was a stroke of genius says Morton because it completely took the argument away from those who believed that if you cure the disease you cure the problem; if you could not cure you could not provide effective treatment and it was felt at that time, except by some very special thinkers as shown above, that nothing could be done but treat the 'symptoms' of the disease and make people safe, warm and keep them fed.

Kitwood's writing and his often theoretical conference presentations struck a chord with practitioners, especially in the UK, hungry for more of the work begun by Stokes and Goudie, and an army of nurse practitioners and a number of psychologists took up the fight.

One of the greatest findings of Kitwood's work was the proposition that certain core conditions existed that created negative reactions in people with dementia, and which he termed 'malignant psychology'. From these he and Bredin postulated, conversely, that there were also indicators of well-being in people living with a dementia and a formulation of positive person work was conceived which has become the dominant model for progressive dementia working and spawned tools to measure these properties, such as dementia care mapping (DCM) and the short observational framework for inspection (SOFI).

Kitwood broke with all convention when he announced that if these positive traits were present in people with dementia, and if the care regime was populated with positive work and negative social psychology was removed permanently, a process of a form of rehabilitation could ensue. This process he called 'rementia'. We return to rementia later as, although it is a concept that has been derided and is much misunderstood, I believe it to be a naturally emergent property when adaptive response principles are married with positive social psychology and stress and negative social factors are removed as much as possible from the care regime.

In many medical practitioners' eyes Kitwood was now fair game for ridicule as he was, they claimed, actually proposing that the terrible and inevitable decline associated with the dementias could not only be stopped but may in some instances be reversed for periods of time if the care regime was correct. This was a sloppy, and possible deliberate misinterpretation of the message that when we get bad things out of the way and allow and facilitate people living with dementia to realise their potential the appearance of recovery and improvement is not only possible but I contend most probable. It is not an exaggeration to state that Tom Kitwood's ideas changed the face of dementia care.

Pre-therapy

Garry Prouty expanded the scope of classical Rogerian therapy (Rogers, 1957) to include work with people whose functioning is severely impaired, and both Dodds (2008) and Smith (2011) have shown how this approach can be applied to those living with a dementia. Such an approach is both in its theory and in its practice opposed to the symptom-centeredness that characterises strictly biological or behavioural accounts and it is expressed in a way that is truly person-centred.

Prouty's work as applied to dementia has excited many practitioners in the field and indeed his books and those on pre-therapy since his untimely death have included examples and ideas of using pre-therapy with those who have short- and long-term cognitive impairments, including those with advanced dementia (Prouty *et al*, 2002; Dodds in Prouty, 2008). Smith has reported the outcomes of the first ever training programme specifically applying pre-therapy to dementia care (Dodds, 2008).

Prouty focuses initially on the six 'necessary and sufficient conditions for constructive personality change' as proposed by Rogers (1957). For constructive personality change to occur, it is necessary that the following conditions exist and continue over a period of time.

● Two persons are in psychological contact.
● The first, whom we shall term the client, is in a stage of 'incongruent', being vulnerable or anxious.
● The second person, whom we shall call the therapist, is 'congruent' or inte-grated in the relationship.
● The therapist experiences unconditional positive regard for the client.
● The therapist experiences empathic understanding of the client's internal frame of reference and endeavours to communicate this experience to the client.
● The communication to the client of the therapist's understanding and uncon-ditional positive regard is to a minimal degree achieved.

Prouty recognised that with diminished capacity the first condition of 'psychologi-cal contact' can be problematic. Pre-therapy, therefore, was initially conceived as a method of facilitating psychological contact, as a precondition of therapy. Without the first condition, the others are unattainable; however, with the first achieved the others are inevitable.

The techniques of pre-therapy are deceptively simple, but the real art consists of using them in practice in a way that may benefit those whose inner world is fragmented or chaotic. Pre-therapy is non-directive; it follows the process of the client. The therapist, however, should not expect to know the client's frame of reference but to work with it wherever it may lead. This is 'empathic contact'.

Prouty's work should be seen as one of the most exciting possibilities for the future development of person-centred approaches to dementia care anywhere in the world, yet it has almost been lost from the current dementia practitioner's vocabulary.

Cognitive stimulation therapy (CST)

Cognitive stimulation therapy is a specific inclusive group work method devised in the UK, chiefly by Aimee Spector, Martin Orrell and Bob Woods. Appealingly, it holds that staff do not require special qualifications or need to attend special training courses and no special equipment is needed. 'All that is needed is for two people to meet with a small group of people with dementia, in a quiet room for 45 minutes, twice a week for seven weeks' (Spector *et al*, 2006).

It sounds straightforward and the techniques, simple as they are, are based around the principles of person-centred work as described by Kitwood (1996, 1998) and in particular look to create conditions of positive self-worth, involvement and inclusion and to create engagement. The core elements were formulated after a large-scale research programme involving over 200 people living with dementia at various care homes and day centres (Spector *et al*, 2003).

Each formal session is recorded and specific observations are recorded for each of the group across four key areas of engagement:

● interest
● communication
● involvement
● mood.

Scores are allocated for the degree to which each attendee demonstrates engagement with these elements and whether this engagement was positive or negative. Scores are on a scale of 1 to 5 with 1 indicating no engagement and 5 indicating positive engagement. The authors recommend two carers per five or six group members.

The CST approach has at its core key principles which the authors describe as being essential (rather than optional).

● **Person-centred**. By this it is meant that both leaders must be grounded in not only an understanding of a person-centred approach but are required to adopt these practices at all times within the group.
● **Respect**. Showing basic respect for each other, discounting, race, colour, religion, ability or disability, and celebrating differences.
● **Involvement**. Incorporating not only leadership but also the principles of tuning in and of allowing space and of encouraging all levels of communication to be used – not dominating procedures.
● **Inclusion**. This is an element where the group leaders need to show their skills by ensuring all are involved equally and that balance is kept throughout the session so that no one leads too much and, more importantly, that no one gets left behind.

- **Choice**. There are 14 types of session described in the manual for workers, but the idea is not to be prescriptive. As skills are developed in delivering these topics new and innovative ways of involving group members will emerge around the basic ideas of using memories, reminiscence and existing cognitive skills together to create better and more profound levels of engagement and reconnection with the self and the sense of self-worth.
- **Fun**. This is what Kitwood may term 'timalation' (1996) – enjoyment through all the senses not just the articulated. The aim of the group is to make participation pleasant, stimulating and fun engagements – to steer away from the dark and into the light.
- **Opinions rather than facts**. The group is not a mini mental exam – it matters little whether people can recall the sitting prime minister or they can spell words backwards; what matters is engagement with memory and reminiscence in all its many facets.
- **Using reminiscence**. Tapping into memories and abilities is central to the group because, as we have shown earlier, not only is it pleasant to tell one's history but it actually has profound therapeutic effects. However, a word of caution should be heeded. With memories come emotions and as in an abreaction where a previous emotional state is re-enacted in the present the group leaders must always be aware that allowing free rein to memories can lead to sad as well as good feelings; all leaders need to be prepared should such an incident occur.
- **Using the senses**. Multi-sense experiences can be dramatic, particularly if one sense has been damaged. Working with preferred senses and sometimes a sense working overtime can be particularly beneficial to group members, so providing things to touch, see, smell, hear and perhaps even taste is encouraged.
- **Always having something to look at, touch or feel**. As indicated above, the preparations for the group are paramount, and all items and equipment should be set up and ready at the start of each session.
- **Maximising potential**. Dementia is a fluctuating and fluid experience – as has been demonstrated by Huub Buijssen (2005) in his short but profound book *The Simplicity of Dementia: A Guide for Families and Carers*. The phenomenon he describes as roll-back memory shows us that just because someone was incapable of doing something yesterday does not mean they will be so again today or next week. CST asks us to never judge abilities beforehand but to work with each group member's full potential.
- **Building and strengthening relationships**. Perhaps the true strength of CST has yet to be realised, but it may lie within the formation of new contacts, in recreating social norms, in allowing sharing of history and in enjoying group

successes within the normalisation context. Being human in all its various shades is what person-centred working requires, and perhaps in providing an arena for relationships to build unconditionally CST has much to offer.

- **Follow-up**. Once the initial programme of CST is completed it is suggested weekly follow-up sessions are maintained for at least a further four months (Orrell *et al*, 2005) and a further 16 session themes are suggested to maximise the ongoing effects of the original works.

Modern principles of dementia caring and a move towards unified objectives

There are a number of organisation-specific principles which have emerged in dementia caring over the last 10 years which differ somewhat from the founding models looked at in the previous section. Together, these principles have influenced the way dementia caring is now developing within the UK.

The need for some commonality in principles has, however, been finally recognised and this has led to the formulation and release of 'the common core principles' developed from current policy and guidance (*see* p. 89).

It is worth looking at some of the more prominent dementia care approaches so as to understand the current direction of caring for people living with dementia and how services for people living with dementia are emerging and synergising. As adaptive response is one such idea, but not a standalone model, the carer's role is to apply its underlying principles and findings within the predominant model or approach. This is not as difficult as it may at first sound as the principles of adaptive response simply seek to provide an answer as to why some people living with dementia respond the way they do to certain built and social environments, specifically those that are stressful or stress-inducing. Armed with this information you may wish to remove or remodel these elements in your caring and as an addition to your core care practices.

The enriched model of dementia care

The enriched model of dementia care has arisen from the combined efforts of those involved in the dementia care development services, which are academic-supported initiatives spanning the UK and in particular from themes emerging over the last 20 years from developments begun by the late Tom Kitwood and the Bradford Dementia Group.

In essence, the model takes as its starting point the Kitwood equation of the experience of dementia and demonstrates the model's relevance to the use of person-centred care planning as the accepted tool of caring which has developed from the nursing process and incorporates these principles.

Bradford Dementia Group Principles for Dementia Care (Tom Kitwood)

- Recognise the uniqueness of each person.
- Focus on each person's abilities and assets, rather than disabilities and deficits.
- Allow the person with dementia to control the action (so far as it is safe and feasible).
- Honour each individual's past.
- Communicate at the feeling level.
- Assume that the words and actions of the person with dementia have meaning.
- Nourish attachments.
- Maintain the integrity of the person's world.
- Promote independence where possible.
- Have a positive and proactive approach to general health.
- People with dementia have the same human value as anyone else irrespective of their degree of disability or dependence.
- People with dementia have the same varied human needs as anyone else.
- People with dementia have the same rights as other citizens.
- Every person with dementia is an individual.
- People with dementia have the right to forms of support which don't exploit family and friends.

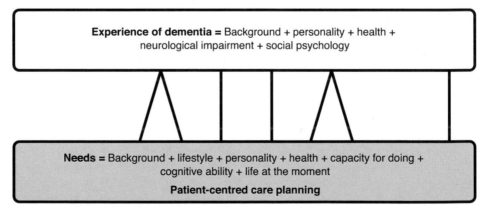

Experience of dementia = Background + personality + health + neurological impairment + social psychology

Needs = Background + lifestyle + personality + health + capacity for doing + cognitive ability + life at the moment

Patient-centred care planning

FIGURE 3.1 The enriched model of dementia care

King's Fund 'Living Well into Old Age' Key Principles (King's Fund Centre, 1986)

Philosophy of domus care (Elaine Murphy & Alastair MacDonald) (Kitwood & Woods, 1996)

- The domus is the resident's 'home for life'.
- The needs of the staff are as important as those of the residents.
- The domus should aim to correct the avoidable consequences of dementia and accommodate those that are unavoidable.
- The resident's individual psychological and emotional needs may take precedence over the physical aspects of care.

Gentlecare (Moyra Jones, 2000)

- The prosthetic model of care focuses on patterns of behaviour and causes of problems.
- Human values, conversation and connection are emphasised by staff whose methods of caring are the major component of therapy.
- Non-invasive tools and techniques are used, with significant reliance on an appropriate person–environment fit; the focus is on the use of human interaction (music, massage, hugs, pets, walks, talks).
- Integration of body, mind and spirit is critical to the care approach.
- Environments are simple, normalised, therapeutic and prosthetic.
- Since many symptoms of dementia cannot be treated, the emphasis is on identifying and supporting remaining function.
- The objective of dementia care is to assist and support the client and the family.
- The social context is vital; professionals, families and communities work in therapeutic partnership.
- All staff are the principal therapeutic agents; their way of caring is the major component of therapy.
- There is a mix of jobs performed in small groups which helps to break down hierarchical divisions between staff groups and foster relationships with small groups of residents who will work alongside these 'pods'.

The EDEN Alternative (Eden Alternative UK & Ireland)

The Eden model uses quite specific terminology and has specific beliefs which are reinforced vigorously within sites using the approach.

- The three plagues of loneliness, helplessness and boredom account for the bulk of suffering among our elders.

- An elder-centred community commits to creating a human habitat where life revolves around close and continuing contact with plants, animals and children. It is these relationships that provide the young and old alike with a pathway to a life worth living.
- Loving companionship is the antidote to loneliness. Elders deserve easy access to human and animal companionship.
- An elder-centred community creates opportunity to give as well as receive care. This is the antidote to helplessness.
- An elder-centred community imbues daily life with variety and spontaneity by creating an environment in which unexpected and unpredictable interactions and happenings can take place. This is the antidote to boredom.
- Meaningless activity corrodes the human spirit. The opportunity to do things that we find meaningful is essential to human health.
- Medical treatment should be the servant of genuine human caring, never its master.
- An elder-centred community honours its elders by de-emphasising top-down bureaucratic authority, seeking instead to place the maximum possible decision-making authority into the hands of the elders or into the hands of those closest to them.
- Creating an elder-centred community is a never-ending process. Human growth must never be separated from human life.
- Wise leadership is the lifeblood of any struggle against the three plagues. There can be no substitute for it.

The experiential model (Power, 2010)

- Each person with dementia has a unique life story and individual needs.
- Although there are cognitive deficits, many complex abilities are preserved, which should be identified and cultivated.
- The brain remains plastic, and new and compensatory learning can still occur.
- The primary task for enlightened care is to cultivate close relationships throughout the care environment.
- The manner in which we provide care can have profound effects on the individual's abilities and well-being.
- Well-being is not dependent on cognitive or functional ability and should be maximised in all people.
- People with dementia can be thought of as inhabiting a 'parallel universe', existing in the same time and space as ours, but with somewhat different rules and

values. We must strive to acknowledge and understand these universes and find a common ground for care.

- We must work hard to find unmet needs and adapt the care environment to meet those needs as far as is safe and practical.
- The world of the person with dementia changes over time, and so we must also change and adapt to their evolving needs.
- We must use creativity and collaboration to create a life worth living for people with dementia.

These collective and developing 'founding' principles come together currently under the English government's new focus on outcomes in dementia caring and have been made expressly clear as the common core principles for supporting people with dementia. The Department of Health has commissioned Skills for Care and Skills for Health to produce new guidance for health and social care professionals who work with people who have dementia. Their latest publication, *Common Core Principles for Supporting People with Dementia: A Guide to Training the Social Care and Health Workforce* (SfC/SfH, 2011a), provides guidance for leaders and managers, commissioners and training and education leaders to develop a workforce that can create dementia-friendly settings and this publication is heavily influenced by the preceding 30 years of thought. It sets out the core principles as follows.

The common core principles for supporting people with dementia

- **Principle 1**. Know the early signs of dementia.
- **Principle 2**. Early diagnosis of dementia helps people receive information, support and treatment at the earliest possible stage.
- **Principle 3**. Communicate sensitively to support meaningful interaction.
- **Principle 4**. Promote independence and encourage activity.
- **Principle 5**. Recognise the signs of distress resulting from confusion and respond by diffusing a person's anxiety and supporting their understanding of the events they experience.
- **Principle 6**. Family members and other carers are valued, respected and supported just like those they care for and are helped to gain access to dementia care advice.
- **Principle 7**. Managers need to take responsibility to ensure members of their team are trained and well supported to meet the needs of people with dementia.

- **Principle 8**. Work as part of a multi-agency team to support the person with dementia.

These common core principles have been developed from current policy and guidance – in response to the first national dementia strategy for England: *Living Well with Dementia: A National Dementia Strategy* (DH, 2009) and the National Dementia Declaration for England (DAA, 2010) and the emergence of Scotland's National Dementia Strategy (2010), along with advice from carers and practitioners. They will support developments which take place to improve the experience of people with dementia and their carers using health and social care services, and are designed to work synergistically along with other guidance such as the *Core Competences for End of Life Care* (SfC/SfH/DH, 2009) and *Carers Matter – Everybody's Business* (SfC/SfH, 2011b)

As you can see there is nothing about the adaptive response approach you have so far read that contradicts the new consensus on how we should care for people living with dementia. In Chapter 4 we present reasons for adopting an approach similar to that proposed above. There we describe stress, its effects and how we as humans react to this both physiologically and psychologically, and begin to relate this to an individual living with a dementing condition. It is hoped that the above context setting has immediacy for carers, showing how you – personally – can make a day-to-day and minute-to-minute difference in the life of someone living with dementia in your care.

4 Stress and **adaptive** responses

When I first created the idea of the adaptive response approach to dementia caring it was necessary, due to the prevailing political climate both within the organisation I worked and the emerging field of dementia as practised by nurses, to base its emergence squarely within nursing theory (although I leant very heavily on the emergence of person-centred theories).

Before presenting my original essay on adaptive response in Chapter 5, in order to provide some context this chapter sets out a short history of the development of the adaptive response approach.

In my review of nursing theory and importantly for me the background and beliefs of the theorists both from the UK and abroad, three models allowed me to express a synergy of my 'understanding of nursing' as applied to dementia care. I synergised these approaches and carried them out religiously with my various teams across the varied sites I managed.

Each of these models had to be capable of expressing both the art and science of nursing and to be malleable enough in order to show a commonality of intention in their applied performance outcomes.

The original theories adapted were those of Martha Rogers (1992), Betty Neuman (1982) and Hildegard Peplau (1952). None of these models or any other singular nursing model in my opinion could be said to be totally applicable to the field of dementia caring. However, the working components of these three theories, when taken as a whole and combined into a singular entity, can begin to forge a culture where basic 'concepts' can become entrenched (and more importantly taught to others).

Adaptive response owes a great debt to these beginnings but also found an expression in a much more diverse and holistic combination of theories from all social sciences and caring disciplines; it also found a synergy with the person-centred care movement and with a care model from Canada in the Gentlecare prosthetic approach of Moyra Jones (2000).

In line with the blossoming realisation that for care to be effective the relationships approach (which involves the person, their family and the care provider) is the way forward I have striven to make adaptive response a working link between all the professional caring agents and their diffuse methodologies to ensure that adaptive response is a fully functional model.

It asserts ways of applying theory daily to our work and is based upon almost 17 years now of daily testing. In my working life, I am in the fortunate position of having many 'test' opportunities and I am happy to inform that, once adopted, the approach seems to be changing lives and appears so far to be applicable to most environments (after making adaptations as illustrated in the final chapter).

My work seems to illustrate that there is a working correlation between applying theories of stress and emotion to changing environments (social and built) and that through the use of systems thinking this approach can be applied consistently to the care of people living with a dementia in care home settings. It demonstrates that social and psychological theories can still be successfully applied directly despite the physical limitation of most dementia care units and that the often-cited demands of practical day-to-day 'management' and the sometimes crippling legislation can be kept at bay by a determined effort to apply humanistic approaches.

Perhaps for me the most important finding of adaptive response in action so far is that when the residents, staff and environment are given equal importance new cultures can emerge and it appears these new cultures are transferrable when the concepts and models are reapplied to new environments.

A brief overview of the adapted nursing models

The theory of unitary human beings – Martha E Rogers

Rogers was one of the first nurse theorists, along with Mary Levine, to discuss the environment as being an intrinsic factor in the life process. Her work moved nursing forward and greatly influenced later nursing thinking.

Central to her concepts is the theme that a 'man is a unified whole person possessing their own integrity and manifesting characteristics that are more than and different from the sum of his parts'. Rogers updated her main theories in 1992 and changed slightly the way she presented her work. This updating was presented in her paper 'Nursing science and the space age' (Rogers, 1992) and had three major tenets:

- Resonancy – the continuous change in energy between humans and their environment.
- Helicy – unpredictable and diverse changes between humans and their environments.
- Integrality – the continuous mutual fields of human and environments processes.

Although Rogers' writing is somewhat esoteric, at its heart it provided the basic understanding that humans and their environment are one and the same, and that it is in the interplay between these two linked entities where the nurse can work most successfully. There is something rather magnificent in Rogers' work, and as our understanding grows about our relationship with the world her theories may again assume an importance and prevalence.

The systems model – Betty Neuman

Many similarities are apparent between the work of Neuman and that of Fritz Perls' Gestalt psychotherapy in that both assume that life exists by attempting to balance the interplay between internal and external factors and both stress a model of intervention based on the balancing of these forces.

Neuman goes so far as to state that the interrelatedness between the person and the environment, in that one cannot be seen as separate from the other, is the direct cause of all behaviour. It is when a stressor is added that the behaviour becomes altered as the organism tries to restore balance (this theme echoes the stress adaptation model of Bell, a cornerstone in my early research which formed some of the tenets of adaptive response, and resonates within the whole of Neuman's work).

Her influence on the adaptive response model is apparent in almost every paragraph as her work suggests that the instant a stressor is identified the nurse should begin to reconstitute balance by manipulating both internal and external factors to restore homeostasis or 'adapted function'.

A word of caution here: later stress research, specifically by Lazarus and his contemporaries, has shown that interpretation of perceived threat to homeostasis is as potent a stressor as an actual stressor itself, and this has changed our understanding of Selye's general adaptation syndrome. However, in principle real or imagined threats work exactly the same way on the human 'stress' response and therefore the primacy of nursing interventions as suggested by Neuman remain equally as applicable.

Psychodynamic nursing – Hildegard E Peplau

Psychodynamic nursing involves being able to understand one's own behaviour in order to help others identify difficulties they experience, and apply principles of human relations to the problems that arise at all levels of experience. Peplau's model is the only model I have adapted that applies specifically to a process – a process of nursing. It takes as its central 'core' the relationship between the nurse and the 'patient' and stands as a direct link with the person-centred movement arising across social care.

It is somewhat paradoxical but somehow typical that psychiatric nursing has adopted Peplau because psychodynamic nursing involves nurses taking on roles to enable the person to move through certain stages of care from illness to recovery. This does not involve much acceptance of the person 'as is', and it is plain to see that a pure application of the Peplau model to dementia caring cannot be possible. The full scope of the nursing cycle as described by Peplau which involves full recovery is just not possible in dementia caring because, inevitably, the process of dementia involves cognitive and physical decline and eventual death, no matter how indelicate or 'old school' that sounds.

However, as we do not accept dementia as an inevitable passive decline nor our role in the caring process as 'passive' either, adopting a model of understanding where both we and the person living with dementia are viewed along a continuum of caring is important. The whole point of adaptive response is about the cycles of awareness of adaptation and adjustment, and therefore this model was adopted mainly for its insistence on the usefulness of allowing carers scope to explore their own feelings and practices. This resulting self-awareness allows us to then adopt new roles when current practices may cease to be effective or if our practice moves beyond a safe and recognisable framework.

Peplau of course offers more, but it is this aspect of recognising where carers and the residents and their families (and indeed the environment) are along a dynamic and shifting continuum that makes her work useful to us as part of the adaptive response.

Introduction to adaptive response

The following is a brief introduction to adaptive response, before presenting my original paper on it in Chapter 5. All other chapters in this book are designed to provide enough background for you to be able to apply the principles of the model in the certain knowledge that its ideas are based on sound evidence.

Adjustment stress and compensation

The term adaptation, as used originally in biology, describes both a trait with a functional role that is maintained and evolved by means of natural selection, and the evolutionary process that leads to the adaptation. Adaptation ensures survival and improvement in the face of changing environmental factors. The concept was eventually taken up by psychologists and renamed 'adjustment'; it refers in this context to the individual's struggle to get along or survive in their social and physical environments.

I wanted to show the biological and psychological consequences of life's experience and the effects of the built and social environments upon them so therefore chose to remain with the descriptive term 'adaptive response'.

Adjustment (or adaptation), therefore, expresses two interactive processes, the internal and the external, and it was within this unified experience framework that I began to develop ideas of adaptation within the broader picture of the dementing experience.

I had two basic questions in mind:

- Is it possible to adjust oneself to fit the given circumstances, or to change the circumstances to fits one's own needs within a 'cared for' relationship?
- Can a person living with dementia achieve or actualise the end-of-life tasks necessary to obtain feelings of well-being, and how can carers assist this process?

Immediately I was struck by how much the above questions demanded.

Erik Erikson (1965), in his seminal work on life stages and the tasks needing to be successfully navigated by people to allow psychological maturity and satisfaction, postulated that in our later and final years we need to travel the road between integrity and despair. To review our past life and become content within our current position is the 'goal' of old age.

But what if you develop a dementia, what if you have to be cared for within an institution and what if that institution regards dementia as the end – is there anything that can be done?

Can you change your circumstances in this instance or is it the work of the institution to change itself to foster integrity within dementia? Will you constantly have to struggle to change the circumstances around you? As your dementia progresses this becomes harder and harder and in all likelihood will be mistaken as behaviour that challenges. Or is it the role of the institution to remove the need for this struggle by recognising and adjusting to allow your adaptation and successful adjustment into integrity within a dementia?

These are challenging questions for the industry, but for me the answers were fairly straightforward; what was not so clear-cut was to develop an explanatory model.

Adaptive response uses Erikson's theories as a starting point for dementia care – care as a prosthetic with the goal of allowing the person to experience, in whatever way is left to them, integrity and adjustment. Even a casual observer will see that these goals are sympathetic to those expressed by proponents of the person-centred approaches. In fact adaptive response has sprung from early lessons taught by Kitwood, Stokes and others as they themselves were grappling with changing the social-care landscape. However, adaptive response, unlike some forerunners, does not attempt to explain dementia or even why people react as they do to dementing. What it does attempt to do is to offer a uniform way of approaching the care of those living with a dementia, in groups, in care homes, as they are, using sound psychological and physiological concepts to reduce the obstacles of social and physical environment impacts.

Its major strength lies in its practical application and its foundation in systems theory. It works in conjunction with nature's laws and allows for feed forward and feedback looping. If things go wrong within systems, as long as you understand the system and it is an open not a closed system, the problems can be located easily and corrected quickly.

Adaptive response considers the internal and external systems of the person as well as those of the organisation as a whole and sees system regulation as the major principle of care within care home settings. Care involves a holistic, 'universal' or synergistic approach. In simple terms, the adaptive response model seeks to meet the needs of the person and to fully compensate for the reduced means to achieve successful adaptation to life's demands.

Adjustment and stress

Any failure to successfully adapt to any given situation leads to stress, whether this is at a conscious or unconscious level. Conscious stress is at one level easier to adjust to than unconscious stress. The processes which tie the body and mind together through the central nervous system (CNS) relate to conscious and unconscious recognition of stress in exactly the same manner – if you think you are going to be attacked or you are attacked the body prepares for fight, flight or freeze in exactly the same way.

Stress, consciously recognised or not, leads to a physical reaction and this reaction not only causes physical responses long term such as heart disease, high blood pressure, ulceration and disorders of the bowel but also causes psychological changes. These include short- and long-term confusion, raised and then reduced acuity and, in the longer term, loss of confidence, self-image and self-belief.

These last three areas are important in that they are also seen as detractors and signs of ill-being in the person-centred approaches. Adaptive response sees these as natural consequences of protracted and unmitigated stressful environments and impacts. Reduce these and a certain degree of 'rementia' is inevitable (more on this in Chapter 6).

This systems approach to the unity of mind and body has a number of benefits to those working in care homes:

- It allows those with limited time and resources to see they are making a difference by being able to physically participate in therapeutic approaches to care even if it is just calming the environment at that one moment.
- The approach is transferable from setting to setting as it is the carers who are required to do the work, and it is easy to teach as it has only a few key principles – there are no obscure or abstract suppositions.
- Carers instinctively know it is 'authentic' because they have all felt the pressures of stress in their own lives and have all felt the out-of-control psychological fear and physical distress that stress exerts.

In this last sense it also helps to break down 'ageism' as it allows everyone to feel a connection with these stress-response systems that are still fully active within the people they are caring for – there can be no hiding behind an us-and-them shield as daily processes and reactions are likened to the carers' own day-to-day experiences. This also helps to break down major 'perceptual' barriers; if older people living with dementia have the same feelings and reactions to stress as we do, surely they cannot be different; if these emotions, feelings and reactions are further compounded by one of the dementia, surely we can no longer see the person as a passive recipient of care and we certainly can no longer ever see them as 'childlike' or as returning to a second childhood!

Awareness and insight

It should be easy to see the benefits of an adaptive-type approach to the care of people living with dementia in its early and mid stages, but what about the more advanced stages of a dementia? When a person's higher cognitive functions are severely compromised is it still sensible to refer to care in terms of psychological goals and models?

Much recent brain research has focused upon the emotional brain and the central core of structures that govern our emotional responses to external stimuli as well as the hormonal cascades that accompany our biological responses. It may come as a surprise that these structures seem to react autonomously, without any conscious effort from 'us', in certain situations and release their cocktail of hormones split seconds before 'our' higher functions even become aware of the external stimuli.

This of course makes sense in evolutionary terms, but we need to be much more aware that these functions, which may in the past have helped to stop us from being eaten, are still very much present in modern brain function.

When an external stimulus is received two functions appear to occur in quick succession: the limbic system reacts and *then* the higher cortical functions access memories, and previous responses stored away in various memory resources, and make appropriate and measured judgements as to how to react in accordance with these 'stored' learned responses.

Of course we just need to think back to times in our own lives when we have done something in quick response that we later look back on and wonder why on earth we did it. Well, that's hormonal hijacking for you. With awareness and training we can have better control of these responses, but we can never completely override these autonomic systems. It is not too difficult to understand why, when damage occurs to higher functions, that the emotional responses of those affected begin to take sway.

Learning Tip 9: Emotional brain in charge

Some people never learn to appropriately control these autonomic urges due to a lack of learning opportunities during childhood, and just as there are individual differences in reaction to stress this will play a role in how the person survives within the dementing experience. It is these higher cognitive functions which dampen down our emotional lability, but it is also these areas that are damaged most during the development of a dementia, specifically Alzheimer's-type dementia. This gradual erosion of higher cognitive function allows the emotional brain to assume ever greater control over reaction and response and to influence greatly the person's ability to adapt on their own to meet social and environmental challenges.

When the emotional brain is in charge, subtle environmental stimuli produce a much more profound effect. When we add hippocampal damage such as that seen in Alzheimer's-type dementia there is massive damage to memory systems and this reduces further the pool of material available for retrieval and interpretation for appropriate responses from the higher cortical areas. Therefore, it is not surprising that the person's responses to unexpected or non-structured stimuli will produce unpredictable and sometimes catastrophic reactions and responses. In short, the ability to adjust and adapt to demands from the external environment (built and social) is severely reduced.

As dementia is almost always progressive, theories of adjustment and adaptation will always resonate no matter what the stage of dementia may be. This is where adaptive response has strength, as we adjust our caring interventions by degree. In the early stages we may simply help to facilitate happiness and attempt to avoid unnecessary challenge, whereas in the later stages we may need to compensate for physical as well as psychological and social challenges even to the point of providing food and drink, safety and comfort.

A further strength of adopting an adaptive response philosophy lies in its clear recognition that as the degree of diminishment of higher brain function progresses so the person as an organism becomes more and more challenged in maintaining biological resources. It takes an awful lot of fuel to maintain system integrity during disease and even more during intense biological activation such as stress.

Stress reactions and body maintenance

About three-quarters of the human body is made up of proteins. The components of protein are amino acids, and these are essential for every aspect of body function, including basic muscle maintenance and repair and maintaining steady metabolic function. Unless the proper metabolic climate exists within the body growth, regrowth and repair do not occur.

In situations of stress and particularly prolonged or repeated stress like that experienced by those living with a dementia who are constantly being hijacked by emotional responses, a huge drain is placed on bodily reserves and particularly on the uptake of amino acids.

Problems often encountered, such as disturbed sleep, further disrupt natural body rhythms which are governed by cyclic hormone releases. When this demand is coupled with the stress response, the body also develops an increased need for carbohydrate by-products which are in effect sugars. So a stressed, ageing and dementing body system now has increased needs for both sugars (carbohydrate) and amino acids (protein), and this produces a carnivorous demand to consume the system's own lean body mass as a means of compensation.

Sugar, in the form of insulin, is a product of amino acids and plays a vital role in regulating both body and brain function and in maintaining a homeostatic metabolism as a whole. When food intake is low, reduced or sporadic, or when the content of food is not well assimilated as occurs under conditions of stress, glucose uptake by the brain is affected. This can lead to confusion, feelings of low esteem and a general malaise – sound familiar?

In dementia care it is a given that people, without assistance, have a reduced ability to sustain their eating and drinking, often due to memory difficulties early on then by sequential processing problems coupled with coordination and recognition challenges. There is of course a price to pay in terms of physical and psychological functioning.

A further effect of low carbohydrate intake and absorption is that the body starts to use proteins for energy (in fact in certain conditions proteins are the body's preferred energy source anyway), and due to calorie restriction this increases the self-cannibalisation of lean body mass. Diet needs to be significantly higher in protein and carbohydrate than we have realised under the above conditions, and lower in fats and salts, to make full use of the protective processes which diet modification can make to the physical and psychological function of the person in your care.

Adaptive response suggest a focus on diet as part of the overall adaptive model which is provided around the person, with individualised meal plans based around the needs of each person. This makes perfect sense when you begin to understand individual differences within a similar experience. Also, if we look at conditions that may further arise within the normal trajectory of dementia, such as that of 'sundowner syndrome', we appreciate that this increased emotional and physical demand, due to increased agitation and the like, will require more fuel to sustain the integrity of the body system. Adaptive response takes into account abnormal requirements such as physical illness or disrupted living patterns and chronic and critical stress. It recognises that these demands need greater energy resources (fuel) and asks that we provide these even to the point of suggesting that when demands are critical supplementation of the diet is provided by artificial nutrient support in the form of calorie-dense, high-protein foods (depending of course on liver and kidney function) other than that which is currently recognised.

It is the emphasis on total function that ensures both the internal and external environments are supported, and it is this true biopsychosocial model that we ask the care provider to offer.

Without this multidimensional approach faulty adjustment and failed adaptation physically and psychologically will persist and you will leave the person unable to self-regulate their environment or make successful adaptive responses to it.

Environmental manipulation and the provision of the prosthetic

The aim of adaptive response is to make the care provider fully aware of the vital role they provide in facilitation of a successful dementia experience in the residential setting (residential meaning social and nursing care provision). The adaptive response approach sees the successful adaptation of the person as being assisted and facilitated by the establishment and this includes the external and internal environments of the individual.

Depending on the person's ability levels, this cocoon of care will range from the simple provision of a place of safety, warmth and comfort through to psychotherapeutic interventions, environmental prosthetics and diet manipulation.

Adjustment and adaptation are the major goals of the model; however, we accept that for some individuals adaptation will not be possible fully due to the progressive nature of the disease process. Therefore, the care practitioner should seek out, at every opportunity, a means of ameliorating this process, and they do this by removing or mitigating attendant stressors – internal as well as external.

If these goals are achieved using a systems approach, every success will be transferable from situation to situation, from environment to environment and from person to person.

5 Adaptive response: the original essay

Dementia is a stressor. Even at its most well lived the dementia syndrome still provides a source of increasing challenge to the resources of the affected individuals and results in a condition of chronic stress punctuated frequently with a series of increasingly acute episodes. At its most purely survived dementia can consist of a regular 24-hour series of gradually more catastrophic, acutely challenging and stressful experiences where relief becomes elusive and tragically less and less frequent.

Put another way, the processes of dementia make the experience of day-to-day living an acute challenge. It is a challenge that I believe can be mediated with educated and timely inputs and where the caring contract may be negotiated to preserve both dignity and quality of life. However, I also believe that without understanding and educated care at various challenging times, the experiences of daily living can prove to become so insurmountable that the person can retreat from 'being' (Kitwood, 1994).

These stressful experiences of living with dementia create an intolerable strain upon psychological and physical body systems and, eventually, through the continuing attack upon its resources, these systems and the attendant immune defences of the body begin to fail.

This failure of the human system to be able to cope with the challenges of day-to-day living and to fight off opportunistic infections, and the resultant damage inflicted on bodily organs and systems, may be one of the major variants explaining the dramatic differences in survivability of the illness.

The premise of the adaptive response model is that armed with the knowledge of human systems and their ability to adapt and adjust, and with a firm application and emphasis on person-centred approaches to dementia care, the experience can be enhanced and living with one of the dementias can be made less traumatic. The findings from many caring disciplines can be fused together effectively to combat this life-threatening reaction to the dementia experience and the adaptive response model is one such multidisciplinary approach.

The rest of this chapter is based on a dissertation presented for the Leeds Metropolitan University Post Graduate Diploma in Dementia Care. It outlines the theories and practical application of the adaptive response model.

Dementia and the effects of stress and unattended emotion upon the human system

Many researchers and medical practitioners have attempted to position stress and emotion in separate contexts. This makes little sense in reality as one is inextricably linked with the other (Lazarus, 1999).

Stress can be said to be positive or negative. But even the most positive of emotions, love, when unchecked can become extremely stressful and cause all types of problematic physical reactions. These are often referred to as psychosomatic from the Greek *psyche–somatikos* which means literally physical illness caused by the mind.

In his most recent update of his own theory on stress and stress reactions, the respected Professor Richard S Lazarus (1999) has presented a new synthesis based on this very position. He has revised the theory of stress and appraisal accordingly, and the involvement of the resultant emotions are shown not as a separate entity as originally proposed, but as an intricate part of the ongoing stress condition.

It is essential for us to understand the basic premise of Lazarus's revised works as it can be juxtaposed for dementia. It is through this new integrated position that we begin to understand that a person will either cope, or not, with the stress of their daily habitat, demands or routine by their personal internal appraisal of how well they are equipped to deal with the challenges presented to them, and in turn this appraisal is associated with its resultant emotions.

What appears to present as little challenge for one person can present as an unfathomable and unmanageable stress producer for another. Internal psychological factors, rather than actual physical ability, appear to be the determinant factor (Selye, 1956).

As human beings we respond to dangerous, threatening or overwhelming situations by subconsciously deploying our most basic weapon of defence: the fight or flight reaction – the release of adrenaline and other hormones to allow our body to protect itself.

If this point of defence is maintained for any lengthy period, cortisol is manufactured and the hypothalamus-pituitary-adrenal systems are persistently activated; this is dangerous to our survival. Another aspect to consider is that this response will occur whether the danger is real or perceived. The same physiological actions result whether thinking about danger or actually experiencing it in real time (Horowitz, 1997).

In the dementia experience periods of doubt, fear and persecution are symptomatic of the losing of memories and abilities. It is pertinent, therefore, to assume that a greater level of overall activation of the adrenal response occurs through these intra-psychic processes.

Defining stress and the stress process

How can we define stress? Stress implies that the environment is felt to be making demands on a person that exceeds their ability to cope (Selye, 1956).

A possible definition is that stress is a situation or condition which places the individual under some pressure, involves adjustment in behaviour and can cause changes which are unpleasant, sometimes maladaptive and even associated with physical damage.

The situation itself is called the stressor and the resulting behaviour as the stress response.

For genuine non-harmful dementia care to become possible it seems essential to always assess the impact another's behaviour and actions will have upon the person. It is vitally important also to remember where there is group living the impact of the person's living environment and their own behaviour on others within it.

If either of these areas can be perceived to have possible stressful consequences that may result in a negative stress response, for either the person living with dementia or those around them, changes must be considered in both approach and the environment itself.

Between the impact of the stressor and the physiological or psychological consequence lies the appraisal.

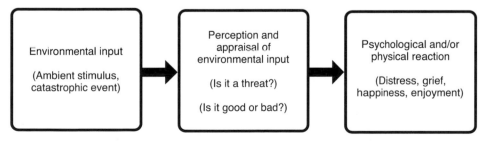

FIGURE 5.1 The three aspects of the stress process (*Source*: adapted from McAndrew, 1993)

It has been demonstrated that unpredictable events are more stressful than those that can be predicted (Glass, 1973) and that when control is felt to be absent the stressor becomes catastrophic.

With damage to regions of the brain thought to be responsible for the storage of memory, people with dementia lose the ability to be able to accurately predict the consequences beyond a stressor. Therefore, they can spend much longer in the appraisal of a stressor than is normal and may feel no ability to control or predict and therefore end their distress.

Time and as much information as possible must be given to the dementia sufferer whenever an assessed stressor is experienced or performed, and a modification to either the caregiver's approach or the environmental load may be required to allow stress deceleration to occur.

The inability to cognitively define consequences creates an intolerable strain for the person living with dementia and can often result in a catastrophic reaction both physiologically and psychologically.

Physiological effects of stress

The body reacts in the first instance to a stressor like an alarm. This alarm call stimulates the body systems to prepare for fight or flight and the sympathetic branch of the autonomic nervous system reacts by releasing adrenaline and noradrenaline.

This leads to an increase in heart rate and blood pressure and an increased blood flow to the brain and muscles. Blood is deviated away from the stomach organs to achieve this and can lead to a feeling of being 'sick' (Tenney, 1997).

If the stress continues the body starts to resist. It burns up its entire energy stores and the person becomes exhausted. Hypoglycaemia can occur at this stage. Body repairs cease and the immune system is reduced; infection and damage becoming much less easy to deal with (Martin, 1997). If the stress continues essential hormones responsible for growth and sex drive may be turned off (Cheek & Rossi, 1985).

At this stage the person feels constantly weary and may suffer repeated illness. If the stressor is removed and the person allowed to recuperate, the system will usually return to normal function (Rossi, 1985). In dementia, however, particularly in the mid and later stages, it is questionable as to whether disturbances in memory will allow a stress-free existence and therefore a return to normal hormonal functioning.

If further stressors are added to this weary and emotionally heightened way of being, the individual enters a third stage, that of exhaustion. Resistance to all forms of stress collapses and there is widespread damage to tissues, often leading to death through infection or stroke (Welch, 1990).

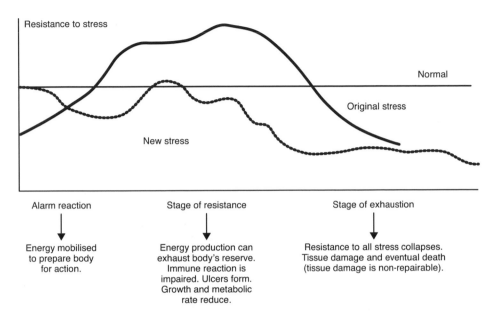

FIGURE 5.2 General adaptation syndrome (*Source*: Selye, 1956)

An elderly person already has a predisposition to many of the above stress consequences. Further exhaustion to the elderly system can prove extremely problematic.

If a person, due to prolonged states of agitation or distress, cannot move out of the stress condition, their immune system may well become greatly suppressed. Their cognitive processes could possibly also become extremely depressed. (This has as much to do with glucose and insulin depletion as to any intra-psychic forces.) This in turn could lead to a condition that moves between personally manageable levels and very confused or retarded thinking that is exaggerated and problematic and which needs external assistance to 'normalise'.

This condition would mimic symptoms exhibited during delirium and may partially be responsible for a percentage of some of the problems that exist in initial diagnosis of dementia when first presented to a GP, for whom direct former observation has not been possible.

TABLE 5.1 The psycho-biology of dementia

Initial adaptive response			Prolonged stress response		
Seconds	Minutes	Hours	Days	Weeks	Years/Decades
Cannon's fight or flight response	Complex adaptive response Mind–body messengers Epinephrine, cortisol etc. Ultradian pulse amplitude Energy mobilisation and use Cognition and performance Cardiovascular tone Cardiopulmonary tone Stress analgesia Immune system Digestion Sexuality Growth		Prolonged stress response Mind–body messengers Addictions Ultradian synchronisation Fatigue Myopathy Sleep Depression Stress hypertension Respiratory problems Anhedonia, alexithymia dissociation Opportunistic infections Psychogenic ulcers Libido		Steroid diabetes Memory and living Psychogenic dwarfism Bone calcification Ageing

Hours after stress

Psychological changes precipitated by stress

The stresses of the changes to psychological functioning associated with brain alterations of the dementia type are immense. Dealing with changes to memory, cognition, recognition and communication produce untold problems and when physical problems of motion and coordination are added the experience appears almost too dreadful.

If stress is added to this equation, which we have begun to reveal is an inevitable consequence of the progression of the dementing process, raised general levels of arousal become a constant feature. Tension, anxiety and depression, which are the features of general levels of arousal (Byrne, 1979), may help to explain aggressive outbursts as a natural consequence of constant arousal and the need to release pent-up energies.

Behaviour may become disturbed not just as a result of the person becoming frustrated in their ability to interpret stimuli appropriately but also through the exhaustion of constant arousal. The person may then experience the feeling of being highly disorientated and, due to reduced coping abilities, reasoning powers may be even further diminished than baseline cognitive assessment and observations would suggest.

Reverse development model

It has been suggested by Perrin and May (2000) that the process of cognitive decline in dementia can be likened to Piaget's developmental theory in reverse. Piaget (1976) suggested that as children mature they go through a number of developmental stages. Perrin and her colleagues suggest that these stages are seen in reverse as the person with dementia attempts to cope with their loss of capabilities. This can be associated with the onion skin metaphor often used in dementia or 'last in, first out'. (Perrin's model is expanded upon in Chapter 7.)

As can be appreciated this model is making assumptions that there is a type of generalised brain deterioration experienced during the dementing process and that this is similar for everyone. It also assumes that the types of ability lost can be linked directly with the 'turning on' of brain ability in the developing child.

I would seriously question any model that attempts to make such broad assumptions. However, this model does provide a framework on which to build a programme for designing types of activity that a person with dementia may be able to perform without outpacing or overtaxing themselves. As Perrin and her colleagues are occupational therapists we see the imposition of a 'world view'; however, this and the Montessori philosophy of 'no-fail activities' sit alongside the ethos of stress reduction.

The model also allows us to see in the context of adaptive response the type of regression and challenge to function the demented person may need to cope with.

It would also seem logical from using a model akin to Perrin's that methods of coping could be found at each stage (adaptation), but that these coping mechanisms would need constant updating and adapting as ability levels decreased. This would again validate the suggestion that adaptation is a constant process in the dementia experience and that the constant need to adjust would produce unavoidable stress-producing scenarios if cognitive ability did not allow the person to make these adaptations.

This idea that an inability to successfully adjust and the person's desire to avoid the stressors this causes may help to explain why individuals develop such dependence on routine and why rituals develop. A type of behaviour is often exhibited when this concreting occurs, which has been characterised by the analogy of the confined zoo animal, where pacing over the same route again and again is evident.

Could this in actuality be a defence mechanism created unconsciously (or consciously) by the individual to avoid the stressor of being unable to predict future outcomes when using other approaches?

This type of coping response in the threat of continued stress can be seen as self-protective, but it can also of itself be damaging and limiting if it persists for prolonged periods. It has been proposed that one of the results of dealing with prolonged stress is a gradual decline into mental illness (Halpern, 1995). It is disturbing to think that some of the more psychotic presentations of the dementia syndrome could be being perpetuated by unresolved stress reactions and that we as professionals are missing the vital clues.

Stress kills. It is our job as professional carers to reduce the stress levels of the dementia sufferer as much as is realistically possible. While not all procedures can be made stress free, we should at all times be mentally assessing our interventions. If they could produce a stressful reaction, we must plan to settle and reassure the person as soon after the event as possible. A person should never be left until you as the agent of intervention have ensured their stress level has been returned to as normal a level for them as possible.

Time is not of the essence but, as we have shown, saving someone's life and sanity is.

The life history and biographical nature of person-centred approaches can help professionals in the formulation of a plan of care based not only on present ability levels but also in assessing the strength of previous coping strategies and abilities and in using these to further strengthen present abilities.

Someone who has never coped well with life's stress and pressure is likely to be more susceptible to the ravages of the dementing syndrome than someone who has shown resilience and durability whatever life has thrown at them.

All approaches to physical, psychological, social and environmental care are to be assessed in the context of the challenges these provide to the individual, and the strength of these challenges are to be measured against the individual's present and future coping abilities.

Where coping abilities are felt to be inadequate, the approach of the carer must include stress-reductionist strategies which, in turn, must ensure than when unavoidable stress is caused, this must be alleviated before any intervention can be said to be 'complete'.

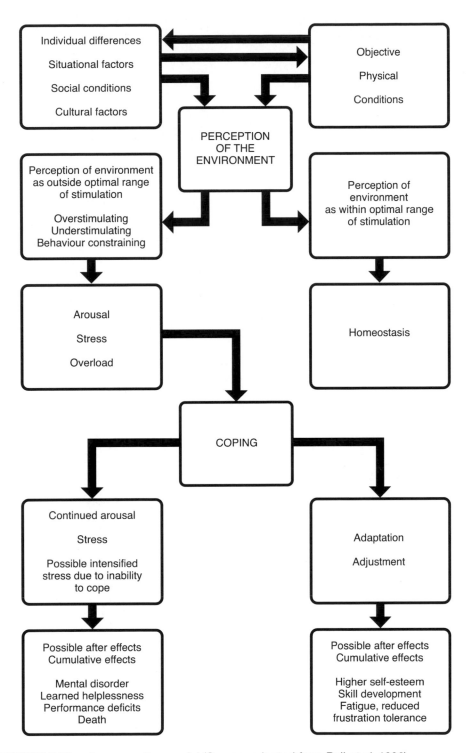

FIGURE 5.3 The stress reaction model (*Source*: adapted from Bell *et al*, 1996)

Learning Tip 10: Dementia and stress summary

Dementia acts as a stressor to the internal system of an affected individual by its alteration in perceptions of the external environment and therefore the individual's reactions to it.

External stimuli from the environment create the opportunity for appraisal. This refers to the person's inner resources and their ability to cope with the presented challenges.

Dementia robs the person of their means of coping successfully with everyday challenges and experiences by reducing their capacity to appraise and predict. This creates stress.

This stress is chronic and is interspersed with acute episodes. Prolonged and compounded stress leads to the state of exhaustion.

This state results in permanent tissue damage, altered ability to cope further, flattened immune system response and to death by either opportunistic infections or by the result of damage done to essential life systems, such as heart, lungs, brain etc.

A caring regime where person-centred 'new culture' approaches are being used can be seen as aiding in effective coping with the external and internal demands of stressors.

CASE STUDY CRITICAL INCIDENT 1: MRS JG, 74 YEARS OLD

Diagnosis
Multi-infarct type dementia.

History
Mrs JG is a widow, and has been for seven years. Her closest relative is a niece who has always been close and visits often but not regularly.

Mrs JG is Scottish but has lived in England most of her married life. She worked as a bookkeeper's assistant, a secretary and as an administrator for a large bank. She retired to enjoy life with her husband who died suddenly from a heart attack.

Mrs JG then lived alone until a series of small strokes made self-care impossible and she was admitted to hospital for assessment. In hospital her condition worsened rapidly and after being in two residential homes she was readmitted with confusion and behavioural problems, which included not eating and incontinence.

Mrs JG's niece was very happy for her to be transferred to our care; however, she was doubtful that her aunt would survive for very long.

On admission

Mrs JG presented as being very frail, underweight and at risk of falling. Her speech appeared pressured and her body posture showed a lot of tension. She refused to eat any solids and was inappropriate in her use of the toilet facilities, often relieving herself where she stood by lowering her underwear and squatting.

She appeared hostile and at times would lash out at fellow residents. She showed marked psychomotor agitation and was dehydrated.

Immediate challenges

- **System integrity**. Increased agitation, tension and stress level all causing an increased demand on body's capacity, coupled with poor nutritional intake and frail condition. It was felt that these factors in conjunction could easily be causing an increase in confusion levels and be leading to some feelings of being overwhelmed, producing such catastrophic presentations as aggression and possible para-suicide in refusing to eat.
- **Failure to eat adequate nutritious diet.** This could already be seen to be causing an acute deficit between system integrity and demand. Increased energy needs due to agitation and tension were not being met externally, hence the frailty of Mrs JG and her likelihood of falling. It was further hypothesised that the decrease in insulin levels would be having an adverse effect on cognition and mood. There was also a risk of infection due to the workload of the kidneys caused by poor diet and fluid intake, and skin integrity was threatened at various pressure sites.

Secondary challenges

- **Aggression**. Mrs JG showed some aggression to other residents and occasionally staff. This, however, was noted to be on physical contact or within her personal space. The aggression was felt to be easily manageable by manipulation of the environment within which Mrs JG resided.
- **Confusion levels**. Within the context of stage of admission it would be

unrealistic to expect Mrs JG to be able to quickly adapt to her new environment or to be able to tolerate the amount of new stimuli provided for her.

Initial system interventions

An assessment was made to ascertain whether Mrs JG had any signs of dysphagia by providing her with a number of differing textured drinks and by the addition of small amounts of highly flavoursome and colourful foodstuffs. (Favourite past likes had been obtained by both interview with the niece and by her being provided with our 'getting to know you' life history questionnaire.) No swallowing difficulties of a functional nature were apparent and although some foodstuffs were untouched, some were taken with gusto; flavoured and textured drinks were also taken well.

Mrs JG was placed on the adaptive response supplement delivery system (ARSDS) and her weight and hydration were assessed on a three-day basis.

Mrs JG was also encouraged to have her drinks and small meals with other residents who had similar ability levels (care streaming) in the hope that the sense of community and the effects of positive modelling would encourage a greater response to eat and drink at mealtimes.

Encouragement was offered at all times and the use of our snack-points was encouraged each time Mrs JG began to wander in an attempt to dissipate her excess nervousness and tensions.

After initial assessment Mrs JD was able to use the lounge area where people with similar levels of ability most comfortably resided. This lounge has specific lighting and decor, as well as aromatherapy diffusers and soft melodic music. Its furnishings are also high enough to provide assistance to people whose musculature has deteriorated due to poor nourishment or frail condition. This allows an extra few inches to help with the initial 'launch' from seated to standing.

Mrs JG was then assessed as to her sleeping habits and it was found that these were often disturbed and that she had a particular problem in getting off to sleep. Various approaches including aromatherapy and relaxing music were tried to ease this problem, also an evening drink, which was high in the amino acid tryptophan. But eventually a three-week period of a mild and non-addictive night medication was prescribed. When this was ended the desired effect of restored energy and sleeping was achieved (Mrs JG now sleeps after her evening milky drink).

The two previously described interventions had a marked effect on Mrs JG's sense of self-worth and on her level of confusion and aggression.

Her energy levels increased so her body stopped using nervous energy and there was a marked reduction in motor activity and in her need to wander.

Her blood sugar levels increased and therefore her cognition and mood increased and hence her ability to tolerate people. As her cognition increased her way finding improved, and guided by the snack-points she quickly made progress around the small lounge area.

Her recent memory deficit, however, still made toilet finding a difficulty. The inclusion of toilet signage discreetly placed near the end lounge snack-point gave the staff a chance to anticipate moves in the general direction of the arrows indicating the way to the toilet. This, coupled with offers of the toilet, made while Mrs JG was involved in exploring, all but ceased the inappropriateness of toilet usage.

Through the use of the 'getting to know you' questionnaires a successful reminiscence programme could be instigated and this helped Mrs JG add some form of attachment to her present surroundings. The use of blending long-term memories with the here and now surroundings created a sense of security for Mrs JG. Her niece joined in these sessions when she visited, which was frequently at first, and this again helped with a blending of the familiar with the new.

These memory lane sessions, which in reality were 24-hour continuous therapy, allowed Mrs JG to be less excluding with her personal space and therefore other people were more forthcoming in their approaches.

Aggression, where not directly aimed at other dementia sufferers, was largely accepted as our problem and not Mrs JG's, and both our approach and the environment were modified to contain its effects. Hugs and kisses were given rather than rebukes where possible and staffs were briefed after any incidents as to the possible casual factors. Detailed scenarios of what other approaches were on offer were given during staff training, and incidents other than very occasional flashes disappeared altogether.

Continuing care

Mrs JG still resides with us. She has had a number of occasions when she has refused to eat – normally – and has returned to the ARSDS. She has formed a number of close staff attachments, and I am lucky enough to be one of them. Her language skills have continued to deteriorate (aphasia), but there are little to no communication barriers as her non-verbal cues are still intact. She appears content with her day-to-day life and appears to be adjusting to the challenges with which she is faced.

Stress and the internal environment

Internal rhythms

Circadian, ultradian and diurnal rhythms are one possible key to understanding fluctuations in the daily performance levels of people affected with dementia.

Each of these pulsatile rhythms causes a cascade of hormones to be released into the system and, as we have already shown, the stress reaction occurring during the person's attempts to cope with the effects of dementia has already begun a series of internal disruptions to these rhythms.

These internal changes may have severely reduced or even turned off vital hormonal production, most of which the internal rhythms are responsible for regulating. These internal rhythms, although disrupted, continue but may become varied in timing (Medina, 1996).

- **Circadian rhythms**. These occur about every 24–25 hours and have two major peaks, the late hours of the afternoon and the early hours of the morning. They affect and regulate body systems and impact everything from heartbeat to the clotting of blood. If certain areas of the brain are affected by dementia or other injury, circadian rhythms disappear completely and variations in function and regulation of hormones occur at totally random times of the day (Mestal, 1998).
- **Ultradian rhythms**. These occur about every 90 minutes and are strongest at night and during sleep. Again these rhythms are responsible for cascading hormones and in enabling the various stages of sleep to be regulated.
- **Diurnal rhythms**. These occur throughout the day and account for people either being morning or night-time performers. As they play a part in consciousness and mental function, these rhythms can cause a severe worsening in abilities in either the morning or the afternoon (Dennett, 1991).

It is important to be aware of internal rhythms when considering the differing ability levels expressed by those people showing excessive swings during the dementia experience. It is also essential that we are aware that at certain times of both the day and the night the person with dementia will be able to perform less well. Conversely, there may be times when the person is at a premium as regards to mental function and physical capability. These times can and should be built into any daily routines in order to maximise the person's ability and experience of their ability. These rhythms will differ between individuals, but most people fall within the norms of circadian function.

The effects on dementia of internal rhythms and their alterations precipitated by stress have yet to be fully explored. However, because this will entail internal temperature monitoring and will need full resident agreement and medical supervision, at present it is not a priority in dementia research or funding. This should not prevent us, however, from using already available research into healthy individuals' reaction to these rhythms, and understanding that changes do occur and that performance is affected at times throughout both the day and night. If we plan for this, we will be encouraging the maximum potential of the person to be realised.

Stress, 'sundowners' and the breaking point

'Sundowner' or 'sundowning' are terms given to a collection of behaviours that occur with some people affected by dementia that are often most pronounced during the early evening period. These behaviours include:

- restlessness
- increased agitation
- wandering searching
- aggression
- shouting
- crying
- indiscriminate incontinence
- increased confusion (Gross & McIlveen, 1999).

It should appear obvious that these are the same type of behaviours we encountered earlier in our exploration of stress and its effects. Could there be a possible link between the disruption to our bodily rhythms, the cumulative effects of stress on the demented person and the behaviours associated with sundowner?

When we couple these biological factors with the progressive damage to brain tissue and function that occurs throughout the dementia syndrome, it would seem obvious that these factors should link together. Also, it seems apparent that this link involves drops in function, with resultant cyclic changes in levels of behaviour and physical and psychological function.

If this supposition is well-founded, it can be postulated that in line with the theory of degrees of dementia (the stage theory), and the effect on personhood and self-image of the social constructs of dementia, that the more positively the dementia experience is lived the less affected by these changes the person would be.

In the physical reality of dementia care, it would appear that those who are engaged in a negative dementia experience are those who tend to exhibit these dramatic 'sundowner' changes.

Based on this as yet unconfirmed position, I would suggest that a model such

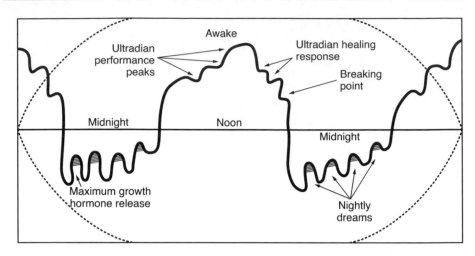

FIGURE 5.4 Ultradian rhythm

as adaptive response, which is based on regulation of stress, and ensuring the adequate provision of sleep and a strengthening of internal conditions by diet, would allow for a re-regulating of bodily rhythms and performance and would remove or reduce the experience of the negative effects of 'sundowner'.

Disturbed behaviours may be the result of altered body rhythm or the effects of unresolved stress upon the person. Helping the person to achieve undisturbed sleep and providing stress-free environments may help in the immediate alleviation of some symptoms.

Sleep, perchance to dream?

Extremely high proportions of people with dementia are reported to have problems with sleeping or with night-time routines. Understanding the way stress and poor sleeping contributes to the person feeling ill or unworthy could also be a starting point for planning our care around the critical or 'breaking points' in the person's daily cycles. Physical and psychological 'tasks' could be manipulated in a person's daily routine to accommodate those times when functioning is predicted to be at its least effective.

It has been suggested that sleep deprivation, less than eight hours per night over a lengthy period of time, causes everything from accident proneness, irritability and depression to the impairment of the immune system and to a greater risk of heart disease and ill-health (Pigarev, 1994).

It has also been found that memory and recall are greatly reduced when sleep is lacking and that glucose reserves are poorly replenished (Concar, 1997). Glucose is required for energy by the brain to maintain optimum levels of function.

Tests at the University of British Columbia by Dr S Cohen (1996) revealed that in IQ tests there was a one-point drop for every hour of lost sleep in healthy individuals.

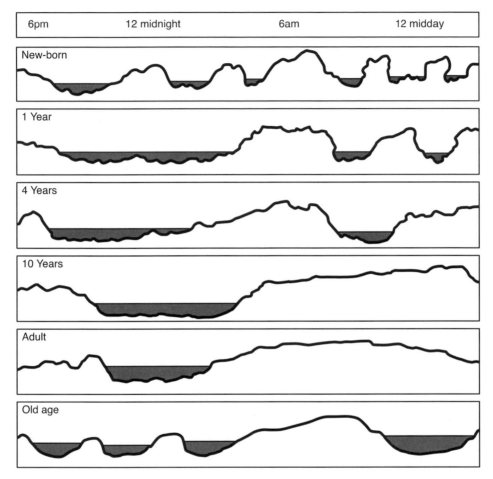

| 6pm | 12 midnight | 6am | 12 midday |

New-born

1 Year

4 Years

10 Years

Adult

Old age

FIGURE 5.5 Sleep patterns at various ages

What of the consequences to someone with dementia?

It would appear that disruption to stage four sleep or 'Deep Delta' sleep may be the most destructive form of lack of sleep. During this stage, the body directs blood flow to the brain and muscles to allow recovery from stress and fatigue. It is also when growth hormone is released for tissue repair and growth.

An interesting piece of research revealing some of the effects of deprivation of stage four sleep found that males actually become impotent from the lack of growth hormone production.

Rapid eye movement (REM) sleep is also of great importance to human function and has been linked with memory, programming (Griffin & Tyrrell, 2004) and the preservation of neurotransmitters (that is, neurotransmitter release is shut down). Interestingly, research has revealed that the two most spared neuro-transmitters during REM sleep are noradrenaline and serotonin (Hobson, 2009).

It would appear also from the evidence that lengthy periods of disturbed sleep are extremely unhealthy and stressful, and that these conditions once again may account for a considerable worsening of the effects of dementia above an expected baseline.

Two ways, therefore, of preventing further damage to the physical systems may be through the direct manipulation of the internal and external environments of the person living with dementia.

Diet and the management of internal stress

Nutrition is a much maligned and misunderstood means of altering both mood and psychological and physical performance.

Nutrition consists of six main areas: protein and lipids, carbohydrates, macro-nutrients, vitamins and minerals. Each plays a vital role in the protection of the elderly system.

Food and nutrients provide the energy and building materials for the countless substances that are essential to the growth and survival of all living things. The manner however, in which these nutrients become integral parts of the body and contribute to its function depends on the physiological and biochemical processes that govern their actions. Disease disrupts these processes, and as continued stress has been shown to lead to disease, stress causes disease.

Diet therapy has long been seen to produce results in the realignment of sys-tems and has been shown to be restorative to some functions (Dodd, 1998). The manipulation of proteins and carbohydrates in particular can have a dramatic effect on the body system and its ability to deal with stress. Diet may make a pro-found change in some instances of dementia, particularly in the more behavioural aspects, and while it can stabilise behaviour and performance it can also help in aiding good sleep. This can be vital to allowing a chance for both stress to be alle-viated and for natural rhythms to be stabilised or even reset.

As rhythms are affected by stress and sleep patterns can be altered it is impor-tant to be aware that some of the weight loss experienced by people in care can be attributed to inadequate nutritional provision in accordance with an increased energy demand over the 24-hour period.

In the late stages of dementia a condition referred to as a non-adjustive fasting response (Mahan & Escott-Stump, 1999) may be present due to the person's inability to eat unassisted or reliance on soft or liquid diets. This state if unchecked will ultimately lead to death through respiratory problems and the suppression of the immune system (Mahan & Escott-Stump, 1999). Meals, therefore, can and should be created during the night where disturbed daytime patterns exist. This may also aid in providing deeper and less disturbed sleep for the periods after eating, particularly when these meals are high in the amino acid tryptophan (Sports Supplement Guide, 1998) as this can induce natural sleep.

Supplements to food can and should also be given at any time throughout the day or night before or after predicted or experienced states of arousal.

Fruit and snacks can be provided in easily visible snack-points (Barrett, 1999). These can be positioned around the home and it should be a priority to keep them well stocked.

Because of some of the effects on memory and attention of the dementia condition people can simply forget to eat or drink. It is important to be alert to this possibility and to ensure that both snacks and drinks are offered freely at both day and night. In instances where food or meals are being missed supplementation should always be considered.

The supplement delivery system

The Caroline Walker Trust has published guidelines for the nutritional requirements of elderly people with dementia (Caroline Walker Trust, 1998). Each meal created from this programme can be designed based on guidance for all the main food groups and essential vitamins and minerals. These menus are high in protein and low in fat. They are, however, generalised and fall short of providing individual interpretations on stressed elderly systems, and they do not account for missed meals.

If a programme like that provided by the Caroline Walker Trust is instigated, the person will be receiving a computer-generated and assessed nutritional package. Three meals per day will provide the optimal conditions for a person to thrive.

However, if meals are being refused or poorly taken it is imperative that supplementation of some form or other be established, and in stress conditions giving six small high-protein meals rather than three large meals has been shown to best preserve and repair the bodily systems (Phillips, 1997). The quick decision to include a supplementation system into the person's daily intake could save a life.

Two supplements the author has used with success to ensure optimal internal function are Met-Rx and Myoplex. These are in meal-replacement sport-supplement formats designed to support athletes during intense training when their stress levels are increased abnormally and their immune systems are suppressed due to their physical and psychological exhaustion. These same internal conditions, we have shown, are present throughout the dementia experience, particularly when the experience is poorly managed or unattended.

Met-Rx and Myoplex are particularly high in protein and their unique proprietary blends are the best sources of protein at present available (*see* Table 5.2). This protein defends the basic skeletal musculature of the person so important for health, strength, mobility and balance. The other ingredients also play a vital role in the prevention of the ravaging effects of stress and can aid cognition.

Metabolic changes brought about by ageing and the effects of stress cause changes to the rate of absorption of the content of food and in the way the body can utilise its properties.

In the tenth edition of the standard syllabus textbook *Krause's Food Nutrition and Diet Therapy* (Mahan & Escott-Stump, 2000), under the sections on old age and dementias, the contributing authors are unanimous in their assertions that specific supplementation should be a standard approach. They further comment that high protein content should be the single most important factor as this will directly compensate for the dramatic loss of nitrogen experienced by elderly people and particularly elderly people under stress or taking in a limited diet.

Both smell and taste are reduced as we age and this is more pronounced in males. The area of the brain damaged by the progress of the syndrome will also have an effect on the person's sense of smell or taste and can remove these abilities completely. This can also be a factor in dementia sufferers neglecting meals and mealtimes.

Presentation of food, therefore, becomes extremely important. Good presentation can mean the difference between the food being eaten or left. Temperature too can be tempting or prohibitive because as sensations decrease so enjoyment decreases. Foods that register in the tart and tangy range may elicit more response than those in the sweet or savoury. Changing abilities will provide the guidelines for individual preferences, and adaptations may be needed over short periods.

Before embarking on a supplement programme exhaust all other possibilities. Supplements are an aid and should not routinely replace food and the experience of dining, particularly with all of its social benefits.

TABLE 5.2 The Met-Rx formula

Serving size 1 packet (72 g)

Amount per serving

Calories 250		Calories from fat 20	
% daily value		% daily value	
Total fat 2 g	3%	Total carbohydrate 22 g	7%
Saturated fat 1.5 g	7%	Dietary fibre less than 1 g	3%
Cholesterol 0 mg	0%	**Sugars 3 g	
Sodium 370 mg	15%	Protein 37 g	
Potassium 900 mg	26%		

Vitamin A 90%	Vitamin C 60%	Calcium 100%	Iron 45%
Vitamin D 60%	Vitamin E 60%	Thiamine 60%	Riboflavin 60%
Niacin 100%	Vitamin B6 60%	Folate 50%	Vitamin B$_{12}$ 50%
Biotin 60%	Panthothetic acid 40%	Phosphorus 90%	Iodine 40%
Magnesium 45%	Zinc 40%	Copper 40%	

Percentage daily values are based on a 2000 calorie daily diet

Calorific values	Fat 9 g	Carbohydrate 4 g	Protein 4 g

In addition each 72 g contains

Chromium 50 mcg	Magnesium 1 mg	Chloride 420 mg	Selenium 30 mcg
Vitamin K 40 mcg	Choline 60 mg	Molybdenum 60 mcg	

No sucrose or fructose added to this product

External stress and its impact: the value of seeing care as a system

When we discuss external environments we include the physical, psychological and social. As we are all part of the external environment to the person with dementia it is ideal that we should be aware of the impact that our interventions and actions can have.

Even though we may have the best of intentions, our actions can be a major source of stress to the person. It is our challenge to develop the skill of promoting interventions that are stress free, or if unavoidably stress inducing that we develop the skill to alleviate these symptoms at the end of the intervention.

'Never be the cause of distress and then leave it unattended. All actions have a consequence; please ensure your actions create calm and contentment as their end product' (Smith, 1997).

The same environment means different things to different people. Depending on a person's background, culture, experience, age and position in life, the same social and spatial conditions are perceived differently and will probably stimulate different reactions (Brawley, 1997). It should be apparent, therefore, that environmental manipulation needs to be a very individual experience, even on an internal level. Many care environments are particularly unhealthy, not only because they feature overcrowding but for the reason the buildings themselves exhibit what has been referred to as 'sick building syndrome'. This refers to the fact that the design of the building and its properties leads to negative responses from those regularly subjected to its effects. These can be lighting, heating, ventilation, space, colour, overcrowding or underpopulation and the generalised combination of any or all of these conditions (Cave, 1996).

Care streaming

One of the ways of applying individualised care in a care setting is that of care streaming (Stokes, 2000). Care streaming in its original concept was about changing the face of dementia care away from the 'one building, all served' philosophy in which people are indiscriminately warehoused, regardless of their abilities, on the strength of the probable diagnosis of dementia.

Care streaming is about individual accommodation for three levels of dementia care:

1   A social model of residential care for those people with degrees of dependency requiring supports beyond domiciliary care.
2   Challenging behaviour units for those people who are disruptive or manifest coexisting psychiatric disturbance.
3   Hospice units for those people in the final stages of gross dependency who are compromised not only by dementia, but also by physical infirmity and frailty. (CareFirst, 1997)

Although the physical reality of care steaming has yet to be realised over any large organisation, a number of specialised care homes where the author was the registered home manager adopted the concept. These units were adapted into three zones, roughly based on the above. Each person was assessed as to their level of ability and then provided with the special adaptations of their living unit.

Each zone was physically assessed as to be meeting the needs of each of its residents while producing positive stress and limiting the negative, as follows.

●   Group A's environment should be entertaining, provide some physical challenges and be constantly a source of mild stimulation.

- Group B should have a protected and safe environment with small areas for individual or small social groups. There should be mild stimulation that can be stopped when overload occurs. Pathways should be clear and lighting should be enough to reduce shadows but not enough to provide glare.
- Group C should have a serene and quiet environment where stimulation is minimal and one-on-one interventions are lengthy and comforting.

Interaction between residents should be facilitated constantly and the good use of the environment will encourage this without unnatural pressures.

Space and stress

Negative and threatening environments can acutely affect an individual. The equations as far as stress production are:

Too much space = negative feelings of fear, abandonment and isolation

Too little space = fear, aggression and suspicion.

Personal space has been calculated at the following values for healthy individuals.

- Intimate (0–18 inches) is reserved for full-contact relationships, such as those involving comforting or lovemaking or occasionally for relationships governed by rules or for heated argument.
- Personal (18 inches – 4 feet) is for friends involved in conversation, where touching may occur.
- Social (4–12 feet) is for business interactions, formal and informal and more formal social interactions, where people are not acquainted and not especially friendly.
- Public (12–25+ feet) would be used for very formal interactions, eg between speakers and audiences, or defensively where interaction is not desired. (Hall, 1966)

From the above, any interactions closer than 18 inches (45 cm) can be assessed as potentially stressful and with a potential for a frightened or hostile reaction.

While personal space is one factor in stress-producing reactions the forming of territorial barriers causes quite another problem. As we have already demonstrated during stress reactions (and especially when coupled with confusion and negative self-image) dependency on routine and structure becomes a major factor of survival.

The recognition of primary, secondary and public territory will prevent unnecessary confrontations and further heightening stress. Rooms, chairs and personal space (which can become extended when confused or feeling threatened) are considered primary territory and an invasion of this area can be seen as a direct confrontation and can heighten aggression or reduce feelings of worth and power if no reaction is possible. Delicate and thoughtful handling of personal space and primary territory must be a major priority in dementia care.

CASE STUDY CRITICAL INCIDENT 2: MR DH, 64 YEARS OLD (DECEASED)

Diagnosis
Early onset Alzheimer's disease.

History
Mr DH developed signs of Alzheimer's disease at around the age of 55 and this had probably been developing for some two or three years. Mr DH had a large family and was a publican. He was originally from Scotland and although resident in England for a number of years, all his children, though being born English, still retained a strong Scottish identity and accent. He was a loyal and vociferous Rangers football fan.

Mr DH had experienced a number of hospital admissions before being admitted to our centre. These admissions along with attempts to settle into previous homes had failed due to Mr DH's aggression.

He had experienced a number of incidences of heavy sedation and his family was extremely depressed and anxious about his care, both past and present.

Mr DH had been a resident of this centre for just over a year when I first encountered him and was given the task of changing practices.

On reassessment
Mr DH was found to be extremely aggressive towards staff and other residents and was also found to be constantly unsettled and wandersome. His body posture was tense and his verbal expressions were generally angry; this, coupled with a degree of dysphasia, made him difficult for staff or other residents to approach or get to know.

His sleeping habits were poor, with nocturnal wandering. He was also doubly incontinent and resistive to help in dealing with it. He suffered from angina and his increased resting rate and constant aggression made his attacks frequent.

He retained memory for his family but would transfer the affection for and name of his wife to his oldest daughter, which indicated that the extent of his recent memory loss was extensive and that he was relying upon past memories to create his present reality (memory roll-back as described by Buijssen, 2005). His wife would sometimes become upset at this and his daughter would approach me in the next six months for help herself in dealing with this transference of affection.

He was obviously hallucinated in both auditory and visual fields and in later life became afflicted with persistent kinaesthetic hallucination as well.

His eating was a problem in the sense that he would eat from anyone's plate and fight over the right to do so. He would also wander if still hungry and take food from those still eating.

He had built up a hostile and territorial relationship with two other gentlemen on the unit and if they met, invariably it would end up with an aggressive exchange.

However, for all these seemingly insurmountable problems, he was very popular with staff and projected a mischievous and engaging personality.

It was through working with people like Mr DH that I began to formulate the way of working that is expressed in this book.

Initial system interventions

It was initially thought that Mr DH's aggression should be tackled as a priority as this seemed to have been a recurring theme in all of his post-diagnosis history.

This was looked at from a number of perspectives, but it was obvious even to non-professionals that the environment and the people mix were probably partly responsible. It also became apparent that Mr DH had a form of tunnel vision and that this was advancing as part of his Alzheimer's pathology.

Any approaches from the side appeared as a sudden intrusion and were met with hostility and startle. It also soon was ascertained that due to the increasing involvement of atrophy to the visual receptor areas of the rear brain that Mr DH could probably only see in shades and had great difficulty in differentiating between distances and depths (spatial agnosia). This of course added to his heightened sense of arousal as he was constantly in danger of having an accident.

Mr DH was a small man and large looming shapes made him anxious and fearful. From his publican background it was revealed that Mr DH had done his own door work and was quite often called upon to protect his property. His reactions now began to make sense to the staff caring for him, and approaches and reaction softened considerably towards his behaviour.

It was also found that in the area where Mr DH was routinely cared for there was a lot of stimulation and external noise. This we appreciated could bring memories to life of the public houses and the type of atmosphere Mr DH had left behind. We decided to try a move to a different daytime environment.

Almost immediately there was a change in Mr DH and in his general posture and behaviour. His body tension began to disperse, although a certain amount of tension never left him, and his facial expression, once so fierce, began also to soften.

Because of the lessening of stimulation in this new environment, Mr DH began to lose his need to eat from or collect others' plates. (This could also be seen as him collecting in the glasses, ashtrays and the like which is a regular part of public house life.) Being in a smaller environment also meant Mr DH could be observed more easily and any confrontations could be averted before they began.

Toileting remained a problem, as the toilet areas were small and for the most part darker than the open spaces. This always caused Mr DH extreme stress and as his Alzheimer's advanced his distress lessened, but this was due to his dwindling sense of self and self-assertion coupled with further losses in awareness rather than any magic cure we found.

In the later and more advanced stages of his dementia Mr DH passively allowed most types of care but still resisted any care to his private areas no matter how carefully and privately this was done. This could well be a sign that even to the very end Mr DH never resigned himself to his disease or there could have of course been other unresolved issues.

Nocturnal wandering was seen as our next challenge as this had an added safety element. An aromatherapy diffuser which contained a combination of ylang-ylang and lavender was suggested by our qualified aromatherapist and a small night lamp that illuminated the new pull-round curtains was also tried.

The idea was to provide a shadow-free environment. Shadows of course could exaggerate hallucination and also create fear on night-time waking. We also attached a wanderguard system to the doorframe, which would alert the staff if the bedroom door were opened from the inside. This allowed the staff to meet and greet Mr DH as he wandered and offer familiarity and security. Within a number of weeks Mr DH stopped wandering at night without any medication other than a hot milky, malted drink before retiring. The heating of milk and the malt allows release of the amino acid tryptophan, a natural sedative.

Some nights Mr DH would lie awake, but he obviously felt secure in his small 'safe' area and did not feel the need to wander or explore.

During his initial treatment plan Mr DH's daughter continued to bath him; however, some sexual transference due to mistaken identity occurred and, after counselling with the daughter, bathing became a staff-assisted activity. The daughter was able to understand the situation with help as she began to have regular access to our service regarding her feelings. Eventually, her mother joined us and this continued until Mr DH passed away at age 69.

Mr DH settled very well on the unit after these initial interventions and remained with us for another five years. During this time he experienced all the ravages of advanced Alzheimer's disease and passed away with pneumonia on Christmas Eve. His family was with him. RIP.

Groups and systems

While most dementia care establishments now work on the principles of person-centred care (Stokes, 1988) and all care is individualised, it should never be forgotten that people living in proximity to each other are classed as groups. We work predominantly with individuals within groups. Group principles must be understood to gain the optimum individual functioning within this context.

Groups can be viewed as systems and we can now present a larger picture of the type of environment that both the person with dementia and the staff member function within when residential care of any form is entered into.

The real secret to good care in care homes

It is the belief of the author that with the professional emphasis being placed very firmly at present upon the person-centred approach to dementia care postulated by the Bradford Dementia Group and the late Tom Kitwood in particular, the realisation that we are nursing people as groups when they are admitted to care has disappeared or at least has become unfashionable.

I assert that without the knowledge of the theory of systems and groups no effective group living can be maintained much longer than the first crisis point. Care from then on will tend to become reactive rather than proactive and will tend to favour the provider rather than the receiver of care.

Karl von Bertalanffy first developed general systems theory, for use in biology, in the 1920s. His work in systems was soon adapted and applied to areas divergent from purely living systems.

The main areas of interest to us in dementia care are in the selective opening and closing of boundaries and in the open or closed flow of information.

Systems work within systems, and although systems can be diverse, a general form is common to all. This form has three functions. A system aims to:

1   maintain its wholeness
2   achieve self-regulation in the face of environmental disturbance
3   progress to higher levels of adaptation. (Von Bertalanffy, 1923)

Systems achieve these functions by opening and closing boundaries and in exchange with the environment.

Using systems perspective, we can immediately see that we are caring within a living and developing environment, and that our social and physical environments will not remain static.

Every action changes the stability of the system and must have a consequence that allows that stability to be re-established. If the consequences cause change, which removes the stability of the situation, a 'breakdown' will be the result. This breakdown can be to the system of care, the safety of the environment, the safety and integrity of the person or to the social fabric of the establishment. Disturbance in the living environment of the person suffering dementia can increase stress in the appraisal and coping mechanisms and this will need the carer's input to re-establish homeostasis.

Groups are social environments that need certain features to function as a stable system. Groups are in a constant state of flux, they are dynamic and are constantly changing, but like all systems they seek to return to stability (Berne, 1966).

When disturbances occur in the stability of the whole group, tensions will be heightened and can lead to crisis points. If successfully managed, these crisis points can actually be useful in that they can allow a situation to become expressed and therefore allow change and a return to stability (Bion, 1949).

All people in the care system need to be cared for as part of the bigger system. Although their care will be individual, the mistake must never be made of thinking care can be provided 'in a vacuum'. All individual care must be seen as integral to reinforcing the stasis of the group or environment. The whole is greater than the sum of its parts.

Adaptive response and groups

Adaptive response is a model of caring for someone with dementia in a group living environment, but it has principles that can be applied away from this setting. However, it is not about treating anyone as any less of an individual just because it takes a societal overview. It presupposes an acquaintance with person-centred care and the concepts of personhood and malignant social psychology. It also presupposes a thorough knowledge of the physical and medical models of dementia and its biological basis.

Adaptive response blends the model of environment, both external and internal, with the psychobiological stress-reactive model of holistic total care.

It sees a person as a system functioning within a larger system. It states that both these environments can be manipulated to allow maintained homeostasis. It uses the manipulation of both the real and perceived environment to enable greater personal function.

It sees real value in nutrition to strengthen internal resources and to manipulate hormonal function and system stability, and it appreciates that at certain points the person will have raised or reduced abilities based on this internal environment.

It proposes a method of using environmental and social psychology to maximise function in the individual and to minimise the negative and destructive elements of the perceived and real environment.

Most of all, adaptive response states that dementia care is not reactive; we do not have to wait for the person affected to make mistakes or to become ill and

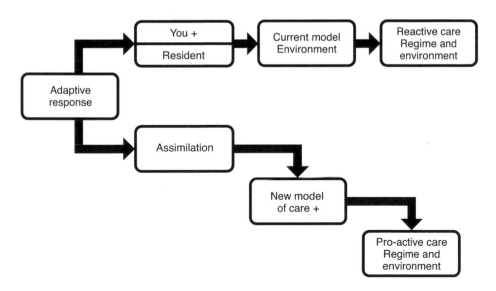

FIGURE 5.6 Adaptive response: proactive care

dysfunctional to use our skills. It hypothesises that given the wealth of multidisciplinary knowledge that exists in related sciences, dementia care can be a proactive service. Dementia care can precede the person and plan for their possible future needs.

Adaptive response is designed to be developed. It says there is a better way. It presumes to be only one part of an answer. It is now up to us as professionals to adapt its principles and assess its assertions in practice.

6 Stress: **concepts**, considerations, appraisal and **stress** thresholds

Stress and its effects

Contemporary discussions about stress started when the word 'stress' jumped from the engineering field to field of psychology in the 1940s (Cooper & Dewe, 2004). However, contemporary scientific exploration of stress only began in earnest during the 1950s, when Hans Selye (1956) found predictable patterns in animals' efforts to adapt when he exposed them to adverse stimuli like extreme temperature and radiation.

Cannon (1914), Selye (1956) and Harold Wolff (1953) would separately explore how the body is a dynamic organism that responds to stimuli to maintain normal body functions and protect itself from the environment, but it was Richard Lazarus (1991) who would change the understanding of stress when he proposed that attitudes, beliefs and expectations influenced how individuals perceive and are influenced by stress.

In the 1960s, researchers began to shift the focus of stress research from physiological reactions to psychosocial factors and this led to studies of stress in the workplace that affect employee stress (Cooper & Dewe, 2004; Jex, 2002) and currently we understand stress as being a combination of physiological and psychological reactions in the face of interpretation (conscious and unconscious) of social and environmental factors.

The physiological and psychological effects of stress were outlined in Chapter 5 and are presented in the panel below in more detail.

PHYSICAL STRESS: EFFECTS OF STRESS ON THE BODY

- Headache
- Chest pains including pounding heart
- Muscle aches and pains
- Back pain
- Clenched jaw and teeth grinding
- Shortness of breath
- Stomach upset – constipation and diarrhoea
- Excess sweating
- Tiredness
- Sleep problems
- Weight gain or loss
- Sex problems
- Skin problems

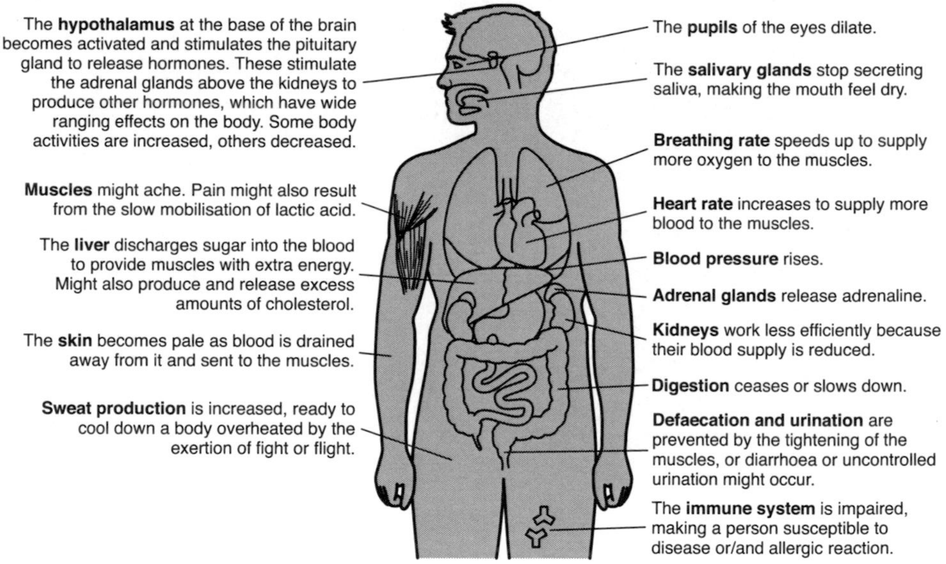

The **hypothalamus** at the base of the brain becomes activated and stimulates the pituitary gland to release hormones. These stimulate the adrenal glands above the kidneys to produce other hormones, which have wide ranging effects on the body. Some body activities are increased, others decreased.

Muscles might ache. Pain might also result from the slow mobilisation of lactic acid.

The **liver** discharges sugar into the blood to provide muscles with extra energy. Might also produce and release excess amounts of cholesterol.

The **skin** becomes pale as blood is drained away from it and sent to the muscles.

Sweat production is increased, ready to cool down a body overheated by the exertion of fight or flight.

The **pupils** of the eyes dilate.

The **salivary glands** stop secreting saliva, making the mouth feel dry.

Breathing rate speeds up to supply more oxygen to the muscles.

Heart rate increases to supply more blood to the muscles.

Blood pressure rises.

Adrenal glands release adrenaline.

Kidneys work less efficiently because their blood supply is reduced.

Digestion ceases or slows down.

Defaecation and urination are prevented by the tightening of the muscles, or diarrhoea or uncontrolled urination might occur.

The **immune system** is impaired, making a person susceptible to disease or/and allergic reaction.

FIGURE 6.1 Effects of stress on the body

EMOTIONAL STRESS: EFFECTS OF STRESS ON THOUGHTS AND FEELINGS

- Anger
- Anxiety
- Depression
- Mood swings
- Excessive worrying
- Forgetfulness
- Lack of concentration
- Negative attitude or apathy
- Sadness
- Feeling insecure
- Irritable
- Restlessness
- Guilt
- Job dissatisfaction

Stress and dementia

A balancing act: good and bad stress

We all think we know a little about stress. We have all been stressed and many of us will have experienced distress, but if you are reading this book it is likely at this point you have managed to return to a normal state of arousal – you have achieved a sense of homeostasis. Life without stress is impossible, but achieving just the right balance between good stress that arouses and stimulates with just the right amount of distress, a state that taxes and challenges but ultimately is not harmful, is a magnificent balancing act.

It is a balancing act that ultimately depends upon how our psychology, physiology, environments and present circumstances act upon one another to allow our 'minds' to remain comfortable and confident that we are not in danger, that we can cope, and in certain circumstances that we can thrive.

A species with predisposition to stress

Of course almost all examinations of stress as a concept begin by telling you about why we get stressed, about why we need stress and about how if we remain stressed over long periods bad things happen to our physiology. Most modern examinations also discuss the differences between modern humans (in evolutionary terms) and our early ancestors who needed a very active system of early alerts to maintain basic life systems, or – in language we all understand – to avoid being eaten.

So by discussing the model of the hypothetical 'triune brain' (introduced briefly in Chapter 2) we perhaps should also start by looking at why we have such a strong predisposition as a species to stress and why this is a good and a bad thing.

It is much too simple to say that in dementia stress is good or bad; it is more accurate to state definitively that too much or too little stress is bad for everyone irrespective of the labels we place upon each other. One thing we can state, however, is that the condition of dementia certainly appears to place us in a very vulnerable place as to the effects of stress.

Perhaps the simplest and most emotive description of the human brain is Paul MacLean's triune brain. The triune model, as the name suggests, distinguishes just three regions: the neocortex, the limbic system and the reptilian brain.

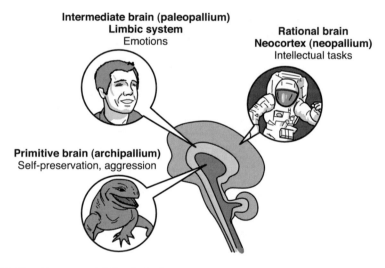

FIGURE 6.2 The triune model illustrated

MacLean (1990) has proposed that our head holds not one brain, but three, each representing a distinct evolutionary stratum. He proposes that each layer of the brain has formed upon the older layer before it as we have evolved over millennia. The theory, although purely hypothetical, does fit very closely with the evolutionary theories of the brain and in particular with evolutionary explanations for our senses, especially with the tricky subject of sight and perception.

MacLean (1990) says that 'three brains' operate like 'three interconnected biological computers', and each has its own special intelligence, subjectivity, sense of time and space and its own memory. These 'three brains' are labelled as if they developed as part of our species' evolutionary journey from the reptile through the early mammals and into modern humans. The neocortex becomes the 'neo-mammalian' brain; the limbic system becomes the 'paleomammalian' system; and the brainstem and cerebellum, the 'reptilian' brain.

Each of the three brains is connected by nerves to the other two, but each according to MacLean seems to operate as its own brain system with distinct capacities.

This hypothesis has become very influential, particularly in popular science and psychology writing, and has forced a rethink of how the brain functions. It had previously been assumed that the latest additions to the brain in evolutionary terms and the highest functioning in terms of cognition, the outer (neo)cortex, dominated the older and lower levels. MacLean has shown that this is not the case, and that the evolutionarily older limbic system, which rules emotions, can hijack the higher mental functions when it needs to.

Daniel Goleman has used this hypothesis to underpin his 'business' best-sellers on emotional intelligence versus intelligence quotient. He also uses the research which shows that the limbic system's early response to threat, or perception of threat, fires up significantly faster than the higher order cognitive 'damping' mechanisms of reason and rationality.

> **Learning Tip 11: Influence of the triune model**
>
> Although usually oversimplified, the triune model has influenced how the general public now thinks about brain functions. The model serves to remind us that stress can be very pervasive and why you must understand that when cognitive abilities are eroded such as in the dementias, you must act as a physical filter to too much or too little stress for those you care for.

Brain changes and adaptive responses

The limbic system, the primary seat of emotion, attention and memory retention, contains the structures of the hypothalamus, hippocampus and amygdala. These structures working together help determine valence (whether you feel positive or negative towards something) and salience (what gets your attention) and they also contribute to flexibility, unpredictability, and creative behaviour.

This area, with its upward interconnections with the neocortex, ensures that brain functions are never either purely limbic or purely cortical but a mixture of both. As dementia begins its destructive pathway through the brain, the way a person experiences life begins to differ from the normal.

It is not just the loss of neurons, or of the mighty 'stuff' that it is now postulated that may lay between neurons, in the synapses where information is transferred from neuron to neuron where our 'personalities' may reside according to the connectome hypothesis, or even the physical shrinkage and loss of tissue mass that changes the way people experience life in dementia. It is also, crucially, the way that these remaining brain areas communicate with each other and respond to environmental demands that is changed and continues to change across the course of the disease.

Learning Tip 12: Constant adaptation

It is important to realise the significance of the above paragraph, as the brain structures change and erode, the brain itself is therefore involved in a process of constant adaptation and as the brain adapts, the ways in which the person experiences the world will become more and more personally subjective.

The individual, therefore, remarkably adapts their abilities day to day, perhaps moment to moment, in order to be able to continue to function and communicate in the world. This is a most remarkable thing about persons living with a dementia – they persist in involvement, in participation and in many cases in active coordination of their environments despite massive amounts of brain insult. So the next time you engage in caring just take an extra second or two to really appreciate the specialness of the person in front of you.

Stress compromises brain function and, as we will see, the equipment required to keep the emotions in check becomes most compromised of all and this can lead to the syndrome of 'overload'.

Importantly for us as carers, we now know through the last 20 years of research that the brain is not fully compromised, effects are not fully global as once thought and certain structures appear to remain intact even in the face of very advanced Alzheimer's disease (Jones & Miesen, 1992–2006). As dementia is progressive this means that compromise comes relatively slowly and we can plan our care based on a 'probable' hypothesis of damage and coping associated with length of time from onset.

Progressively lowered stress threshold (PLST) model

A model that greatly mirrors the proposition of care featuring an awareness of the need to adapt our responses is that of the progressively lowered stress threshold model developed by Hall and Buckwalter (1987).

The PLST model is used to assist formal and informal caregivers in understanding behaviours and planning of care for persons with dementia. The model addresses three dimensions of a dementing illness and the interaction of these dimensions across the disease process:

1   Losses associated with cognitive decline and their accompanying symptom clusters
2   Behavioural states
3   Stage of the disease process.

Losses accompanying cognitive decline are clustered into four groups:

1   Intellectual losses
2   Affective or personality losses
3   Planning losses
4   A progressively lowered stress threshold.

The model focuses on the fourth cluster by postulating that progressive cerebral pathology (as seen in people with dementia) is accompanied by a progressive decline in the stress threshold. A reduced tolerance to stress is reflected in the altered proportion of behavioural states.

I agree with Hall and Buckwalter's suggestion that as the stress threshold declines over the course of the disease there is a progressive reduction in normative behaviours and an increase in anxious and dysfunctional coping behaviours (such as agitation).

In adaptive response I am building on this hypothesis by suggesting that care regimes based around this knowledge may compensate for the overload effects of stress on someone living with dementia. If the hypothesis is correct, we are absolutely required to assist in this reduction more and more as the person gradually loses more and more control over their built and social environments.

Hall and Buckwalter also show that during the course of a single day the threshold for stress significantly rises and falls. As I have shown in Chapter 5, there may be a number of integrated factors that impact this fluctuation. One is our body's own natural rhythms and the other is environmental overload.

In care homes there are some features that appear universal – such as breakfast, dinner and evening meal – and not surprisingly these are usually 'group functions'.

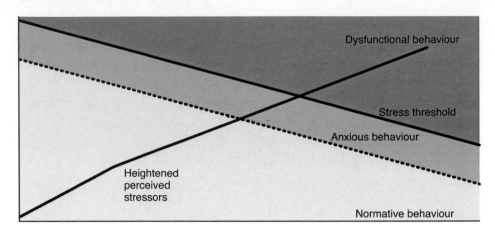

FIGURE 6.3 PLST model: reduction in normative behaviours and increase in anxious and dysfunction behaviours

These are times when people not only are challenged by the demands of using utensils and navigating limbs and tools but also by the demands to socialise in an 'acceptable norm' while filtering out the distractions of noise and hustle and bustle.

It should at this point come as no surprise to you that we see some catastrophic behaviours around evening meals and that often this is blamed glibly and without much actual evidence on the 'sundowning' syndrome.

Behaviours that challenge arise in many people living with dementia around this evening timescale. I suggest it is our regimes that often precipitate these reactions. When our natural rhythms dictate our lowest natural threshold for dealing with environmental demand we, in care homes across the world, at this very same vulnerable time, launch into the complex multiple demands of the evening group meal.

Rementia and adaptation

In Chapter 3 we touched on Tom Kitwood's proposal that, given the right care conditions, a halt (even reversal) of decline in persons with dementia was possible, a rehabilitation process he called rementia. It seems entirely logical to me that under research conditions the physiological as well as psychological basis for rementia could be proven. I am hypothesising that by manipulating the reduction and control of stressors in the built and social environments of those living with dementia significant improvements in quality of function, which would directly equate to improvements in quality of life through better coping, are entirely possible in line with Kitwood's assertions.

The person's dementia does not 'get better'; however, their ability to 'cope', to function and to normalise their reactions in line with demand would all improve. By simply altering the environmental demands we alter the stress threshold.

Dementia Care Mapping (DCM) and PLST

Bradford Dementia Group worked with the British Standards Institute and a panel of healthcare experts in the UK to develop the guidelines for Dementia Care Mapping. It is a method for improving care practice for people with dementia. Taking the view of the person with dementia, the DCM tools help staff teams to develop person-centred practice and to improve care for residents.

A quick look at the enhancers and detractors indicated in the latest version of DCM shows clearly the correlation between detractors as stressors and the enhancers as control of stressors or prevention of stressors by the care regime.

Detractors:
- intimidation
- withholding
- outpacing
- infantilisation
- labelling
- disparagement
- accusation
- treachery
- invalidation
- disempowerment
- imposition
- disruption
- objectification
- stigmatisation
- ignoring
- banishment
- mockery.

How many of us could fail to be stressed and distressed in a world where the above were common features?

Enhancers:
- warmth
- holding

- relaxed pace
- respect
- acceptance
- celebration
- acknowledgement
- genuineness
- validation
- empowerment
- facilitation
- enabling
- collaboration
- recognition
- including
- belonging
- fun.

Conversely, how many of us could fail to respond and act differently in a world where the above were the common defining features?

So what is DCM really mapping? Although it fails to account for it explicitly, it is measuring the features of the care regime as an indicator of the stress threshold the built and social environments impose upon the individual recipients (inclusive of the malignant psychology of Kitwood explicitly).

While the PLST studies referred to earlier regarding stress thresholds and the effect of decreasing tolerance to stress across the 24-hour cycle are not explicitly accounted for within DCM, there is a need to clearly show the time of assessment within the 24-hour cycle. (DCM does ask for timings of observation periods to be made explicit but no direct correlation is drawn with biological occurrences within the internal environments of those observed – a detail perhaps open for inclusion in the next version.)

An important assumption of the PLST model is that all behaviour has meaning, which is our current hypothesis for behaviour that challenges in dementia and that, therefore, all stress-related behaviour has an underlying cause (Hall & Buckwalter, 1987). This also correlates strongly with the work of Stokes and Stokes and Goudie as previously described.

The model identifies the following six factors that contribute to stress in those with dementia.

1   Physical stressors (eg pain, discomfort, infection)
2   Misleading stimuli or inappropriate stimuli

3   Change of environment, caregiver or routine
4   Internal or external demands that exceed functional capacity
5   Fatigue
6   Affective response to perceptions of loss. (Hall & Buckwalter, 1987; Hall *et al,* 1995)

Assessment of the temporal patterning of agitation over a 24-hour period reveals that persons with dementia usually experience relatively few stressors in the early morning hours. However, as stressors accumulate, the person begins exhibiting anxious behaviours such as loss of eye contact and increased psychomotor activity (eg restlessness). Without intervention, stressors continue to accumulate until the stress threshold is exceeded, usually by mid-afternoon, resulting in severe agitation characterised by cognitive and social inaccessibility (Hall & Buckwalter, 1987). In the preceding chapter I demonstrated with physiological examples some of the contributing factors for this agitation.

The person living with dementia then cycles between states of anxiety and severe agitation if the stress threshold is repeatedly exceeded and this vulnerable state rises and recedes at certain times of the daily cycle.

A similar hypothesis for people with mental health needs is being assumed as part of the three-year Hearts and Minds project for mental health service users in South London (Riches, 2012).

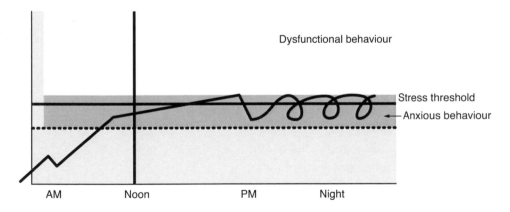

FIGURE 6.4 Stress over the 24-hour period

If we were to use this data and add the assumption of adaptive response that we have a duty to intervene and control the stressors and then to plot our interventions – adaptive responses – we would presumably wish to apply therapeutic intervention in a way illustrated in Figure 6.5.

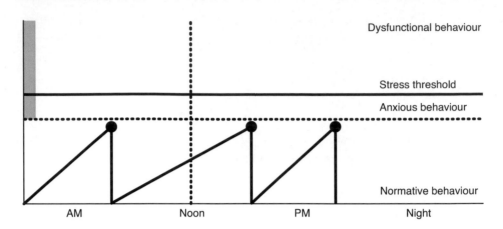

FIGURE 6.5 Therapeutic intervention during the 24-hour cycle

The person is assessed for breaking points in their daily life within the care home and where these points become known interventions are planned by the care teams in order to prevent the person experiencing arousal leading to stress threshold breach.

Cyclic interventions based around this model account for the effects of too much stress by facilitating high-functioning lives, but intervening before too much stress becomes a problem. Conversely, by understanding the theory of too little stress the staff would offer stimulation during those parts of the day where boredom and lack of stimulation could lead to the need for catastrophic behaviour in response.

Care in care homes then becomes proactive rather than reactive and begins to approach a therapeutic regime desired but so often absent in modern care.

Principles of the PLST model and therapeutic interventions

The six principles of the PLST model, according to Hall and Buckwalter (1987), provide the foundation of care for the person living with dementia.

1   Maximise safe function by supporting losses in a prosthetic manner.
2   Provide unconditional positive regard.
3   Use anxiety and avoidance to gauge activity and stimulation level.
4   Teach caregivers to observe and 'listen' to patients.
5   Modify environments to support losses and enhance safety.
6   Provide ongoing support and assistance for informal and formal caregivers.

These principles are used to equip caregivers with the knowledge and skills to recognise the subtle behavioural changes indicated by heightened anxiety and arousal in those in their care in an effort to provide timely and appropriate intervention.

Efforts to establish effective means of behavioural management for the person living with dementia is done in an effort to diminish the adverse outcomes experienced by both the person and their caregiver.

The premise of adaptive response is that we can respond before negative behavioural responses arise. In essence we try to eliminate the necessity for these behaviours arising by controlling the built and social environments. When and if these reactions do arise we have an understanding of the controls we must exert to assist in rapid de-escalation of the stress threshold.

Stress and the development of dementia

'Stress, like Einstein's theory of relativity, is a scientific concept which has suffered from the mixed blessing of being too well known and too little understood' (Dr Hans Selye).

Why does an understanding of stress and its effects matter? Stress and the body's reaction to stress is likely to turn out to be much more important a concept in dementia than the mere controls we may be able to exert once dementia has developed.

I have long thought that much of the development of Alzheimer's in particular may be found to be a natural immune response to an unnatural coping ability to stress oxidants in the brain – toxicity, if you like, to stressful events. How often have we heard the story of the wife or husband whose spouse dies suddenly and the person then seems to develop all the signs and symptoms of Alzheimer's disease?

A link between stress and the development of dementia has been hypothesised for 30 years or more. However, recent research from the University of Kuopio in Finland has also found a link that suggests that the effects of long-term stress may be one of the major causes of dementia. The stress-release hormone cortisol entering the bloodstream regularly and circulating through the brain is thought to kill cells, leading to Alzheimer's. The research found that patients with high blood pressure and high levels of cortisol resulting from stressful lifestyles were three times more likely to develop Alzheimer's than those who did not have these features.

It is likely that these 'type A' personalities continue to react to stress negatively once they have the disease and this may again be a factor, as I suggested earlier, that leads to some of the variation in survivability of the disease and the severity of the disease in individuals.

Professor Clive Holmes of the University of Southampton is investigating how the stress we are all affected by may become a risk factor for the development of

Alzheimer's. He believes that something such as bereavement or a traumatic experience – possibly even moving home – may be a potential factor. Understanding this is the 'first stage in developing ways in which to intervene with psychological or drug-based treatments'.

Interestingly, in the context of this book and the adaptive response approach, Professor Holmes revealed they are looking at two aspects of stress relief – physical and psychological – and the body's response to the experience.

Other emerging research confirms that stressed middle-aged women are 65 per cent more likely to develop a dementia. Scientists at Gutenberg University in Sweden found those who complained of repeated periods of stress, including irritation, anxiety or related sleeping problems, were significantly more likely to develop dementia in old age than those who led worry-free lives (Johansson *et al*, 2010).

Unique brains and responses

I have introduced the concept that stress affects the brain and the mind, and by that you may conclude that I am stating for our purposes that brain and mind are one and the same. However, it would be hard for me to outline an argument within this short volume that they are completely separate entities. I am fascinated by philosophical arguments that although one appears to arise from the working of the other, the mind itself may be a different property from that of chemicals, electricity and inherited DNA.

Each brain as we have previously stated is slightly different from another, and some brains like Einstein's brain are remarkably different from others, and this is one more reason to constantly see the uniqueness of each individual in your care.

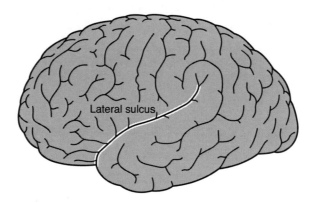

FIGURE 6.6 Lateral sulcus

Studies of twins and savants also show clearly that different brains produce different people with different skills and multiple intelligences.

If the way we think and interpret the world are the result of our mind operating out of the physical processes of the brain and its anatomy, it follows that different brains produce different minds and that minds develop from the interaction between the brain and the outside world – the nature/nurture argument.

What is now becoming apparent, however, is just how much this ongoing outer world interaction can actually shape the physical structure and function of the brain itself. While this book does not have the capacity to explore this concept fully I would urge readers to research this subject further as it is acutely critical for acceptance of the adaptive response premise.

We can see that we have different brains and that our 'minds' will also be different. This means we will all react differently and assess and respond to our environments differently based upon just how different we are from each other. The same stimuli will be interpreted differently by different people and they will react accordingly. This is true of stress and true of the experience of dementia.

How on earth did we ever operate a care system that essentially treats everyone the same just because they have the same diagnosis?

Responding individually to social and built impacts

Responding individually to social and built impacts has implications for us as carers of people living with a dementia.

First, the person's stress response system will be triggered by anything that creates a state of arousal or alarm and their automatic defences will be activated whenever they perceive challenge in their environment and we know with the losses and changes to memory that almost every 'new' social interaction and almost all environments will produce challenges.

Second, the research of Lazarus and later stress researchers building on his theories has shown that these threatening or challenging events actually don't even have to take place or be real. Often it is enough simply to imagine them for the stress response to fire up. So someone experiencing roll-back memory could begin imagining terrible scenarios simply by their memory not syncing with the evidence of current experience.

Someone wakes at night and sees two strangers in their bedroom; they believe they have woken in their own bed in their own house where they lived with their wife for the last 50 years. The stress response will be activated intensely and this is likely to be a scenario that happens multiple times during the night – most nights.

No matter how caring you are as one of these two intruders, for the person you are the cause of their stress response.

Adaptation to stress

The system triggered by stress is called the alarm system. Its purpose is to alert us to any threat or challenge so that we can be better equipped to deal with it. But difficulties arise when we are threatened over and over again, or when we are constantly challenged, or when we begin to live in a perpetual state of emergency. When this happens, what was designed as a protective agent begins to be harmful to us. This is when ordinary stress begins to damage us.

If our bodies are repeatedly held in a constant state of alarm, they soon begin to show this as a reduced stress threshold, with damaging consequences. So-called psychosomatic disorders, which have both physical and psychological causes, are often consequences of this loss of stress resilience.

In addition to damaging the body's defence systems, stress can also lead to illness by disrupting normal physiological functions more directly and damaging the tissue of the body. There is an even more subtle way in which stress can cause illness. The high level of adrenaline sparked by stress reduces our ability to rest. It cuts down on our apparent need for sleep, and creates poor eating habits. This, in turn will take its toll by causing further illnesses and damage.

Another factor that complicates the stress picture is that of 'hidden stress' or, more accurately, 'hidden stressors'. Sometimes we cannot always feel distress even when we are, in fact, experiencing it. This is because we are all born with an amazing human trait – that of adaptability.

This is the negative side to adaptability. Our bodies can adapt to circumstances that in the long run are harmful to us, such as when we carry too much stress for too long a period of time. We can see this in stress that raises blood pressure. The blood pressure goes up and stays up, and it will not come down very easily again. It is all a part of our adaptation capabilities, only here the adaptation is destructive.

When you experience a lot of stress for a long time, your body adapts to this prolonged stress by keeping you in a protracted state of 'fight, flight or freeze'. Furthermore, our adaptation to higher stress arousal can occur in response to stressors that we don't even know exist or, at least, don't recognise as stressors. They influence us at the unconscious level, causing our bodies to react with elevated blood pressure or muscle tension, even though we are oblivious to what is causing stress.

Recent research has illustrated how chronically activating the stress mechanism can damage the immune system, the cardiovascular system and even the brain (Norden, 2007).

Although most brain research takes a functional perspective, this fails to look at work by Lazarus and others which clearly shows that the way people emotionally experience and interpret the world 'has a profound effect on our physical and mental health'. Research is showing the damage stress can do to the human system and this is important because we have shown that people living with a dementia due to difficulties understanding and controlling their environments often cannot control the stress reaction this brings. Thus, even where there is no danger, damage occurs from continuously activating the stress mechanism when no real danger exists; this damaging stress is caused by perceptions and reactions to stressful events, not by the events themselves.

Norden (2007) explains that genetic and environmental factors influence how people experience, interpret and react to perceived stressors. Children develop coping skills based on their personality and temperaments, and these coping skills are carried into their adult lives. Coping skills vary between individuals, and factors such as family, culture, religion and context add to developing coping strategies. These coping strategies appear to 'influence how people interpret events as stressful or incidental, and reactions to perceived threats become habitual' (Hart, 1995).

An important insight gained from systems thinking into adaptation is that the human is an active being who grows and thrives by solving problems, not by avoiding them, so stress must be present at some level for a healthy organism to thrive.

Contemporary stress research tends to consider environmental factors as annoyances and threats that need to be fixed, reduced or eliminated so that people can achieve a stress-free state before the stressor causes the system irreparable damage.

Systems theory (see next section) seems to provide a more complete understanding by saying that efforts to reduce or eliminate stress completely are not only wrong; they may be exacerbating the problem. Adaptive response states that when a person can no longer deal healthily with life's challenges we should facilitate compensation.

Rather than seeing stress as a negative force, adaptive response sees stress as a vital catalyst for growth and survival for individuals, organisations and societies. Systems theory recognises that the lack of stress, a state of equilibrium, means death to a biological system. Excessive and prolonged stress, however, is the condition that harms the organism and that is when we must step in with compensatory strategies.

Dealing with individual responses to stress

Stress has different meanings for different people; different people respond differently to stressful situations. However, just as people interpret and respond to experience through individual perspective, adaptability practices may ultimately be individual. It is those people who have always struggled with the stress of life who are likely to become much more vulnerable than others when they are confronted with the changes and challenges of a dementia-type illness.

It is only by applying person-centred approaches that this individuality will be recognised and acted upon.

Important findings that provide insight into how to deal with individual interpretation of stress is that panic attacks are triggered by known events and that they are a consequence of misfiring the fight-or-flight mechanism. Identifying and understanding 'triggers' in the case of panic attacks can help to reduce anxiety and thus stress. This is achieved by providing a sense of predictability as the foundation for effective coping.

Understanding the mechanics of conditioning and triggers allows us to look for indicators of stress-inducing stimuli and to then removing or adapting them (perhaps to a stimulating rather than disabling extent).

Schwarzer and Taubert (2002) discuss a cognitive-transactional theory of stress that recognises the reciprocal and continuous interaction between the individual and the environment which helps us understand how we can intervene within this interaction when needed.

In this framework, stress is how people appraise and interpret environmental events that they perceive will tax their resources or threaten their well-being and this may be on a conscious or unconscious level. Building on this stress framework, Schwarzer and Taubert proposed a proactive coping theory, which provides functional strategies that use goal-oriented and long-term behaviours to allow people to anticipate and handle perceptions of stressors positively.

Put simply, this means that people can learn to mitigate stressful situations by understanding the way they interpret them. Our premise is that when this can no longer be achieved by the individual an external buffer is required.

Due to the complexity of stress, especially in social contexts, coping cannot be understood by simply understanding and managing fight-and-flight and rest-and-relax modes. Viewing stress through only one perspective provides an incomplete picture that limits adaptability; but a dynamic systems perspective seems to provide a more complete assessment that integrates elements of many theories.

It is clear that the consequences of stress are the result of the dynamic interaction of environmental factors, severity, length and association of events, and the individual's perception – particularly of their interpretation of their ability to cope.

A person's perception of events is influenced by the physiological, psychological and spiritual state of the individual, which is moderated by the social environment the individual finds themselves within.

Perception determines whether the individual considers events as insignificant, a challenge, or a threat. Perception also determines how a person musters their coping strategies, although as dementia advances this becomes much more of an unconscious reaction.

The reaction then influences the result; that is, whether the person adapts or declines. Decline decreases the individual's ability to cope and adapt, and threatens damage to the individual's psychological, physiological and spiritual well-being. This is likely to lead to a continuous threat to their coping abilities, and as the system fails to adapt to changing environmental demands it atrophies.

This understanding of stress as an adaptive process lets us see the importance of thinking about ways of intervening in a systematic manner and the following section looks a little further at systems.

Systems thinking and applying a care programme

One of the things that changed the way I practise and has been a liberating influence is working with an understanding of systems perspectives (there is not really a unified theory of systems, more a set of collective principles).

A general description of systems thinking is the process of understanding how things influence one another within a whole entity. In nature, this may be elements of an ecosystem interacting in interdependent ways; in organisations, it may be the interaction and linkages of people, structures and processes that work together to make it healthy or unhealthy. Systems thinking has been defined as an approach to problem solving, by viewing 'problems' as parts of an overall system; it sees components of a system in the context of relationships with each other and with other systems, rather than in isolation.

This section offers a short primer of systems thinking and how you may use this approach when thinking about applying an adaptive response approach within your care centre.

Systems and systems thinking to make the change

'No man is an island entire of itself; every man is a part of the main. ... Any man's death diminishes me because I am involved in mankind, and therefore never send to know for whom the bell tolls; it tolls for thee.'

—John Donne (1572–1631)

A system is an entity that maintains its existence and functions as a whole through the interaction of its parts. The behaviour of different systems depends on how the parts are related, rather than on the parts themselves. Therefore you can understand many different systems using the same principles.

Systems form part of larger systems and are composed in turn of smaller subsystems.

The properties of a system are the properties of the whole. None of the parts has them. The more complex the system, the more unpredictable the whole system's properties; these whole-system properties are called emergent properties – they emerge when the system is working.

Breaking a whole into its parts is analysis; building parts into wholes is synthesis. You gain understanding through both analysis and synthesis. When you take a system apart and analyse it, it loses its properties. To understand systems you need to look at them as wholes.

Detail complexity means there are a great number of different parts. Dynamic complexity means there are a great number of possible connections between the parts, because each part may have a number of different states.

Each part of a system may influence the whole system. When you change one element, there are always side-effects.

Systems resist change because the parts are connected. However, when they do change it can be sudden and dramatic. There will be particular places where you can effect large changes with very little effort once you understand the system. This is known as leverage.

Thinking in circles

Systems thinking is thinking in circles rather than in straight lines. The connection between parts forms feedback loops. Feedback is the output of the system re-entering as its input, or the return of information to influence the next step.

There are two types of feedback:

● Reinforcing feedback is when changes in the system come back and amplify a change, leading to more change in the same direction. The system moves away ever faster from its initial point. Reinforcing feedback can lead to runaway exponential growth.

- Balancing feedback is when changes in the whole system feed back to oppose the original change and so dampen its effect. It leads to less of the action that is creating it. Balancing feedback keeps the system stable and resists attempts to change it.

All systems have a goal – even if that goal is only survival. The goal is its desired state, where the system is at rest and balanced. Balancing feedback acts to reduce the difference between where a system is and where it should be. It drives the system towards a goal.

Feed forward is when prediction or anticipation of the future influences the present in a way that leads to a self-fulfilling or self-defeating prophecy.

There is almost always a time delay between cause and effect in systems. The feedback loop takes time to complete. The more complex the system, the longer the feedback may take to appear. If not taken into account, time delays can lead to overshooting and oscillation, or if the effect is badly underestimated can lead to a complete failure of the system.

Mental models

Mental models are the ideas and beliefs we use to guide our actions. We use them to explain cause and effect, and to give meaning to our experience.

Our mental models themselves form a system. We need to understand our own mental models because we use them to make sense of other systems.

Mental models are created and maintained in four distinct ways.

1   Deletion: selecting and filtering experience, blocking out some parts.
2   Construction: creating something that is not there.
3   Distortion: twisting experience, reading different meanings into it.
4   Generalisation: one experience comes to represent a whole class of experiences.

There are a number of factors to consider, however, that will produce misleading feedback.

- Regression. Extreme events are unrepresentative as a basis for prediction and misleading if a change towards the average is taken as evidence for the effectiveness of a course of action.
- Time focus. Unfocused effects can occur any time after their presumed cause.

Focused effects are limited to a particular time horizon. Unfocused effects are not reliable evidence.

- One-sided experiences. These are where only one result is memorable, anything else being a non-event.
- Two-sided experiences. These are where any result is memorable. Two-sided, focused experiences provide the best feedback for mental models.

Cause and effect

In systems, causes are relationships between influencing factors rather than single events.

Systems thinking exposes three mistaken beliefs or fallacies of change management.

- Cause and effect are separate and the effect comes after the cause.
- Effect follows cause closely in time and space.
- The effect is proportional to the cause.

Closed systems are isolated from their environment.

Chaos theory deals with complex systems where a small change in the initial conditions can make a huge difference. Complex systems therefore are not predictable. However, there may be some simple rules at the heart of very complex systems.

- To deal with complex systems, define the boundaries of the system. Look for attractors (stable states where the system tends to settle).
- To change a complex system, destabilise the old attractor state. Create a new attractor state.

Moving beyond logic

Logic alone is inadequate to deal with systems. Logic cannot deal with self-reference, where a statement refers to itself. To solve the paradox of self-reference, you need a systems view, or metaposition, outside the frame of reference.

The best leverage points for change are often the mental models that are supporting the structure of the system. To effect positive changes we often need to change the way we initially think and develop a new perspective.

New perspectives

A perspective is a point of view. Systems thinking looks at how experiences relate, how they go together to form the greater wholes. It is important to have many different perspectives to get as full a picture as possible and to widen your mental models.

There are two fundamental perspectives:

1   An objective view is looking at a system from outside it.
2   A subjective view is looking at a system from inside it.

Systems thinking uses both views.

Which view you adopt depends on how you define the boundary of the system you are considering. There can never be final objectivity, because you can never stand completely outside the system of which you are a part.

The subjective perspective divides into:

● your own perspective from the inside out, and
● someone else's perspective.

Your mental models, and those of others, are also part of the system.

Solving problems using systems thinking

Systems thinking suggests some useful questions to ask, and as we explore alternative ways of looking at assessment to achieve positive results a little later this perspective is illustrated.

The first questions are:

● What do I want?
● What have I got?

In trying to achieve the goal a balancing feedback loop has been set up, which is driven by the difference between what you have now and what you want. It is best to always be explicit about both of these positions.

Second, you need to ask:

● What stops this problem from being resolved?
● How is this problem being maintained?
● What am I doing that is maintaining this problem?

These questions will get to the structure of the problem without blame.

Third, you need to look at the feedback you have.

● What are my results so far?
● What have I learned from them?

Lastly, look at the mental models you are holding about the problem.

● What am I assuming about the problem?
● What am I assuming about the people or processes involved?

Learning Tip 13: Applying a systems perspective

Systems thinking or using a systems perspective should form your attempts to introduce an adaptive response model into your current caring practices. You should always see the residents and yourself as occupying a unified space within the larger system – when you make a change to one part of the system it will change other parts of the system and you must be ready for this.

When applying a systems perspective you will need to be able to see the connections within the overall system. You should never simply expect to change just one aspect of practice as the bigger picture must be appreciated; otherwise, you will simply knock the system out of sync.

Your efforts must be ongoing, and just as using an adaptive response approach allows you to see the care process as a biopsychosocial process so you should see the care home as an open system.

The truth about systems is that they are only as strong as their weakest parts and any changes you make must account for these weaker areas. Changes will take time and the efforts you exert will very likely have a delayed impact. Because they will need to work through the various loops of the system the final results will only be visible at some future point, but to get to that future point you must get started right now!

What does it mean to use a systems programme in dementia care?

The label 'task orientation' rears its head when we see the word programme, and rightly so – we would be horrified at programmes such as 'toilet rounds' or 'feeding' and 'bath times' in today's healthcare systems. (They still exist, and if they exist in your system you now know what to get beginning on changing.)

So why has a programme approach made such an impact in Canada, Italy and America if it's such a bad thing? Should we even discuss care programmes in a book such as this or would that be turning back the clock?

If we think about it we are all programmed. When we rise, we wash, dress, sometimes eat and head for work where we do the very 'tasks' that fulfil our job description. We return home and hopefully unwind with social activities or maybe we care for the family. We go to bed, we sleep. Then we rise …

We don't feel as if we are task orientated; we feel we have a system or routine that suits us. It may seem as if we are doing what most everyone else of working age is doing but actually it's unique to us by the connections and people who populate our system.

If that system changes in ways beyond our control we try to correct it; it traumatises us until we do. If we can't correct what went wrong we feel loss, we feel angry, depressed, helpless and out of sync even if it is just a small part of our routine that has been altered. We now know, using a system perspective, that one small change will in fact change all connections and that making one small change requires adjustments across the entire system.

When someone develops a specific form of dementia they go out of 'sync' within their lives too. Things change beyond their control. They lose the ability to put things right without help and because dementia is predominantly but not exclusively associated with old age, they also feel that the end has just driven into sight.

When the system cannot be put right and the person moves too far out of 'sync' for them to continue their normal lives, they come to live with us – in a care home. Ask yourself this question: at the end of your working life do you want to choose, right now, to live in a nursing home? I didn't think so.

We may think it best for someone who can no longer cope to have help and live in a care establishment. Sometimes this can be the case and people choose to live happy and productive lives in care establishments, but the predominant attitude to care homes is that of dread. It is also never as easy as a simple admission – between developing symptoms and being admitted to care a thousand and one losses are experienced by the person.

Not least – in person-centred terms – is the loss of self. Self is considered the essential ingredient in the personhood model of dementia care. The self is the part of you that is different from me. It encompasses your personality, your hopes, dreams and wishes and your unique life history. When someone develops dementia this does not change.

It is proposed that in the process of dementia the failing of brain processes and the death of some structures causes the structure of mind to retreat or alter somewhat, allowing a person's sense of self to be damaged or lost. When this process occurs the person feels fear, dread and extreme sense of loss. We have all at one time or another asked the old question 'Who am I?' and if we accept the mind as a product of the brain or as arising from within it, damage to this organ may indeed begin to change this internal representation of 'self'.

Meeting needs

Much problematic behaviour can be seen in the context of this loss of selfhood. Some cognitive behavioural approaches to behaviours that challenge have been tried and they have had some level of success. However, an approach that combines psychotherapeutic working with environmental modification has proven to be most successful in the removal or modification of behaviours that are problematic to both the person experiencing dementia and to the care staff dealing with these behaviours.

The approach involves the use of resolution work (Goudie & Stokes, 1989) as we have discussed in Chapter 3, and more recently the Colombo Approach, rather affectionately called the Newcastle Model after its region of origin (James, 2006).

With resolution work the approach is to meet needs and not manage problems. In dementia care when we talk of 'problem behaviours' we are usually describing one of two things: behavioural deficits (acts of omission) and behavioural excesses (acts of commission). In terms of dementia acts of omission are those dependent actions we observe and wish were not present, and acts of commission are acts of independence we observe that lead to worry or distress and which we also wish were not present.

Incontinence may fall into the first category whereas wandering or striking may fall into the second. In our terminology we can very clearly see the 'model' of our care.

Referring to behaviour problems or problematic behaviour is a negative assessment of someone. Referring to needs or to the behaviour itself as being the challenge is a more positive reframing, and this is much more in line with an adaptive response philosophy. 'Mr Brady is withdrawn' could well be restated as 'Mr Brady needs companionship'. The medium is social contact, the need is the person living with a dementia and the solution lies with us.

Learning Tip 14: Reframing behaviours

If 'Mr Brady is incontinent' becomes 'Mr Brady needs to achieve dignified relief every three hours' we are left with a positive action plan from a seemingly negative starting point. This reframing of behaviours is characteristic of a listening and learning approach to care which we must adopt to perform person-based assessments.

If we apply this needs-based approach to some of the more common behaviours expressed in the dementia syndrome we can find genuine attempts to communicate.

So immediately we have become person-centred in that the need belongs to the person but the problem belongs to us. As carers we must find the solution to the need. We must change the physical and social environment to fulfil our role as carer.

If we really look at some of the possible causes for both behaviours of commission and behaviours of omission, we as caregivers must understand that it becomes our role to formulate plans to enhance, relieve or compensate these attempts to communicate.

Dementia causes many areas of difficulty, from simple memory loss to problems of judging depth and distance, from mistaking words to seeing objects that don't exist and from feeling very depressed to being constantly active. But dementia also causes the person to doubt their place in the world, to lose their significance.

A counselling approach, therefore, should always run alongside any interventions in dementia care. Person-centred approaches advocate the principles of Carl Rogers and his client-centred (person-centred) approach, and Garry Prouty (as we mentioned briefly in Chapter 2) has applied these principles to those with much reduced capabilities with broad success.

So it should never occur to us that because someone does not appear to see us or hear us that they are any less worthy of being involved in communication or offered stimulation.

If we treat people as objects, eventually they will react in that way.

After looking at dementia, person-centred care, stress and the adaptive response model we can see the need to be constantly seeking ways to compensate for negative arousal through manipulation of the built and social environments (systems), areas we can control as they are mostly within our powers to do so. Therefore, the final two chapters will discuss these two areas that directly impact on the well-being and reduction of stress upon this growing and vulnerable population.

7 Manipulating the social environment

Activities, occupation and the forming of therapeutic relationships

It is vital that older people feel worthwhile, that they have a sense of self-importance and control and that they feel they can contribute and hold influence over their own lives.

If we look closely at those people living with us, and then assess which areas of their daily contribution to the life of the care home we could enhance to meet the above needs, without a doubt it is the level and degree of activities and occupation.

Activities need to be designed to meet the basic need for inclusion and involvement, and each person individually needs to be meaningfully occupied. Activities should not be childlike, should be in groups and individually, and should be created around a strengths-based model. Everyone should have a meaningful assessment of their abilities to participate within an activity and occupation programme, and then this should be tailored to the person's specific needs. I personally like to use the Pool Activity Level (PAL) tool devised by Jackie Pool for occupational profiling (*see* www.jackiepoolassociates.org/pal), and this would fit with the information that follows as I have used a theory from Tessa Perrin so this approach and tool can be adopted.

This does not imply I feel the Perrin model is fully realised, but as a metaphor for understanding the approach I describe as care streaming, where individuals are able to live in small groups with others based on similar strengths and abilities, it is as good a starting place as any.

What is meaningful occupation?

Occupation does not only mean a 9–5 job. It means any purposeful activity that provides a sense of accomplishment and fosters self-worth.

Does activity then differ from occupation? Yes and no, in that both imply doing, but one implies a 'greater payback' emotionally. Activities for older people have historically focused on play, such as bingo, word puzzles, draughts and the like. But what do we do when a dementia has progressed and abilities to perform cognitively demanding tasks are severely diminished?

The stage theory of occupation (a developmental model)

One of the most well-known figures currently working in dementia care is the occupational therapist Tessa Perrin. She and others who follow her occupational models work in applying stage thinking to occupation and activity in dementia, and this thinking may be one of the models we can apply that will make activity work productive for those in our care by applying adaptive response thinking.

Simply put, her 'developmental model' offers Piaget's developmental theories in reverse. This model was outlined briefly in Chapter 5 and is expanded upon below.

Piaget was, among other things, a psychologist who was interested in cognitive development. After observation of many children, he posited that children with normal development (that is, without any cognitive disability) progress through four stages and that they all do so in the same order. These four stages are described below.

- **The sensorimotor period (birth to 2 years)**. During this time, Piaget said that a child's cognitive system is limited to motor reflexes but the child builds on these reflexes to develop more sophisticated procedures. They learn to generalise their activities to a wider range of situations and coordinate them into increasingly lengthy chains of behaviour.
- **Preoperational thought (2 to 6 or 7 years)**. At this age, according to Piaget, children acquire representational skills in the areas of mental imagery, and especially around language. They are very self-oriented, and have an egocentric view; that is, preoperational children can use these representational skills only to view the world from their own internal perspective.
- **Concrete operations (6/7 to 11/12)**. As opposed to preoperational children, children in the concrete operations stage are able to take another's point of view and take into account more than one perspective simultaneously. They can also represent transformations as well as static situations. Although they

can understand concrete problems, Piaget would argue that they cannot yet perform on abstract problems, and that they do not consider all of the logically possible outcomes.

- **Formal operations (11/12 to adult)**. Children who attain the formal operation stage are capable of thinking logically and abstractly. They can also reason theoretically. Piaget considered this the ultimate stage of development, and stated that although the children would still have to revise their knowledge base, their way of thinking was as powerful as it would get.

Adaptation: assimilation and accommodation

In Piaget's theory of development, there are two cognitive processes that are crucial for progressing from stage to stage: assimilation and accommodation.

- **Assimilation**. This refers to the way in which a child transforms new information so that it makes sense within their existing knowledge base. That is, a child tries to understand new knowledge in terms of their existing knowledge. For example, a baby who is given a new object may grasp or suck on that object in the same way that they grasped or sucked other objects.
- **Accommodation**. This happens when a child changes their cognitive structure in an attempt to understand new information. For example, the child learns to grasp a new object in a different way, or learns that the new object should not be sucked. In that way, the child has adapted their way of thinking to a new experience.

Taken together, assimilation and accommodation make up adaptation, which refers to the child's ability to adapt to their built and social environment.

It is worth noting that it is thought now that not every child reaches the formal operation stage and that developmental psychologists now debate whether children do go through the stages in the way that Piaget postulated at all.

Whether Piaget was correct or not, however, it is safe to say that this theory of cognitive development has had a tremendous influence on all modern developmental psychologists and it is relevant to our model and specifically may help with using assessment to plan activity and occupation within a centre.

Perrin's model demonstrates three types of ability level that spans four stages of dementia: early, early to mid, mid to late and late.

(The validity of this model may be doubted; however, as a way of simply explaining the need to apply varying activity and occupation programmes for those living with a dementia, it is hard to beat the applicability of the approach.)

One of the problems of course when using a stage theory is that most people, most of the time, will either be in two or more categories simultaneously and thereafter constantly fluctuate between grading determinants. But as you can see from Table 7.1, a delineation of this sort can prove helpful when designing for ability. However, using the term care streaming, where people are cared for in smaller groups based around shared abilities and weaknesses, allows us to be accurate in our caring. (The Pool Assessment Tool is an excellent resource in achieving this methodology.)

TABLE 7.1 Perrin's formulation

Developmental stage	Reflective	Symbolic	Sensorimotor	Reflex
Stage of Dementia	Early Dementia	Early–Mid	Mid–Late	Late Dementia

Source: Perrin and May (2000).

If we use these broad areas to look at the type of abilities suggested for each of the three main groups we find the following:

TABLE 7.2 Nature of stage and abilities suggested for the three main groups

Early dementia	Early to mid stages	Late-stage dementia
Aware of others and broad environment. Equality of relationships and able to adapt to the world	Increased inward focus and relates the world more to self than self to the world. Perceives their environment as shrinking and becoming more dependent in relationships	Inwardly focused with environment shrunk to a very narrow focus (bubble)
Flexible of thought and able to handle multiple stimuli		Dependent on other with the world within (me). Little evidence of structured thought, loss of language with little evidence of symbolic use
Deductive reasoning with good use of language	Concrete in thinking. One stimulus at a time. Lack of direction in thinking. Language impairment, increased reliance upon symbolic representation	
Nature of activities	Nature of activities	Nature of activities
Goal directed, rule orientated	Increasingly inappropriate with loss of rules and goals	Imitative and reflexive, circular and repetitive
Competitive	Symbolic and representational	Sensorimotor
Cooperative		Solitary/one to one

Source: Perrin and May (2000).

Learning Tip 15: Creating win–win situations

One of the most important aspects of designing activities or creating meaning-ful occupation is ensuring that the person is not outpaced; that is, avoiding any intervention that is too fast, too complex or too difficult for the person to cope with at any point in time. Outpacing can result in the person being left lost, floundering and feeling helpless and belittled. This is not what we are aiming for.

What we are aiming for is a match. With the correct use of assessment and the right choice of activity or occupation we have a win–win scenario. I consider that the model put forward by Perrin will go a long way towards creating rewarding win–win situations.

An explanation of developmental stages

As discussed, Perrin and May (2000) have suggested applying Piaget's theory of development in reverse. This helps us when we look at counselling needs in that we may be able to see some of the related fears as being associated with the loss of certain abilities. We may also be able to appreciate that the cognitive ability to explore situations or circumstances in relation to life stages may no longer be pos-sible, and that we should move from a counselling relationship to that of helper or carer.

The stages we will explore are that of reflective, symbolic, sensorimotor and reflex. These stages, as demonstrated above, are progressive and correlate to a specific stage in the advancement of the dementia syndrome.

The reflective

This stage begins as the first effects of the dementia syndrome begin to occur. At this stage mental capacity is still fully functional for planning, organising, working together with others to achieve outcomes and to make decisions made on memory and foresight.

One's position in the world is still fluid and many options remain open. Language skills remain and the relationship with the world remains positive and dynamic.

The symbolic

During this phase, as in the reverse of Piaget, there is a lessening of conceptual thought and language begins to be affected. Attention begins to narrow and the environment becomes less global and may even be seen as threatening, as thinking becomes concrete. Reasoning becomes less effective and is often distorted by the impression that the world now impacts on the person rather than they themselves being able to manipulate the world. The person becomes more egocentric and the use of symbolism is strong. Multiple stimuli now create confusion.

The sensorimotor

By now even symbolic representation has begun to diminish and the person begins to function more and more at a basic and reactive level.

The world now begins to appear through the various senses, though these may be damaged due to the ageing process. Although activities can still be performed, they are often performed on 'instinct' with little understanding behind function. Speech is now only reminiscent of clear language and there is little evidence of directed thought. Object relation and the use of specific transitional objects are strong features of this stage.

The reflex

This is the late dementia stage which some mistakenly refer to as being 'vegetative'. If we use the developmental model we can see this stage as being akin to the stage of childhood before the brain has developed its special skills but is nevertheless still a functioning tool.

In this stage we find that function is reflexive and reacts directly to the input from the outside world with little evidence of knowledge of separation between the person and the world in which they exist. 'Where do I end and where does the world begin?'

The world has become closed at this stage and 'living in a bubble' would be a good analogy for the person's level of relationship to the outside environment. Eventually, even this level of functioning recedes and the person retreats even further into themselves. Depending upon neurological and other system damage, in the later stages of severe dementia only random neurological signs are evident.

Using the developmental model with adaptive response models

Throughout this chapter, for practical application of adaptive response, you will find reference to the above stages of need. In each of the areas where we care for the person with dementia we allude to the ability level of the person; this model helps us to look at a disability and plan our activity/occupation accordingly.

The disability model is a 'best practice model' for dementia care as it focuses our assessment on not only what the person cannot do, but also on what the person can.

Using the reverse developmental model enables us to work within the framework of adaptive response while offering help, be it counselling, activity or meaningful occupation. So, in accordance with the developmental model discussed above we can begin to match activity to ability levels.

TABLE 7.3 Matching activity to ability level

Early Stage	Early–Mid	Late Stage
Nature of activity	*Nature of activity*	*Nature of activity*
Goal directed	Increasingly inappropriate	Intuitive/reflexive
Role orientated	Rules difficult to follow	Circular/repetitive
Competitive	Little ability to compete	Sensorimotor
Cooperative with group	increasingly solitary	One-One

		Types of activity	
Games	Music	Massage	Singing
Sports	Dance	Cooking	Rocking
Quizzes	Art	Rummaging	Holding
Discussions	Movement	Balls, bubbles	Squidging
Crafts	Drama	Balloons	Non-verbal
End-product tasks	Pottery	Gardening	Stroking
Newspapers	Spiritual	Snoezelen	Cuddling
Reality-orientated	Reminiscence	Dolls, soft toys	Dolls, soft toys
Planning	Story telling	Folding	Snoozelum

Source: Perrin and May (2000).

Learning Tip 16: Using blended theories in dementia care

It is time to add understanding to your physical working tasks as this is where the real beauty and pleasure of dementia care begins. You now have a number of converging theories regarding the person you care for and it may seem you need to pick those you find more relevant or that you have understood better.

As you become more skilled and as your education around dementia and dementia caring progresses, your application to your working practices of many blended theories will increase your enjoyment of your work. Remember, in a system approach it is all about seeing the whole picture not reducing it to its parts.

The following sections introduce two more theories that are essential to understanding the essence of why adaptive response thinking came into being.

Learned helplessness

The basic belief that underlies all our interventions with service users is that we believe everything we do is to the benefit of the person. The theory of learned helplessness, however, tells us that this may not always be so.

In 1967, American psychologist Martin Seligman, and colleague Steve Maier, carried out behavioural experiments involving responses to stimuli. It was discovered that by inflicting painful electric shocks to dogs, and by rendering them so that whatever action they took they could not avoid the pain, the animals learned effort was useless and began to simply receive the shocks. This was the case whether there was a possibility of avoidance or not (Seligman & Maier, 1967).

The dogs suffered without trying to save themselves. Seligman commented that they had learned that responding and reinforcement are independent. Seligman described this state as 'learned helplessness'.

You may wonder what an experiment such as this has to do with the care of people in care environments. The answer could be a case of life or death.

The theory of learned helplessness has been further extended to humans (but not by experiments with electricity I hasten to add). It would appear that not only do people need to expect some control over their life and their environment but they actually need control. The effects of having no perception of control over events and destiny, Seligman believes, are truly dramatic (Seligman, 1975).

He believes that the effect of having no control over life events can lead to stress, depression and even death. He makes this chilling link after observing the effects of Voodoo curses and on the death of service users in nursing homes. In both cases the persons seemed to have resigned themselves to a complete inability to exert any influence over future events and outcomes and both died. They had learned that they were helpless.

The implications of these findings seem to indicate a direct link with what we can do for the people in our care and what we should not. If the perception of helplessness and of not being able to influence events leads to stress, depression and death, the act of empowerment takes on even more significance in our caring strategies.

Can instilling a sense of control enhance physical and psychological well-being?

There are authentic reports and studies that indicate reducing learned helplessness does lead to more positive outcomes from illness and that even mortality rates have seemed to be reduced (Langer & Rodin, 1976).

While relevant to all nursing, the theory of learned helplessness must carry even more importance in the field of older person care and in particular the older person living with a dementia-type syndrome.

A person once admitted to a care home often has no control over this event and even less in the subsequent days and weeks. They lose their home, their routine, their family, lifestyle, food choices, favourite TV programmes, privacy and in some cases even dignity and identity. We, without often even realising, control all of these elements and we are unwittingly and unthinkingly contributing greatly to the beginning of feelings of learned helplessness. The admission period into a care home must be seen as a very distressing and possibly destructive time, and we must all become aware of this and begin adapting our responses from this very minute.

In nursing homes in particular, 'helplessness' is often assumed, unlike 'real life' where the opposite is true. People are expected in real life to be able to cope. It is suggested by Posner (1994) that it is a disadvantage to have abilities in a nursing environment, as nurses are equipped to deal better with incompetent behaviour. Incompetence and dependency are rewarded by nurses with more time and with more physical and psychological contact. Competent behaviours are often ignored as the nurses feel of more use dealing with the dependent.

One experiment conducted by Langer and Rodin gives a very clear indication of the effects that perception of control had on a group of nursing home service users. One control group was given an intensive discussion on increased responsibility and the process for decision making. They were then given the opportunity to choose a small plant and were informed it was their task to look after it as their own over the coming weeks and months.

A second control group had a plant placed next to their bed and were informed that it was the staff's job to care for it.

Three weeks later it was found that the first group were happier, more mentally alert and more active than the comparison group. Differences were maintained over an 18-month period.

The most exciting thing about this experiment is how easy and simple it seems it is to ward off the effects of learned helplessness.

It would seem that one of the issues Nystrom and Segesten (1994) have identified as being detrimental to good psychological health is the 'power' differences between staff and service users in nursing establishments. The above experiment could serve as an example. Some carers would think to involve the resident in a decision such as that of caring for a plant, while others would just automatically assume the plant would die without their care.

They point out that the powerful in the establishment (the nurses or carers) need to refrain from defending their powerful positions and to allow its redistribution.

To make full use of the theory of learned helplessness it is essential that nurses and carers examine our reasons for feeling more useful when engaging with residents' physical rather than psychological needs and why we feel the need to manage the system rather than assume our position within it.

Learned manipulation

But can all maladaptive responses and reactive depression in care be attributed to controlling and physically orientated nurses and carers and be explained by the theory of learned helplessness? Could there be other possibilities?

White (1959) contends that some residents use passivity and dependence as a tool to manipulate staff and therefore alter their environment. Service users may have realised that the more dependent they are the more staff time and attention they will be allocated.

This is a very different position from being out of control and unable to influence anything; in fact, this could easily be seen as effective adaptation.

Staff should be very careful, therefore, not to label behaviours that seem non-productive as learned helplessness. This could just as easily be termed 'learned manipulation'. These residents are successfully manipulating their social environment. This view is strongly supported by other authors who have examined the care and nursing home environments.

The other problem with only a superficial understanding of the theory of learned helplessness is the effect on the resident when staff begin to expect more than can be actually achieved. Nurses and carers could be expecting greater involvement by individual residents in the belief that this will ward off stress and depression, or slow down generalised deterioration.

Learning Tip 17: Too much or too little?

Overtaxing of the person can be as damaging as not extending them, and both it would appear can have far-reaching consequences. It is hoped your understanding of dementia and stress will now allow you to assess each situation systematically and then plan how you will approach each situation as part of an overall approach.

The theory of learned helplessness is a valid and important addition to carers' knowledge; however, there is a fine line between doing too much and doing too little. The carer must consider the implications of their intervention very carefully, at all times.

Always expect more but be prepared to accept less. Always encourage independence but never avoid dependence. Always look beyond the obvious but be prepared to accept that sometimes it will be as it is.

Human relationships and the therapeutic relationship

One of the most difficult areas of our practice to become really skilful in is the arena of forming mutually beneficial human relationships.

What is meant by 'mutually beneficial human relationships'? Any mutual benefit serves both parties equally, and human relationships refer to an equality of role, where both have basic, intrinsic rights and respect.

Very few relationships in life have these qualities, so it is not something that you would generally be expected to form without some guidance, support and training.

This section is designed to allow you insights into the techniques and methods of some basic therapy so as to enable the roots of this kind of relationship to germinate.

Counselling

Counselling is a technique that can be learnt by almost anyone. It has some basic rules and beliefs, but if you are a person who can listen without prejudice, you can offer counsel.

To offer counsel does not mean to give advice, although I would argue that in dementia counselling certain advice might need to be imparted. It does not mean to give solutions and it does not mean the imposition of strict goals or targets. It also means to offer space and time for change to occur, to offer an impartial and listening ear and offer reflection. It also involves trust.

One of the goals of counselling that needs to be modified is that of *resolution*. For many people with progressive conditions resolution is just not realistic. Some aspects of past relationships or problems, however, may be resolved, but on the whole the key difference in offering counsel to any person (especially if dementia is present) is to offer *validation*. To offer acceptance of the person with all of their current and past lot is to offer validity to their life and to add hope to their future.

Resolution therapy

Resolution therapy was introduced in Chapter 3. The term was first used by Graham Stokes and Fiona Goudie to describe the forming of healing relationships in dementia work. However, it has since become synonymous with behaviour that challenges.

The idea of resolution therapy is that once an effective pathway has been achieved between the carer and the person living with dementia the fundamental 'isolation' and 'fear', conscious or unconscious, can start to be resolved and that past issues of loss and abandonment can begin to be addressed.

A major outcome of resolution therapy is the forming of effective communication, and this in turn allows resolution therapy to be seen as an adjunct to pre-therapy (or contact work) developed by Garry Prouty.

Prouty developed a position, as we have, of performing whole-person work (a systems perspective) (Prouty *et al*, 2002). This is an important point when performing therapeutic work with those considered in advanced stages of cognitive decline. Pre-therapy assumes the existence of an internal as well as an external world: still functioning and coexisting – perhaps damaged or altered but maintained. I would consider this one of the necessary conditions for working with people living with a dementia; we must have unconditional positive regard for the whole person, not simply a reductionist model of disease.

It is this positive regard for the internal and external experiences and the combined approach advocated by pre-therapy contact work that allows us to place pre-therapy firmly within the current biopsychosocial model of dementia care and puts it within the reach of everyone working in dementia care.

It truly is a person-centred approach; it also builds upon the continuum from validation and resolution work to adaptive response.

This is a substantially deep prospect and one that needs some explanation.

Attachment, loss and separation

The theories of attachment separation, anxiety and loss were introduced in Chapter 3. They were most fully explained by John Bowlby in his volumes of work

Attachment and Loss (1969–82). These views were formed through observing and performing clinical research with children, their carers and the institutions and environments in which they were living or being raised.

If we propose to adopt the theory of intellectual and psychological regression proposed by Perrin and related to the work of Piaget for our model, these studies provide us tremendous opportunity for our approach to care.

Attachment theory can be attributed to John Bowlby, but he would be the first to admit that he owes debts to both Freud and Jung and their initial interpretations of relationships between children and their parents, particularly the mother.

Basically, attachment theory states that once a relationship has been established between child and parent/mother, the child feels terrible stress and loss at separation and deep joy at connection.

In times of stress or loss this sense of separation can be exaggerated and the person throughout their life looks for parent or mother substitutes to replace or attain this feeling of comfort. Persons who experience loss and separation early in life often find themselves constantly searching for effective 'mothers' throughout life and can often exhibit 'catastrophic responses' to stress or loss in their adult life.

In cases of dementia, using the theoretical framework of past life predictors, attachment theory allows us to see patterns and formulas for the person's possible reaction to the losses of the syndrome.

Learning Tip 18: Searching for security

In dementia the losses are many and grave. It is possible to see relationship formulation and searching and disruptive catastrophic behaviour in new lights when using attachment, separation and loss as frameworks for person-centred working.

Many people while undergoing the transformation to self-image caused by a dementia syndrome revert to a 'search' for these figures of security. It is easier to understand these attempts to achieve security and comfort when we use an attachment framework.

One of the major factors in survivability of the dementia syndrome is the handling of stress, both internal and external. If we as professionals can understand and begin to meet some of the causes for internal stress, such as the need for the 'mother' substitute, and then address the external stress by providing prosthetic environments, we could produce better and more fulfilling lives for those so affected.

Bowlby found that the younger the child (the less intellectually developed) the greater the need for attachment. He discovered that when this relationship was threatened or removed the child became anxious and distressed. If the relationship was not restored quickly the child would engage in some destructive or self-destructive conversion behaviours and that apathy and depression (withering) inevitably would follow.

Death has been shown in some studies to occur in very young children when these separation conditions are extended.

It is not too difficult to envision the acute losses of late-stage dementia as seen in Perrin's hypothesis as facilitative to the subconscious re-emergence and activation of these deep early-childhood needs.

Bowlby also showed that substitute figures would be sought and that feelings would be 'transferred from one person (object) to another and that these feelings could be as strong as to the original attachment'. Many of us have found residents that become deeply attached to us or another carer, sometimes following us around and seemingly becoming distressed when we are not around or when we attempt to leave. Many have had residents who cling to us or grab our hands and attempt to 'suckle'.

How many of us also have felt deep paternal or maternal feelings activated within ourselves by these regressed behaviours?

Accepting these findings, we can see that as dementia progresses and as memory deteriorates along with other necessary components of psychological function involved in formation and continuation of relationships that attachments and transference of feelings may become quite commonplace.

The more dependent a person becomes as the dementing process progresses the greater the need for substitute relationships providing comfort and assurance.

The use of resolution in the 'soothing' of these displacements can now be understood in the context of its original goals of 'communication and relationship' and as being the desired result.

If we can communicate within these feelings of need and loss and the need for attachment in a productive and non-destructive manner we will have succeeded in the basic aim of resolution.

Validation therapy

Validation working (Feil, 1972, 1982) was introduced in Chapter 3. It is another form of therapy that is designed to communicate at this deep level with people in what could be described as 'confusional states'.

Validation was based around ideas of psychoanalytical thought, particularly

Freudian concepts. This reliance on analytic thought has brought validation much criticism and in its purest early interpretation a lot of this criticism can be seen to be justified, as some analytic principles do seem to be confused, particularly attempts to combine Freudian and Jungian concepts. However, at the most basic level validation therapy, the acceptance of one human being by another within their present reality and accepting of their present level of ability, has little that can equal its central message.

Validation serves not to try to contradict or 'orientate' the confused person. It accepts the person in whichever state of reality they now function and serves to resonate within that dimension.

Validation works particularly well with people who are in later stages of dementia and who are no longer able to function successfully within externally 'accepted' timescales.

The following approaches include some new views on assessing and programming for successful care.

Modelling: the 24-hour approach to assessment

The technique of 24-hour assessment is not new; it has been used by various therapists and medical professionals for some time now. However, we can use neuro-linguistic programming (NLP) techniques to map behavioural responses to the challenges faced by a person with dementia over a specified timeline. We can then extrapolate the type of adaptive behaviours the person has used to achieve their goals.

We should at the end of this process have an idea of:
- what the person was trying to achieve (their goals/needs)
- what the person used that was successful and what was unsuccessful
- how we can change the environment to exaggerate the adaptive behaviours that were successful
- how we can change the environment to diminish the experiences that created difficulties, frustrations and stress.

We will check these assessments against the possibilities available to us to create a plan of care over a 24-hour period. This will be relayed to all staff involved in the delivery of the programme. Care plans will be devised to demonstrate these constructive prosthetic techniques and changes.

Before we can begin we need to understand why we are using this approach to assessment and care delivery.

Very little real progress has been made in the field of dementia care at the coalface over the last decade. Although we have changed our vocabulary and new ways of looking at people with dementia have emerged, when push comes to shove people resort to care strategies they feel best suit the situation and in cash-pressed times these are task driven.

Often these strategies are self-created, or based on scant information but with best intentions. They do get the person with dementia through the day, but they often don't make any real changes to the person's experience and future behaviour.

One of the missing ingredients for good care practice is a solid and applicable assessment process. Without a baseline that shows what can and cannot be achieved, all care practices are cobbled together from various backgrounds and models – in short they serve little purpose in a crisis.

Neuro-linguistic programming

As the field of dementia care begins to mature untried and new ideas will enter the established ways of doing things. One of these ideas which has yet to enter the fray is that of neuro-linguistic programming. One of the reasons for this may be the seeming simplicity of NLP and its techniques or perhaps its supposedly pseudo-scientific background.

In fact there exists empirical data to confirm the premise of NLP and what may seem simple in two-day 'quick-fix' training programmes turns out to be a very sound and complex system of psychology. So could there be another reason why NLP has not entered the field? NLP has been termed the science of excellence, but it is also something much broader: it is the art of understanding subjective experience and, moreover, the art of devising strategies to change these subjective experiences – for the self and other – for the better.

Understanding subjective experience

Subjective experience includes what goes on inside your mind, as well as in the outside world. Nobody really knows how anybody else thinks let alone what they think. We each think we know reality. So-called 'experience' therefore differs enormously from person to person. We each perceive the world in which we live uniquely and subjectively. We see things differently. We have our own values, attitudes and beliefs which together make up our 'mind-set' (Adler & Heather, 1999), which may not make sense to other people. The way some people think and behave does not always make sense to us.

NLP accepts this and sets out to understand subjective experience in order to help individuals do what they do better.

In the field of dementia many behaviours and 'mind-sets' seem foreign to us. We observe someone trying for hours to go through the same locked door, wandering from place to place with no apparent purpose, talking about things that bear no resemblance to what they are engaged in or where they are and we don't understand why.

We try desperately to communicate to that person that this is the way it is, but they don't seem to understand. The fact is of course that your subjective reality and their subjective reality are so disparate that they really cannot comprehend.

If the person can no longer communicate effectively in the medium we are all used to, it is up to us and not them to make the effort to change. NLP is one option to allow us to do this.

Adaptive response ascertains that we need to create prosthetic social and built environments that work with the person and not against them.

Some of the principles of 'Gentlecare' (Jones, 2000), introduced in Chapter 3, are very similar in theory. Gentlecare, however, includes charts and recording instruments to help the carer cope with the application of the principles of the model.

This chapter reflects this approach and also that of Dr Graham Stokes, who believes very firmly that assessment is the key to understanding and therefore designing care approaches for people with dementia.

How can NLP help?

NLP looks at analysing behaviour and looking at the emotional attachments this behaviour may contain. A person will not change a negative behaviour if they are receiving an emotional feedback from its completion. Even negative emotional attachments are seen as better than none by our nervous system, which works instinctively on feedback.

Feedback is the key to understanding the application of NLP techniques to dementia care. We need to ascertain what feedback is maintaining behaviour in the person being assessed. In other words, what is the person trying to achieve? A person who constantly wanders is achieving some aim – discovering what the underlying aim or goal is may be the key to modifying, eliminating or at least understanding the behaviour.

In dementia care I don't believe we should want to change all reactive behaviour. If I get angry I may shout or I may retreat into a safe space to prevent a 'blow-up'. If we see this type of behaviour as a reaction to the dementia instead of part of normal behaviour, we take away the 'escape' for that person. This could be dangerous and will most certainly add to the frustration and stress of the person and will almost undoubtedly lead to maladaptive behaviour.

In this case the feedback will be relayed to the person with dementia from the environment and the care regime and even though this will be negative it will lead to a responsive behaviour in turn. This responsive behaviour is likely to constitute a repression of expression or an aggressive outburst. This would be seen, in person-centred terms, as a natural consequence of a malignant culture.

What type of assessment will give us productive feedback?

For any assessment to be productive it must be relevant. In the case of dementia it must be relevant to both the person experiencing the behaviour as well as to the person producing the behaviour (carer and cared for). It should also be a comprehensive and unbiased assessment – a tool that looks at the positive aspects of behaviour as well as the negative.

For example, a person may be disorientated in their environment (negative) but still mobile (positive); a way of using this information would be to compensate for the disorientation while emphasising the mobility of the person. Way-finding tools and strategies may be employed that help to level up the playing field. We therefore exaggerate the positive (the person can still get to where they can now find their way) while de-emphasising the negative (the featureless environment now has colours, directions and signage).

Assessment also needs to use all the senses available to both the assessor and the assessed. In dementia certain senses can be lost, dulled or even exaggerated by the changes in brain connections necessary for the brain to continue to navigate its way through daily living while coping with the insidious damage it is suffering. The brain is complex and as has been shown time and time again is a plastic organ; it can adapt to much more damage than we would imagine while still functioning relatively well.

One of the very reasons dementia presents so differently in different people is this fantastic ability to adapt. Based on the neural connections that have formed (and these are formed by life experiences as well as development), the person with dementia may still be able to carry out intricate pre-learned skills while being unable to locate their own front door.

Many of these skills have been learned via more than one sense; for example, playing the piano involves kinaesthetic (feel, touch), auditory (sound, pitch, vibration) and visual (colour differences, distance, texture and appearance) senses. In fact it is almost impossible to learn any skill with merely one sense alone.

Therefore, when someone attempts a task they employ all their senses to accomplish it. It follows that if we want to help someone complete a task we should do so using all their and our available resources (senses, memory, unconscious learning and environmental conscious and unconscious cueing).

NLP gives us a blueprint for detailed observations

Using the 24-hour principle of 'Gentlecare' assessment we 'map' the person during their day from waking to sleeping and, depending on their level of need, the activities of care involved during non-waking hours too. In effect we end up with a detailed picture of what the person does in their life and the obstacles they face to create fulfilment of each day.

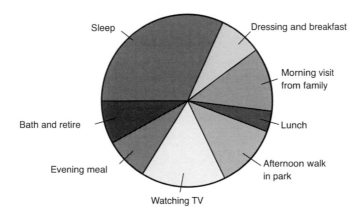

FIGURE 7.1 The 24-hour map

What type of things do we assess?

At first this assessment process is time consuming, because we will need to assess the performance of each aspect of the person's day. We are trying to build up a picture of what is important to the person and not what is important to the system or the model. As Milton Erikson, the famous clinical hypnotherapist, once commented, 'Do not fit the person to your theory – with each new person invent a new theory.'

It would seem pointless to allow a person to struggle for an hour to fasten two buttons on their shirt (no matter how person-centred that may be) if what is really important to the person is not that their buttons are in the right holes, but that they are eating breakfast after a long and restless night. Conversely, of course, if the person's self-esteem rests with having the ability to fasten those two buttons at any cost, you would be wrong to try to divert attention elsewhere.

So the assessment should be relevant to what is important to the person. It also needs to be practical. We cannot justify claiming that the real need of the person is to be at home if their husband/wife or family are no longer able or willing to cope, no matter how much we wish it to be so.

If the practicalities of the situation revolve around physical care, we should be assessing how this impacts upon the person. However, if the practicalities involve a person destroying the environment around them, the emphasis of assessment should be on why.

Four basic stages of the assessment process

The assessment process has four basic stages, as follows.

1   Discover what the person wants.
2   What are they doing to get it?
3   How are they doing this?
4   Change whatever is preventing the person from succeeding.

We will explore each area in some depth and then look at ways in which we can use this information to create real, effective and lasting changes to the lives of those in our care.

1 Discover what the person wants

How do we discover what another person wants? We have already decided that we cannot know what another person thinks so how do we assess for what they want? It may be as simple as asking the person, 'What do you want?' but it usually is not that straightforward.

We need to observe what the person is attempting to do and we need to interpret their actions. However, unlike validation, we do not place one model of theoretical interpretations upon actions. If someone is trying to put something in their mouth we may assume they are hungry, they are stimulating themselves or they are searching for comfort. We would not immediately interpret this in a Freudian sexually symbolic manner.

If someone is pacing the floor we may assume they are trying to leave, but they may have started the journey knowing where they were going and become lost or they may have unmet attachment needs or they may need the toilet.

So we need to follow the actions through to their conclusion. Is there a clue in the way that the behaviour ends? Shown the toilet, does the person then use it? When a nurse comes into view does the person become less anxious and seek the nurse out?

We need to look intricately at the behaviour to understand the meaning beyond.

- What initiated the action? Was it the person or the environment?
- Who was involved? Did the action carry a beginning, middle and an end? Was someone else involved?
- Is the action repetitive? Does the person appear stuck? Do they become unstuck when assistance is given?
- Where did the action take place? Has it happened in this place before?

This assessment may need to be performed a dozen times until you feel you understand the behaviour being exhibited and the drives behind it. The results will be worth it.

2 What are they doing to get it?

Just what is the person actually doing in an attempt to achieve their goal? Remember the person may have a goal in mind but because of the areas of function that are damaged by the progress of the syndrome they may have different ways of achieving this end than you or me. It may also be true that the person is prevented from meeting their aims by their illness and then reacts to the frustration this causes. At present we need to know what they are doing.

- How does the person get their actions done? Are they completed successfully? If they are not completed successfully what stops them from being so? Is it intention or action that is affected?
- Has the person the physical means to achieve their goals? Are goal-orientated behaviours being subjugated into inappropriate actions?

3 How are they doing this?

We now need to break the actions down into stages. All actions have a beginning, middle and an end. How is the action initiated – how does it start? What happens next, in the middle, near the end, how does it conclude?

If we can find the person's goal, learn how they are trying to achieve it and break it down into stages. We should be able to reconstitute it into more effective parts.

The above steps 1 to 3 are shown on the assessment form below, which concludes with step 4: changing whatever is preventing the person from succeeding.

24-hour goal-orientated assessment

RESIDENT'S NAME .... DATE.................

D.O.B. ....

This assessment is not meant to be interpretive. You should record what you see, not what you think you see. Remember we all see the world differently. We are trying to find out how this person views their world and how we can make this world easier to live in.

DISCOVER WHAT THE PERSON WANTS

What is the person attempting to do?

What does the person want to do?

Describe what they appear to be doing.

Is the person using tools to achieve their aim?

Is the person enlisting others to help?

Has the person been successful in their actions?

WHAT ARE THEY DOING TO GET IT?

Is the person able to achieve their goal?

What appears to be stopping them?

In what way is the person trying to achieve their goal?

Who initiated the actions towards the goal?
Is there a physical reason the person cannot achieve their goal?

Is the environment preventing the goal being attained and if so how?

Where did the action take place?

HOW ARE THEY DOING THIS?
What seemed to start the action?
What did the person do first?

Describe the stages of the person's action in detail
1.
2.
3.
4.
5.
6.
7.
8.
9.
10.

Did the person achieve their goal?
What stopped them?

How?

What did they do next?

In order to fully appreciate the experience of another we must try to look inside their experience. To do this we need to consider all the senses:

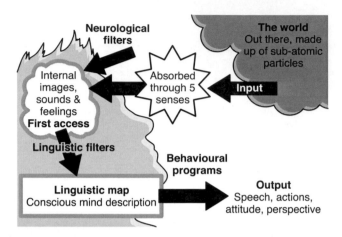

FIGURE 7.2 The NLP map

Visual	*Sight*
Auditory	*Hearing*
Kinaesthetic	*Touch/feeling*
Olfactory	*Smell*
Gustatory	*Taste*

HOW ARE THE SENSES INVOLVED IN THIS EXPERIENCE?
In what way did eyesight affect the person's performance?

In what way was hearing involved in this action?

In what way was the kinaesthetic system involved in this action?

Was smell involved in this action?
If so, how?

Was the taste system involved at all in the action?
How?

**USING ALL THE INFORMATION COLLECTED HOW CAN WE MAKE THIS
PERSON'S EXPERIENCE LESS STRESSFUL AND MORE SUCCESSFUL?**
The action/actions we wish to make a positive difference are:

We can enhance the sensory experiences of the person in the following ways:
V
A
K
O
G

In what ways can we help with the sequencing of the action?

Can we change or enhance the environment? How?

Would this person benefit from staff having extra training in the areas we have
shown need assistance?

In what areas and by whom would this be best achieved?

Assessment completed by................................   Date ....

How does the goal-orientated behaviour fit into the person's routine?

The next stage in our assessment comes at looking at how this goal-orientated behaviour fits into the person's lifestyle: their activity over 24 hours.

We will express this as a hierarchy, which will show how much over the 24-hour period the person is involved in each activity of living.

This should also display to us quite graphically how the person is not being engaged or involved in any meaningful activity. By meaningful, remember we mean to the person, not to us. We might think that meaningful activity is going outside and playing with a dog or cat. For someone whose reality has been reduced to enjoyment of warmth and food this type of activity would be highly unlikely to cause positive reactions.

Each person with dementia has different ways of viewing their world. We must attempt at all times not to thrust our reality onto another individual, particularly one who is by definition vulnerable.

Once again an individual is assessed over a 24-hour period and the results are this time presented in the form of a graph indicating the time spent in engaged activity or occupation.

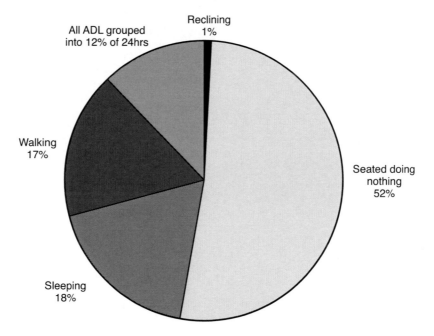

FIGURE 7.3 Typical breakdown of a day and night

Learning Tip 19: Create diagrams

You can create your diagrams and graphs at any time, then use them to inform your colleagues of states within the current system that need changing. Imagine creating a 24-hour record and then showing this as a clock face which showed that all a person really did all day was get up and be brought to a lounge where they remain for 14 hours, only occasionally being taken to a toilet or fed in their chair in that lounge before returning to bed. Imagine if this was their life seven days a week.

Would you want to start now to change that system?

Stress threshold profile

You can also use this type of mapping to create a stress threshold profile. Each person is observed over a period of 24 hours and recordings are made of the 'catastrophic' events evident during the assessment. They are recorded on the stress profile graph (*see* Figure 7.4).

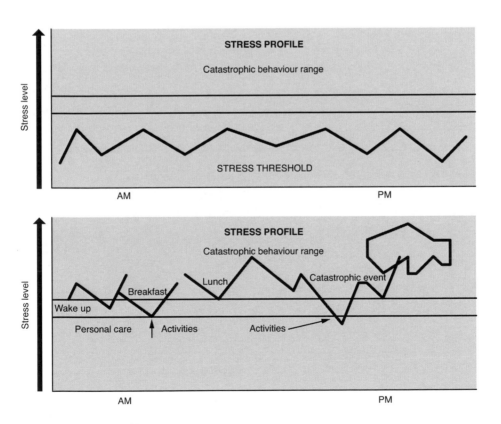

FIGURE 7.4 Stress profile

Once you can see graphically what activities are affecting the person within their day-to-day living it will be easier to start changing the systems that are maintaining these behaviours.

Behavioural mapping

Once again an individual is assessed over a 24-hour period and the results are this time presented in the form of a graph indicating the time spent in engaged activity or occupation.

THE 24-HOUR DAY
BREAKDOWN OF ASSESSED MEANINGFUL ACTIVITY
Make a note each hour of the activities the person is engaged in.
12 MIDNIGHT
1 AM
2 AM
3 AM
5 AM
4 AM
6 AM
7 AM
8 AM
9 AM
10 AM
11 AM
12 NOON
1 PM
2 PM
3 PM
4 PM
5 PM
6 PM
7 PM
8 PM
9 PM
10 PM
11PM
12 MIDNIGHT

The preceding chapters have covered the history of modern dementia thought and have shown the processes of dementia across the biopsychosocial domains. We have covered internal factors and introduced novel ways of looking at our physical and psychological engagement as a protective and therapeutic response to known and unmet needs and we have briefly discussed the manipulation of the external physical environment. The next chapter looks more specifically at our ability and requirement to use the built environment therapeutically – to turn it into a prosthetic. This is examined on the macro and micro levels.

You may feel there is little that you can do personally to influence the architect of the next new care home, although there is much to influence them in the research literature. However, that does not make you a passive participant within this new environment. In fact if you have read this far you now accept caring passively in dementia care as an abdication of responsibility. You will be pleased to know that any environment can be made into a prosthetic. With or without massive funding, armed with the knowledge contained in these closing chapters you will meet your goal, which is to protect the individual from the negative effects of the built environment through adaptations you can make individually or as a care team.

8 Manipulating the built environment

Environmental prosthetics

'Prosthetic' a. the replacement of a missing bodily part with an artificial substitute b. an artificial part such as a limb, eye, or tooth

2. Another word for prosthesis: via Late Latin from Greek: an addition, from prostithenai to add, from pros- towards + tithenai to place

(Collins English Dictionary –
Complete & Unabridged 10th Edition, 2009)

Most buildings are designed to meet a rather specific requirement of use. Care homes and hospitals are designed to fulfil an institutional purpose, a purpose which does not enrich life for persons with physical disabilities, memory, perceptual or behavioural challenges.

Most buildings, especially those designed to hold large numbers, disable the person living with dementia and lead to a level of challenge and stress that often increases the symptoms of their illness. This leads staff to become controllers rather than facilitators and to thus offer care and medication regimes that seek to remedy institutionally created responses – sadly further disabling those we seek to help.

Understanding how our built and social environments disable and distress those in our care is the first stage of removing these barriers.

It would seem sensible and necessary, therefore, to design or redesign our environments using a 'model' that considers the abilities of the person living with dementia, as well as their disabilities, and which facilitates the ability of the staff group to care for people in these environments where their remaining abilities are enhanced rather than challenged.

Using built and social environments to decrease physical and psychological limitations and to enhance abilities is termed 'prosthetic' and for our purposes in this chapter we will examine how we can use environmental prosthetics to enrich lives within the framework of adaptive response.

Taking account of the syndrome

When beginning to think of design for individuals or groups of individuals living with dementia it should be an essential starting position to become intimately knowledgeable with the subject itself.

To recap, dementia is a descriptive term given to a collection of signs and symptoms (a syndrome) that are the predominant feature of over 100 different but related conditions and diseases (Jacques & Jackson, 2000). It is a process predominantly, but not exclusively, of advanced age.

Risk factors for developing one of the dementias rise sharply from 1 in 20 at the age of 65 years to a 1 in 4 possibility at the age of 85 years and over (Adams & Clarke, 1999). The most prominent and lasting feature of dementia is a severe and progressive disruption of memory. This disruption occurs across all areas of memory use and affects creation, recall and storage.

In most cases the process of dementing is progressive and terminal.

Based on the evidence of the degree of dementia in varying age groups, most large-scale dementia design should therefore be geared towards the older individual. As such, design must also account for the varying needs of the older, oft times frail, intended population.

Older body systems have a predisposition to present in a number of distinct ways as they age. Before we design with consideration to meeting the needs of persons living with dementia, design must also address the general requirements of older persons and what it is they require from built environments.

By taking this route design will present a 'home' that begins with a basic living environment that can be mastered by all. It is only at this point that we can begin to provide specific adjustments or additions that will allow the built environment to adapt to the more specific needs of the person with dementia by the use of prosthetics.

Buildings are not designed with the intention of constructively supporting cognitive impairment.

Many cognitively impaired residents also experience diminished capacity in one or more of the following areas:

- Memory for facts: names, numbers, and sequences.
- Action and motion: ability to balance, coordinate, swallow, and manoeuvre utensils.
- Emotion: capacity to match emotions with situations.
- Social behaviour: ability to relate to people in conventional ways, need for smaller groups.
- Judgement: ability to plan, anticipate, change behaviour midcourse, override situations, and anticipate danger.

As more and more healthcare settings attempt to serve a resident population that consists of large numbers of people living with Alzheimer's disease in particular, and other related dementias, and for longer periods, it is becoming increasingly clear that design is not just an incidental concern but integral to a well-balanced approach for the provision of dignified caring for this vulnerable and discriminated population.

Major profits will still be made by care operators spending more on adapting environments, training staff and supporting relatives: in fact, perversely, this investment will increase profits in the future as more people are able to choose where they 'purchase' their care.

Cognitive impairment

Physical problems experienced as we age are now becoming acceptable within society but, to most of us, depression and dementia, the most significant other contributors to loss of function in the old, are not acceptable. As individual competence decreases, social stigma grows and the personal, social and physical environment becomes increasingly important in determining well-being.

The primary focus, therefore, for those designing for dementia and old age should be to maximise the capability within the built and social environments to support remaining abilities and facilitate residents and their families carrying out meaningful and relevant life-affirming activities.

Careful design planning can facilitate mental functioning, minimise some areas of confusion, decrease real and perceived stress and allow individuals to function more independently at whatever level they may be able. Further consideration can make these places good for staff and attractive to relatives and friends.

The number of disabled older people is expected to grow rapidly, and they will form a larger percentage of the total elderly population in the future because of the changing age composition of the population and particularly the higher proportion of people living to 85 years or older. We should embrace these statistics not wince.

Eighty per cent of older people suffer from chronic limitation of mobility. Forty-eight per cent have arthritis, 29 per cent have hearing loss, 17 per cent have orthopaedic impairments, and 14 per cent have vision problems. To that list add incontinence, sensation loss, respiration, and cardiac difficulties.

Unfortunately, I could not find in my literature searches a similar list of percentages for all the really wonderful and positive contributions older people make. Perhaps this speaks volumes about our consumerist twenty-first century perspective so let me reverse the above: 52 per cent do not have arthritis, 71 per cent do not have hearing loss, 83 per cent have no orthopaedic impairments and 86 per cent have no vision problems. Most will not be incontinent, have minimal sensation loss and will have either few or well-managed respiration and cardiac difficulties and will manage well with chronic limitation on mobility – and most will be incredibly loved and respected heads of extended families and the overwhelming percentage will not experience dementia in their lifetime.

Supportive care environments: messages from current evidence

Many care home residents face multiple challenges, but strong accumulating evidence suggests environments can be designed, or redesigned, to provide support, enhance and simplify lives, and most importantly make life more enjoyable.

Key aspects of successful care schemes across extra care and care/nursing homes are:
- specialist design for a specific population; that is, dementia
- having adequate useable social space within the building as a whole.

The physical environment has a wide range of impacts on outcomes for residents, staff and visitors.

Pleasant, homely and easy to understand environments which offer opportunities for residents to improve their functioning can increase independence, mobility and encourage food and fluid intake.

Important design priorities that assist vision and way finding in dementia care environments are lighting, signposting, the use of colour, the use of colour contrast, and the use of artwork and memorabilia.

There are a lot of guidelines, recommendations and examples of good practice relating to the design of buildings and living environments for people with dementia. However, much of the information is anecdotal and, although it might be helpful, is not as yet proven (Smith *et al*, 2004).

Small or large scale?

There are pros and cons regarding the size of buildings. Larger schemes can be disorientating and confusing but are more likely to be able to provide a wider range of amenities and facilities and in reality attempting to push the care industry into providing smaller, more normal environments will not work as the staffing costs will make providing care unaffordable.

The 'housing' element is, however, as important as the care aspect and there is emerging evidence from small-scale UK studies of the following.

● Adequate spaces for gatherings of both large and small groups should be provided.
● There should be provision of baths as well as showers.
● Schemes should appear welcoming to relatives and friends.

Fleming and colleagues' recent literature review of the design of physical environments for people with dementia concluded that little is certain (Fleming *et al*, 2008) and that findings from studies existing to date support the previously published 'consensus of views' on principles for designing dementia-specific facilities (Marshall, 2001) which concluded that care accommodation for older people living with dementia should:

● compensate for disability
● maximise independence, reinforce personal identity, and enhance self-esteem/confidence
● demonstrate care for staff
● be understandable and easy to orientate around
● welcome relatives and the local community, and
● control and balance stimuli.

Fleming *et al* (2008) also conclude that the currently available evidence also strongly supports the use of:

● unobtrusive safety features
● a variety of spaces, including single rooms
● the enhancement of visual access, and
● the optimisation of levels of stimulation.

Baker (2002) highlighted the importance of having a communal room or space which is suitable for relatives and friends to meet should they wish. Likewise, Evans and Vallelly (2007), in their literature review of 'Best Practice in Promoting Social

Well-Being in Extra Care Housing', concluded that features that are welcoming for friends and relatives should be incorporated.

Tilly and Reed (2008) support the view that homely and pleasant environments that provide opportunities for residents to improve their functioning and walk around with minimal risk lead to more independence in daily activities.

Reducing stress and improving well-being

Evans and Vallelly (2007) demonstrated that the layout and design of a scheme can impact on social well-being, and Chimes (2007) also stated in his design features for older people with dementia literature review that there were evident positive correlations between built design features and quality of life. He cautioned, however, that it is difficult to establish whether it is the design features that improve well-being in most cases because other factors, such as the social environment and philosophy of care 'that are difficult or impossible to extrapolate', may influence outcomes.

It is important here to draw from the views of Chimes two important observations:

- Design features have not been proven to increase well-being in care.
- Philosophy of care and the social environment may influence the outcome of research into the impact of design on well-being.

We must assume Chimes refers to negative care philosophy and social environments as relating to Kitwood's malignant social psychology as the negating factors within the environment as opposed to the direct impact of building design, which has been well studied and well published in literature relating to sick buildings and architecture.

I am also not sure that the evidence is so inconclusive as to whether built environments affect the quality of life and specifically the well-being of those living within them. If we consider that a building is only any good if it serves its purpose, studies need to contrast the lives of those living in adapted facilitative environments as opposed to those living in regular care home designs before any conclusions can logically be drawn.

Which design changes are debatable and which are not

Before we discuss some of this supporting literature I think it is important to note the difference here between what we do know and what we do not. I don't think, for example, that at present we know enough to definitively state that using various coloured doors to differentiate bedrooms is helpful or not.

The argument seems to hinge on memory and that an individual will remember their room better if the doors remind them of when they were younger, perhaps a child, and the family door. However I think that argument is flawed in a number of ways in practice.

Not everyone living with dementia in care will have memory that rolls back to a specific fixed point in time. Also, with our present multi-ethnic society, childhood experiences differ widely. I think we may also have points in our memory – probably better accessed by their emotional resonance than a specific timeline – where many coloured doors may feature throughout differing 'fixed points'.

Also, if we accept the argument for time-specific memory of coloured doors, how can we be sure in a care home where there are say 30 beds on one corridor and therefore five blue doors, five red doors, five yellow doors and so on that just one specific red door will be relevant? Perhaps this approach simply encourages people to explore five red-door options before finding home?

More understandable is the argument for highlighting toilets and bathrooms and disguising exits and other doors people do not need to be attracted to. If each same-coloured door explored leads to a toilet, that seems to me to have real value and relies on retained and existing abilities rather than on a hypothetical, possibly intentional blurring of what we know about the many different forms and functions of memory.

Arguments for redundant cueing make use of retained abilities and an understanding of brain science as do the use of smells and colour and the deliberate use of design to highlight contrast and depth.

I don't think we need to argue about signage either, except perhaps the design of the signs – signage has been used to assist people to find their way around large buildings and spaces for many years now so the argument seems won. We understand that in a strange place even with full cognitive ability people need to be shown the way – it lessens stress and leads to more desirable outcomes, thus it enables and not disables.

The counter-arguments based around the aesthetics of care homes – 'we don't want it to look institutional' – show a misunderstanding between institutional and functional. Buildings that have the same carpets, colours, wall fittings and so on are institutional despite their pleasant looks whereas a building with signs and other prosthetics that assist people in finding their way around are functional. Make the signs pretty but don't omit them. That's not care; it is business.

Success factors

The extra care housing literature review, *Raising the Stakes* (IPC, 2007), determined that evidence exists for the following success factors to be built into extra care design:

● adequate space in schemes as well as in each unit
● design being closely aligned to address the needs of the scheme's population, including specialist design for dementia.

Joseph's (2006) review of the literature looked at the relationship of physical environmental factors to resident and staff outcomes in a range of different types of long-term care settings. Key findings were that the physical environment has an impact on outcomes for residents, their family, and staff in terms of:

● resident quality of life
● resident safety
● staff stress.

His excellent review identified several studies which showed that different aspects of the physical environment can have direct impact on quality of life and well-being in a wide variety of ways, including:

● improved sleep
● improved orientation and way finding
● reduced aggression and disruptive behaviour
● increased social interaction
● increased privacy and control
● improved links to the familiar
● increased physical activity
● increased resident safety
● reduced falls
● reduced infection
● reduced 'walking around' and unsafe exiting.

Criteria for designing dementia care settings

There are several issues that complicate the provision of long-term care for those living with a dementia. As a cognitive disease, dementia manifests itself in behavioural and mental difficulties, but it does not necessarily lead to physical disability until the later stages and for some death arrives from other complications of old age long before mobility has been compromised significantly. This means that the traditional medical model of nursing home care may not provide for the needs of the resident living with dementia. Where an environment remains non-adapted it may lead to unnecessary over-reliance on restraint, locked doors or medication.

Special care units (SCUs)

In response to the rising numbers of residents living with dementia in particular care homes, specialised care units are emerging internationally as a means of managing the complex care associated with dementia.

Special care units have grown from the belief that residents living with dementia require specialised care and perhaps, regrettably, that people without dementia will be happier if they are separated from the trauma of 'living with those experiencing the more distressing symptoms of dementia'.

The intent is not to segregate but to encourage and support the optimum quality of life for all residents. The intention is similar to care streaming and arises from the recognition that one size does not fit all.

Residential long-term care for persons with dementia is different from the care required for a person who has skilled general nursing needs. It requires a focus on the biopsychosocial needs of the individual, and provides specific therapeutic activities designed to maximise remaining cognitive and physical abilities. Appropriate dementia care settings should provide a specialised physical environment that enhances and supports individualised care specific to those residents living with a dementia.

The environment of an ideal SCU is designed to enhance care by creating a warm, bright and cheerful 'homelike' atmosphere, and by including 'wandering' space, special lighting designed to eliminate shadows, and wall coverings that serve as a reminder of a more homelike setting.

Individual resident rooms are personalised by including many personal treasures and possessions, to make them more comforting and more comfortable, and recently the use of memory boxes has been an important addition to further personalising while at the same time orientating both residents and their families.

A therapeutic milieu is a distinguishing feature of SCUs. Creating such a milieu involves meeting needs in a way that reflects compassion, patience, understanding and creativity and by providing a safe, pleasant and clean environment.

Activities are emphasised as a way to provide stimulation for residents' physical, cognitive and social skills, and they are provided in a manner that supports the dignity and lifestyle of the individual and assists in maintaining that lifestyle.

Virtually all special units have some type of alarm system that alerts staff when residents leave the unit. As dementia special care settings evolve, these design elements have emerged as the basis for prototypical design. Innovative trends that raise the level of special care design involve getting away from gimmicks to focus on designing settings that work functionally and facilitate adaptation (Alzheimer's Association, 1992).

Sloane and Mathew (1991) have identified some of the trends.

- In housing, a smaller number of people in a less stimulating, and therefore less confusing, setting is definitely preferable.
- The cluster or pod design reduces institutional care settings in size and scale to something that more closely resembles a home environment, and it allows for a variety of different groupings and activity spaces.
- Architects are incorporating outdoor spaces in the overall design plan by adding more doors and by making the outdoor areas accessible to residents from a number of locations.
- Courtyards are recent innovations that provide gardening opportunities, bird feeders, outdoor seating for residents and opportunities for other additional programme activities.
- Private areas where disruptive or distressing behaviours can be cared for within one-on-one settings are the norm, and separate activity spaces for groups that need special attention are empowering to the staff.

In addition, designers, working with staff members, are creating interesting opportunities for activity and stimulation such as pictures for reminiscing, wall-mounted panels that attract touch, or cabinets made with various and interesting hardware, doors and drawers made for opening.

Efforts are also being made to individualise orientation to assist with effective way finding for residents and this is stimulating the discovery of more effective orientation methods or cues.

Learning Tip 20: Changing the way people function

Real excitement comes in understanding that when we change the way the environment functions, we can significantly change the way people function within that environment – especially people with dementia.

Principles of design for dementia

The Dementia Services Development Centre at Stirling University has suggested 10 basic principles of design to aid persons with dementia cope in their living environment (Table 8.1).

TABLE 8.1 Principles of design to assist those with dementia

Small, local and domestic	See and be seen
Form is more important than colour	Space to move about
Different rooms for different functions	Lots of cues
Single storeys are always more preferable	Control the stimuli
Toilets should be visible at all times	Good staff facilities

Source: Dementia Services Development Centre (2008).

Chapman, Gilmour and McIntosh (2001) have added to these specifications and have stated that buildings for persons with dementia should:

- make sense
- help way finding
- provide a therapeutic environment
- provide a safe environment
- minimise staff stress. (Chapman, Gilmour & McIntosh, 2001)

Likewise, Brawley emphasises that physical design features can be seen to potentially compensate for the impairments of persons with dementia in the following ways. They:

- assure safety and comfort
- support functional abilities
- assist with way finding and orientation
- prompt memory
- establish links with the familiar healthy past
- convey expectations and elicit and reinforce behaviour
- reduce agitation
- facilitate privacy
- facilitate social interactions
- stimulate curiosity and interest
- support independence, autonomy and control
- facilitate the involvement of families. (Brawley, 1997)

Cohen and Weisman add one more critical criterion that seems to have been absent in the previous guides:

- The building should adapt to changing needs. (Cohen & Weisman, 1991)

This last component may prove to be the most pertinent for the future development of the field and allows us scope to design for differing needs within the same footprint. As new builds require both land and finance the modification and adaptation of existing buildings offers an immediate and cost-effective route to meeting many current and future needs.

By redesigning our environments for people living with dementia we can build in different features which become more applicable as the various disease processes mature, thus future proofing our care homes for:

● a decrease in residential-type service requirements
● an increase in physical frailty
● the advancing of the disease process through active mobility to dependent immobility and towards a 'good' and dignified death.

Brawley and her contemporaries have rightly suggested that design for dementia should be designed around ability and not disability. This then becomes the starting point for adaptations within the care home, because once we understand the abilities as well as the disabilities of persons living with dementia we are better able to design our environments to enable rather than disable.

This desire to create prosthetic environments, based around abilities, now provides an operational definition which will guide the use of adaptive-response applications to the built environment.

Designing for ability

It is difficult to conceptualise the challenges that dementia presents. Designers cannot experience dementia firsthand and because of its progressive and degenerative nature, people do not recover and then become able to describe the entire experience of what it is like. However, based on research and anecdotal evidence of lives well lived within built environments, the following adaptive principles are to be considered.

A three-tier living environment

If each area of the care environment is designed to compensate for the degree of strengths and abilities of its residents, allowing a smooth transition to the next, more care-dependent zone with the onset of increasing need, the design achieves the otherwise impossible task of allowing the person to remain at the care site and experience the same care staff and surroundings. They receive environmental compensation not from moving accommodation but from the accommodation itself changing and modifying within the same but progressively more adaptive prosthetic environment.

The first area of the building will have design features that compensate for the basic generally acknowledged difficulties of ageing such as the provision of level walking surfaces (cardiac and respiratory), assistive door handles (arthritis and weakness), highly contrasting gross features (failing and non-discerning sight diminishment) and call assistance technology, as well as having specific design innovations that will compensate for the losses in dementia illustrated within the first level of the stage theory model.

The second and third area accommodations will have many of the first area features but will gradually introduce more staff-assisted features. In the case of level three accommodations, the unit will have larger bedrooms featuring automated beds and monitors while self-access kitchens, a feature of the first two areas, will be removed.

Also at level three accommodation bedrooms will feature overhead hoist tracks and all areas will allow wheelchair access. Bathrooms will be larger and feature hoists as standard (Coons, 1996). There will be a heavy reliance on natural sunlight throughout all areas and staff facilities will be separate from the living areas of the residents, thus accommodating the proviso that staff need as much consideration as those in their care (DSDC, 2008).

There are a number of reasons for creating stage theory living plans, not least the idea that adaptive and prosthetic environments support the contentions of this book, but further because insight is maintained long into the dementia process (Jones & Miesen, 1992–2006).

To house people together, with deeply contrasting cognitive abilities, simply because they have an arbitrary diagnosis of dementia, is in the view of the author fundamentally and ethically wrong. Persons who retain insight in the early and middle stages of their illness will have demonstrated to them, on a daily basis, just by observing their residential compatriots, just exactly what their future holds.

Designing the whole environment: the body systems approach

Older body systems have a predisposition to present in a number of distinct ways as they age. Before the designer can consider meeting the needs of the persons with dementia they must also address the general requirements of older persons and what it is they require from built environments. By taking this route the designer will present a 'home' that begins with a basic living environment that can be mastered by all. Only at this point can they begin to provide specific adjustments or additions that will allow the built environment to adapt to the more specific needs of the person with dementia.

In assessing the ways in which the effects of ageing on the human form will dictate design essentials it might prove beneficial to adopt a body systems approach. This will allow the design specification to accommodate macro needs and then introduce micro needs 'desirables' based on a reconstituted 'whole'-person approach.

The essence of the field of design for persons with dementia should be focused then upon producing environments that accentuate the abilities of the person and compensate, as much as possible, far more than on any failings (Netten, 1993).

Brawley (2001) has suggested that architects and interior designers have 'an obligation and a responsibility' to understand the changes which occur during the ageing process and how these may impact on the person's ability to cope with living environments.

Designers for dementia therefore need to understand not just the effects built environments have on independence and dignity in older populations, but specifically on the population of persons with dementia where these elements are already severely threatened (Kitwood, 1987).

Adopting the above design approach affords a close review, system by system, of the normal ageing process of human beings. Failure to account for any of the changes of ageing in body systems would lead to an immediate negative and progressively magnifying impact from the environment, thus creating future disability.

These normal ageing effects will be briefly illustrated here and further examined to encompass abnormal ageing. Finally, the needs of the person with dementia will be considered in respect of the needs generated for dementia designers.

Vision

Human beings receive a wider range of information through the eyes than through all the other senses combined and it is therefore not surprising that persons use sight to learn from and to navigate around and within their own world (Dana, 1992). Vision is the primary sense and therefore all design considerations should be cognisant of this fact.

Changes to the eye with age include:
- lessened ability to adapt to changes in light levels
- sensitivity to glare
- loss of detail from the environment
- losses in the field of vision and lack of depth perception
- an inability to perceive contrasts clearly
- lessening of colour awareness.

Hearing

Like sight, hearing is one of the first senses to be affected by the ageing process and the deterioration in these two most vital senses begins as persons enter their forties.

Changes in hearing occur in a number of ways:

- high-frequency sound becomes less obvious
- less sensitivity to lower pitched sounds
- background noise becomes less easy to separate from that in the foreground.

Persons with hearing loss constantly strain to hear and this can lead to frayed tempers and agitation levels as well as to tiredness and headaches. Constantly having to ask other people to repeat conversation or questions can lead to avoidance and isolation in the affected person. Poor environmental acoustics can lead to avoidance and further acceleration of disabilities.

Smell and taste

As people pass the age of 65 the senses of smell and taste decrease. The loss of smell can seriously damage the enjoyment of eating as dining is, physiologically, mostly about smell (Bedell, 1994). Failure to enjoy food can lead to an avoidance of dining and a slide into depression.

Mobility

Humans become more sedentary as they age and this directly affects their muscular strength and size. It is also the reason for a steady decline in the motor skills so important for successfully negotiating the environment. Women in particular are prone to osteoporosis – a bone-thinning disease – which makes them especially vulnerable to painful fractures, particularly of the hip, wrist or spine (Johnson & Slater, 1993).

Arthritis affects one in seven people over the age of 65 and often appears more prominently in the weight-bearing joints, affecting all areas of mobility. There are two main types of arthritis:

- Rheumatoid arthritis often occurs as early as the mid-forties and is an autoimmune system disease that attacks the body's own tissue as if it were foreign.
- Osteoarthritis is more directly linked to ageing and involves the deterioration of cartilage. Hereditary and weight factors are also linked to the development of osteoarthritis.

Not only is arthritis painful but also its limits on mobility can lead to depression, isolation, disinterest in the activities of everyday living and stress and distress.

Depression

Loss of self-esteem, loneliness, stress, anxiety and boredom become much more prominent in the older population as they are forced to deal with retirement, death of spouses, relatives and friends, and the decrease in their previous ability levels (Hamilton, 1993).

For older persons living in nursing homes the incidence of depression has been reported to lie somewhere between 15 per cent and 50 per cent (Streim & Katz, 1994).

Abnormal ageing

Most of the special features of disease in the older population are a result of the structural changes that occur within the body with ageing (Eliopoulos, 1980). The basic maintenance and repair of tissue becomes progressively less efficient with a drop in physiological performance capability in most organs.

There is a loss of nephrons in the kidney, which results in a loss of renal function. Hepatic function also decreases. There is neuron loss in the brain, with slight size shrinkage, degenerative changes in the autonomic nervous system and with a reduction in nerve conduction velocity. All these losses affect performance and increase with age.

Changes to lung elasticity lead to a diminished ability to utilise oxygen and cellular loss in the pancreas accounts for the development of diabetes. There is acceleration in athermanous changes, which results in a predisposition to strokes and ischaemic heart disease. Cellular loss in the conductive tissue of the heart produces an increasingly high incidence of sino-atrial and atrioventricular node dysfunction. Deposits of amyloid in the heart leading to major health complications and death are also a result of the sedentary lifestyles adopted by many frail older persons (Forciea, Lavizzo-Mourey & Schwab, 2000; Rolak, 2010).

Further, the stress of day-to-day living produces harsher effects on the older person and they develop a decreased ability to cope with changes in their external environment.

Changes in the body's ability to deal with stress or infection result in many elderly persons experiencing transient but debilitating periods of confusion (Rolak, 2010). Temperature regulation also becomes impaired and hypothermia becomes a risk for many older persons living alone or in group housing and care homes. Postural hypotension is also a feature for many older persons.

One is hardly ever dealing with just one disease process in the older person, and it has been claimed that if there is a diagnosis of just one disease process occurring in the older person, at least one other is being missed (Martin, 1997).

When designing or suggesting the addition of assistive technology for persons experiencing a dementia-related illness, it is essential that these more common factors of the normal and abnormal ageing process be accounted for. Failure to do so will create only a temporary solution to general health needs where, should a person experience physical as well psychological illnesses, they may need to be transferred from the environment they have become accustomed to and enter a building designed specifically for physical care only. The move into hospital and the resultant stress is something many people will not recover from fully.

Designing buildings and their internal environments to meet all future physical and psychological possibilities, as well as those of a more immediate nature, would prevent the dichotomy currently experienced where persons have to use different facilities for differing needs (Cohen & Day, 1993).

Issues specific to dementia pathology

The design remit for the adapted buildings outlined in this chapter made a specific claim that the *design should accommodate three levels of group function*. Although it is not the reality that dementia pathology fits neatly into any stage theory, nevertheless, the use of models of distinct stages of function does help to allocate care, design and funding to like client groups (Stokes, 2000).

The type of disabilities faced in living area one, where technological compensation may be helpful, will be:

- Impairment to memory capabilities, particularly in working or short-term memory.
- Impaired learning: the inability to lay down new environmental maps (the process where we internally digest and store landmarks and the like from the existing environment for repeating journeys, such as finding our way around new towns, streets and buildings).
- Impaired levels of reasoning: these may lead to increased frustration and feelings of worthlessness or self-doubt (Parkin, 1999).
- A decreased ability to deal with stress from both daily living and the environment due to the above factors and an increasing tendency to rely upon information from the senses (Ballard *et al*, 2001).
- In living area two there would be more likelihood of the development of compensatory type behaviours and for the need to adopt behaviours that challenge to compensate or display unmet needs.
- The environment would need to be less stimulating than in area one but this

must never be allowed to remove stress to the point where lack of stimulation becomes problematic.

● More prosthetics would be required in this area as senses would be more affected by the disease progression and picking up clues from the environment of what is expected must be enhanced and exaggerated.

● Area three should take on the features of sanctuaries with colours, music, lighting, odours and so on which are used to calm and soothe

The Alzheimer's Association has suggested a three-stage model of need that may prove to be helpful in designing for heterogeneous groups within the overall intended home model (McKhann *et al*, 1984) and that helps us with our use of care streaming.

The adaptive design elements of the care home can be much more fully provided if at each stage the intended living area expressly reflects the major needs of each prospective tenant.

Although the stage theory proposed by the Alzheimer's Association is somewhat crude, the distinctions it draws between the varying abilities of the person at each stage of their illness indicates the need for design elements that would dramatically differentiate between those required by a person after four years of illness and those required after a further 12 years of disease progression and would follow closely the guide for areas provided above.

First stage: two to four years leading up to and including diagnosis

Symptoms

● recent memory loss begins to affect performance
● what was the person just told to do?
● confusion about places – gets lost on the way to work
● loses spontaneity, the spark and zest for life
● loses initiative – can't start anything
● mood/personality changes and person becomes anxious about symptoms, avoids people
● poor judgements – makes bad decisions
● takes longer with routine chores of daily living
● trouble handling money and paying bills.

Second stage: two to ten years after diagnosis (longest stage)

Symptoms

- increasing memory loss and confusion with a much shorter attention span
- problems recognising close friends and family members
- repetitive statements and movements
- restless, especially in afternoon and at night
- occasional muscle twitches or jerking
- perceptual-motor problems
- difficulty organising thought, thinking logically
- can't find right words – makes up stories to fill in blanks
- problems with reading, writing and numbers
- may become suspicious, irritable, fidgety, teary or playful
- loss of impulse control – wont bathe or afraid to bathe, trouble dressing
- gains and then loses weight
- may see or hear things that are not there
- needs full-time supervision.

Terminal stage: one to three years

Symptoms

- can't recognise family or self in the mirror
- loses weight even with a good diet
- little capacity for self-care
- can't communicate with words
- may put everything in mouth or touch everything
- can't control bowels or bladder
- may have seizures, experience difficulty with swallowing and suffer persistent infections.

Adapted from *Care of Alzheimer's Patients; a Manual for Nursing Home Staff* (Gwyther, 1985)

As can be gleaned from this simple if somewhat outdated descriptive model, persons with dementia go through a number of differing ability and disability levels as their dementia progresses. Differing conditions within the dementia spectrum also offer differing levels of challenge and opportunity. For instance, while a person with Alzheimer's disease may progressively lose almost all previously held abilities across the activities of daily and instrumental living, the person experiencing multi-infarct type dementia may only lose ability in the functional areas of the brain damaged by the infarct (Dawbarn & Allen, 2001). They may therefore retain much function in other areas and retain much enjoyment of life in many areas until natural death. Dementia design needs to encompass these differing ability levels.

Of course the prohibitive factor in designing for so many individual needs in one specific client group is cost (Judd, Marshall & Phippen 1998).

But as dementia is as individual as every person who experiences it, the need for variety and individual preference must run through the whole design.

Choosing to create three or more areas that differ in their ability to provide new levels of progressive support seems one such way of curtailing excessive costs while increasing choice.

If each built area is designed to also run separate but adjacent to each other, with only scant restriction between each area, individuals will tend to migrate to the environment that offers the most stimulation or provides the least challenge, and this is entirely consistent with the adaptive response ethos.

Recommendations and conclusions: the adapted environment

It has been shown that stress reactions are based on appraisal (Lazarus, 1999) and that mild levels of stress are productive while high levels of stress are destructive (Rossi, 1985). Older persons and particularly persons experiencing dementia have a much lower stress threshold than their younger counterparts. Dementia design needs to facilitate effective appraisal while minimising the stress involved in so doing.

Each specific area needs to be designed to house people who are gently stimulated by its effects and not overstimulated or stressed by them (Horowitz, 1997). This can be achieved by considering the areas over and above the normal, or even the abnormal, effects of ageing that are brought about by the dementia experience and then designing each individual facet to specifically meet them.

Technology currently available and recommended in the government's dementia strategy (*Living Well with Dementia* – DH, 2009) will aid and exaggerate certain sense-specific functions in all three areas of living accommodation. Telecare should be a consideration in all care facilities as should the inclusion of orientation and cueing signage and colour schemes.

- Floor surfaces can be made to vary in texture, giving textural clues as to position or potential hazards.
- Lighting can reduce glare and produce less shadow than normal buildings allow.

- Aromatherapy or smell diffusers can be installed to 'mark' areas specific to the intended function of the room or of that particular environment.
- Speaking clocks, calendars and touch-sensitive computer systems and television screens can dispense information both audibly and visually with minimum need for complex understanding capacity or new learning.
- Kitchens can be fitted with heat-sensitive cookers and time-sensitive microwave ovens that turn themselves off after designated timescales. Kettles that are cool to touch and the installation of both heat and smoke detectors ensures safety. All water dispensers will be thermostatically locked, keeping temperatures at safe levels, and baths can be fitted with anti-flooding technology that turns off the water supply when a certain depth of water has been dispensed.
- Colour and space can be controlled to provide maximum contrast and furniture and fittings will be of a style that portrays a 'homelike' environment and not that of an institution.
- Wall decor will be created for the same effect.
- Doorways may be sensitively alarmed but not locked and the surrounding perimeter fencing can be closed to exit except by code. This allows freedom but also offers a timescale for intervention should safety become an issue for certain inhabitants.
- Signage within the units can be of a design that shows information but does not label the user as incompetent or 'childlike', and the use of signage can be increased or decreased depending on user need. Toilets, bedrooms, dining areas and so on can be signed, as they are in any restaurant or shopping centre, and 'you are here' wall displays can give immediate positional identification about how to get to or from each area.

Individual features to be incorporated within each area:
- Entrance and exits will act as transition areas, allowing space for greeting and saying goodbye to loved ones, orientation, meeting other residents and leaving and entering the home. The area should have as much light as possible and contain vital information like way-finding display panels that give clear indications of where to go next and the purpose of the building (Brawley, 2001). Punch pad or night locks are available and mimic individual home security. Bleepers and alarm bells should be avoided as these stigmatise, startle and anger users. Alarm systems that display to staff in separate areas that people are exiting are preferable (Brawley, 2001).
- Living rooms can have furniture arranged in small clusters with coffee tables and other low-level furniture placed away from thoroughfares (Cohen & Day,

1993). Cosy talking and reading areas with appropriate lighting can also be provided and the windowsills in all areas should be low enough to allow seating and high levels of natural sunlight to enter (Brawley, 2001). Too much empty space giving the feeling of lobbies is to be avoided (Judd, Marshall & Phippen, 1998) and hearing for deaf systems should be installed as standard. Televisions, video, DVD and audio systems should be available but not played throughout the day as background as this confuses persons with dementia and disrupts audio systems for the hard of hearing (Bayles & Kaszniak, 1987; Stokes, 2000). Taped music should be strictly avoided. Lighting should be glare free but dim-mable for evening activities and cosy conversation.

- Kitchens should be family size (Brawley, 2001) and provide familiar but safe to touch features. Signage should be prominent in the kitchen with spotlights and colour coding on most items. Lowering of work surfaces with less shelf depth aids with both limited mobility and memory/visibility. Under-counter shelving and access storage should be minimised. Smart cookers turn themselves off and induction cook tops (such as those made by General Electric) have no exposed coil, open flame or heated surfaces (Cohen & Weisman, 1991). The addition of work surfaces, tables and chairs creates a social setting where occupants can gather and socialise in safety and in small cosy groups (Judd, Marshall & Phippen, 1998).

- Dining rooms are often the contact place for many otherwise socially isolated occupants, but if the room does not lend itself to social inclusion mealtime will become dreaded rather than anticipated as in so many good homes (AIA Foundation, 1987). Dining areas should not be designed as huge central facili-ties away from living accommodation and residents' rooms. Ideally, they will be small, well lit but homely and be within easy reach of cluster bedrooms and living rooms (Coons, 1996). Tables should be small and individually lit and the area should only be used for socialising while eating (Brawley, 2001).

The principles for the dining area should be that it provides a place where people:
- can converse as well as enjoy the sensory stimulation
- experience a quiet environment where stimuli not focused on the task at hand is minimised
- enjoy a family/home-like smallness
- experience less distraction and have as long as they wish for the experience.

Hearing for the deaf devices should be standard and menu boards and individual menu cards need to be highly visual in nature. Matt surfaces are preferred for decor and two-sided 'sticky' place mats and adaptive cutlery can be provided for those with coordination, depth perception or motor-control deficits.

- In bedrooms, individual clock projectors can be installed which allow time and date to be highlighted and visible during the night and early morning; speaking calendars and clocks can also aid orientation. Windows should have low sills and be able to allow lots of sunlight to enter the rooms. Blinds and time-controlled self-close/open curtains can be installed (Edinburgh Project, 2001).

- Rooms should be spacious and where possible be furnished with the person's own belongings or personal choice of colour schemes and decor. The installation of private bathing facilities in rooms garners much argument with some advocating health and safety precautions as a precluding factor and some citing privacy as an essential feature (Ohta & Ohta, 1988) but the modern building could encompass both in-room showers systems and communal bath areas. If shower rooms are to be installed these need to be designed so that they can be closed off inconspicuously when required.

- Doorways should allow visual access into the room from the outside to help with orientation and identification but should narrow to provide a 'normal' outlook from inside. Adequate bedside lighting and TV, hi-fi, video and DVD equipment can be optional and can be controlled from one multipurpose control box. Computer access can also be available that allows one-touch information on the facilities, whereabouts and timescales of the unit's operations. Personal addresses, emergency numbers and email can all be accessed through this one resource. This control centre can also program night and daytime alarms, shower/bath fills, curtains opening and closing and set room temperatures.

- Call buttons and two-way voice contact can complete the unobtrusive inclusion of many facilities to make living as independent as possible within the security and safety of the bedroom. Beds will vary in protection levels within each unit from no-protection normal beds to hospital beds with side protectors and up/down swivel and tilt in-place controls. Mattresses for pressure care will be introduced as dependency grows and these will be individually assessed as to need.

- Doors can be locked, swing ranch door style or feature safety locks which open from the outside in emergencies to allocated staff but keep unwanted visitors out. This increases the feeling of security and sanctuary many persons living in group accommodation report as being vital to low stress levels (BUPA survey, 2002). Bathroom doors and bedside lockers and the like should also be fitted with personalised locking devices (*Care Homes for Older People* – DH, 2003; *National Care Standards* – Scottish Government, 2007), and safety locks can be used for this purpose.

- Corridors will be kept to a minimum in the overall unit design, and walls will feature regularly spaced visual clues and markers to allow for way finding. The unit itself will feature an inclusive pod-shaped design and have access and egress from at least three points. Each end of walking routes will feature a sit-down reading and socialising area and feature both couches and individual armchairs.
- The main entrance exit hallway will not feature these sitting/reading/socialising areas in line with the suggestions that areas be specific for their purpose (DSDC, 2008).

Ethics and other user considerations

The ASTRID guide to using technology within dementia care has considered the ethical position of persons with dementia and their rights to receive, sometimes unknowingly, assistive technology (ASTRID, 2000). It states that ethical issues arise in dementia practice irrespective of the use of assistive technology but that assistive technology should not be seen as a quick fix. The guide offers a series of questions to be asked regarding an ethical approach to the use of assistive technology.

- What is the problem?
- What action has been tried to resolve the problem?
- Is technology being considered?
- What are the alternatives to technology?
- What technology is going to be used?
- When will it be reviewed?
- Who will review it?

One of the great failings of dementia care is that we cannot as yet understand the changes to brain structure and the personal understanding this affords the individual from an inside perspective. We are always outside looking in.

It would appear that the use of assistive technology and design will become more prominent in dementia care as more is understood about the effects on coping and self-esteem that may be delivered by adaptation of living environments and the provision of day-to-day technological assistance (ASTRID, 2000).

Increasing technological application must not be seen as a replacement for human aid and contact and in closing this book it may be pertinent to review the guidelines of the ASTRID project for using assistive technology in dementia care.

ASTRID GUIDELINES 2000

- Technologies should be used to enhance rather than replace human social contact.
- The individual needs and preferences of people with dementia and their carers must remain at the centre of any proposal to use assistive technologies.
- Technologies should be applied only where they can benefit the person with dementia and are supportive of appropriate care arrangement.
- The usefulness of assistive technologies is variable and is dependent on the needs of those who use them.
- Technologies should be reliable and user friendly.
- Technologies should be cost effective and used to complement existing provision.
- Information provided by telematics services should be regularly updated, accessible and relevant to the needs of those using the service.

Using technology and design elements to create user-friendly specific adaptations to new builds gives a degree of surety in that all service users and purchasers will be aware theoretically beforehand the facilities they will have available.

Altering and adapting already built environments requires much more sensitive approaches than simply inserting a clock that speaks. All technology must be seen to be beneficial to the person with dementia and not as a cost-saving or an easy option for time-strapped staff.

Adapting the environment should be as commonplace in dementia caring in the future as locking doors is currently!

Applying adaptive response approaches to advancing care options should always include new technology and new approaches to care and where this is pertinent we should adapt our own mentality to all new advances – not to do so would deny the very essence of the adaptive response model.

I hope as we now close this book you have enjoyed the journey – we started deep in the brain of someone living with dementia and ended up discussing the ethics of the very external artefacts of assistive technology. For a book that aimed to use a biopsychosocial approach, however, you could have expected no less.

I set out to challenge myself by writing this book and I have set you challenges during its reading. I am on a journey to continue improving and changing lives and if you now join with me I think we have met the challenge of adaptive response together.

References

Adams T & Clarke CL (eds) (1999) *Dementia Care: Developing Partnerships in Practice*, Balliere Tindall, London.

Adler H & Heather B (1999) *NLP in 21 Days: A Complete Introduction and Training Programme*, Piatkus, London.

AIA Foundation (1985) *Design for Ageing: An Architects' Guide*, The AIA Press, Washington, DC.

Alzheimer's Association (1992) *Guidelines for Dignity: Goals of Specialized Alzheimer/Dementia Care in Residential Settings*, Alzheimer's Association, Chicago.

Alzheimer's Society (2008) Dementia infographic, online, www.alzheimers.org.uk/infographic.

Alzheimer's Society (2012) Dementia infographic, online, www.alzheimers.org.uk/infographic.

Alzheimer's Society and Dementia Care Matters (2003) *Building on Strengths: Providing Support, Care Planning and Risk Assessment for People with Dementia*, Alzheimer's Society, London.

ASTRID (2000) *ASTRID: A Social and Technological Response to Meeting the Needs of Individuals with Dementia and their Carers*, Hawker Publications, London.

Baker T (2002) *An Evaluation of an Extra Care Scheme: Runnymede Court*, Hanover Housing Association, Estover, Plymouth.

Baldwin B & Capstick A (2007) *Tom Kitwood on Dementia: A Reader and Critical Commentary*, Open University Press, Maidenhead, Berkshire.

Ballard CG, O'Brian J, James I & Swann A (2001) *Dementia: Management of Behavioural and Psychological Symptoms*, Oxford University Press, London.

Barnes C, Mercer G & Shakespeare T (1999) *Exploring Disability: A Sociological Introduction*, Polity Press, Cambridge.

Barrett J (1999) 'Snacks as nutritional support in dementia care', *Nursing Times*, 95, pp32–3.

Bayles KA & Kaszniak AW (1987) *Communication and Cognition in Normal Aging and Dementia*, College Hill/Little Brown, Boston.

Bedell T (1994) 'The scent of a memory', *Age Wave: More Life*, 1 (3): pp34–5.

Bell PA, Greene TC, Fischer JD, *et al* (1996) *Environmental Psychology*, Rinehart and Winston, Fort Worth, Texas.

Bender M (2003) *Explorations in Dementia: Theoretical and Research Studies into the Experience of Remediable and Enduring Cognitive Losses*, Jessica Kingsley Publishers, London.

Bowlby J (1969–82) *Attachment and Loss*, Hogarth, London.

Berne E (1966) *Principles of Group Treatment*, Grove Press, New York.

Bion WR (1949) 'Experiences in groups: III', *Human Relations*, 2 (1), pp13–22.

Brawley EC (1997) *Designing for Alzheimer's Disease: Strategies for Creating Better Care Environments*, John Wiley & Sons, New York.

Brawley EC (2001) 'Environmental design for Alzheimer's disease: a quality of life issue', *Aging and Mental Health*, 5(Suppl 1), ppS79–S83.

Brooker D (2004) 'What is person-centred care in dementia?', *Reviews in Clinical Gerontology*, 13, pp215–22.

Brooker D (2007) *Person Centred Dementia Care: Making Services Better London*, Jessica Kingsley Publications, London.

Brooker D (2010) *The VIPS Model and the Importance of Life Story Work*, National Life Story Conference, Leeds, UK.

Bryan K, Axelrod L, Maxim L, *et al* (2002) 'Working with older people with communication difficulties: an evaluation of care worker training', *Aging and Mental Health*, 6, pp248–54.

Buijssen H (2005) *The Simplicity of Dementia: A Guide for Family and Carers*, Jessica Kingsley Publishers, London.

BUPA survey (2002) [Care home security], BUPA Care Services, Leeds.

Byrne DG (1979) 'Anxiety as state and trait following survived myocardial infarction', *British Journal of Social and Clinical Psychology*, 18 (4), pp 417–23.

Byrne EJ, Lennox G, Lowe J, *et al* (1989) 'Diffuse Lewy body disease: clinical features in 15 cases', *Journal of Neurology, Neurosurgery and Psychiatry*, 52, pp709–17.

Cannon WB (1914) 'The emergency function of the adrenal medulla in pain and the major emotions', *American Journal of Physiology*, 33, pp356–72.

CareFirst PLC (1997) *Dementia Care Strategy*, internal memo, CareFirst PLC, UK.

Caroline Walker Trust (1998) *Eating Well for Older People with Dementia*, VOICES (Voluntary Organisations Involved in Caring in the Elderly Sector), London.

Cave A (1996) *Inclusive Accessible Design*, RIBA Publishing, London.

Chapman A, Gilmour D & McIntosh IB (2001) *Dementia Care: A Professional Handbook*, Age Concern England, London.

Cheek DB & Rossi EL (1988) *Mind-Body Therapy: Methods of Ideodynamic Healing in Hypnosis*, Penguin Books, New York.

Cheston R & Bender M (1999) *Understanding Dementia: The Man with the Worried Eyes*, Jessica Kingsley Publishers Ltd, London.

Chimes (2007) [Design features] Information supplied by Chimes Interiors, UK.

Cobban N (2004) 'Improving domiciliary care for people with dementia and their carers: the raising the standard project', Innes A, Archibald C & Murphy C (eds), *Dementia and Social Inclusion*, Jessica Kingsley, London.

Cohen S (1996) 'Health psychology, psychological factors and physical disease', *Annual Review of Psychology*, 47, p113.

Cohen U & Day K (1993) *Contemporary Environments for People with Dementia*, Johns Hopkins University Press, Baltimore.

Cohen U & Weisman G (1991) *Holding on to Home: Designing Environments for People with Dementia*, John Hopkins University Press, Baltimore.

Concar D (1997) *Mind Travellers: Unravelling the Mysteries of Sleep*, New Science Publications, IPC Specialist Group, London.

Coons DH (ed) (1996) *Specialized Dementia Care*, Johns Hopkins University Press, Baltimore.

Cooper CL & Dewe P (2004) *Stress: A Brief History*, Blackwell Publishing, Oxford.

DAA (2010) *National Dementia Declaration for England*, Dementia Action Alliance, online, www.dementiaaction.org.uk/info/3/national_dementia_declaration

Dana (1992) *The Dana Guide to Brain Health*, The Dana Foundation, New York.

Dawbarn D & Allen SJ (2001) *Neurobiology of Alzheimer's Disease*, 2nd edn, Oxford University Press, Oxford.

Dementia Services Development Centre (2008) *Best Practice in Design for People with Dementia*, Dementia Services Development Centre, University of Stirling, Stirling.

Dennett DC (1991) *Consciousness Explained*, Little, Brown & Company, Boston.

Department of Health (DH) (2003) *Care Homes for Older People: National Minimum Standards*, 3rd rev. edn, The Stationery Office, Norwich.

Department of Health (DH) (2009) *Living Well with Dementia: A National Dementia Strategy*, The Stationery Office, London.

Dodd JL (1998) 'Nutrition in aging', Mahan LK & Escott-Stump S (eds), *Krause's Food and Nutrition Therapy*, Saunders, Philadelphia.

Dodds P (2008) 'Pre-therapy and dementia care', Prouty G (ed), *Emerging Developments in Pre-Therapy: a Pre-Therapy Reader*, PCCS Books, Ross-on-Wye.

DSDC (2008) *Best Practice in Design for People with Dementia*, Dementia Services Development Centre, University of Stirling, Stirling, Scotland.

Eden Alternative UK & Ireland, online, www.eden-alternative.co.uk (accessed December 2012).

Edinburgh Project (2001) [Project information], Edinburgh University, Scotland.

Eliopoulos C (1980) *Geriatric Nursing*, Harper & Row, London.

Erikson E (1965) *Childhood and Society*, WW Norton & Company, New York.

Evans S & Vallelly S (2007) 'Never a dull moment? Promoting social well-being in extra care housing', *Housing, Care and Support*, 10 (4), pp14–19.

Feil N (1972) *Summary of 1972 Research Data. Presented at the 25th Annual Meeting of the Gerontological Society*, December 1972, San Juan, Puerto Rico.

Feil N (1982) *Validation: the Feil Method*, Edward Feil, Oregon.

Feil N (1993) 'Validation therapy with late-onset dementia populations', Miesen BML & Jones GMM (eds), *Care-giving in Dementia: Research and Applications*, Tavis/Routledge, New York, pp199–218.

Ferri CP, Prince M, Brayne C, *et al* (2005) 'Global prevalence of dementia: a Delphi consensus study', *The Lancet*, 366, pp2112–17.

Fleming R, Crookes P, *et al* (2008) *A Review of the Empirical Literature on the Design of Physical Environments for People with Dementia*, Primary Dementia Collaborative Research Centre, University of New South Wales, Sydney.

Forciea MA, Lavizzo-Mourey R & Schwab EP (eds) (2000) *Geriatric Secrets*, 2nd edn, Hanley & Belfus, Philadelphia.

Fossey J & James I (2008) *Evidence-based Approaches for Improving Dementia Care in Care Homes*, Alzheimer's Society, London.

Gilleard CJ (1984) *Living With Dementia: Community Care of the Elderly Mental Infirm*, Croom Helm, Sydney.

Glass AJ (1973) 'Lessons learned', Glass AJ (ed), *Neuropsychiatry in World War II*. Washington, DC: Office of The Surgeon General, US Army, pp989–1027.

Goldsmith M (1996) *Hearing the Voice of People with Dementia*, Jessica Kingsley Publishers, London.

Goudie F & Stokes G (1989) 'Understanding confusion', *Nursing Times*, 85, pp35–7.

Griffin J & Tyrrell I (2004) *Dreaming Reality: How Dreaming Keeps Us Sane, or Can Drive Us Mad*, HG Publishing, UK.

Gross R & McIlveen R (1999) *Bodily Rhythms and States of Awareness (Aspects of Psychology* series), Hodder & Stoughton, London.

Gwyther LP (1985) *Care of Alzheimer's Patients: A Manual for Nursing Home Staff*, American Health Care Association, Washington, DC & Chicago.

Hall ET (1966) *The Hidden Dimension*, Doubleday, Garden City, N.Y.

Hall G & Buckwalter K (1987) 'Progressively lowered stress threshold: a conceptual model for care of adults with Alzheimer's disease', *Archives of Psychiatric Nursing*, 1, pp399–406.

Hall GR, Gerdner L, Zwyart-Stauffacher M & Buckwalter KC (1995), 'Principles of non-pharmacological management: caring for people with Alzheimer's disease using a conceptual model', *Psychiatric Annals*, 25 (7), pp432–40.

Halpern D (1995) *Mental Health and the Built Environment*, Taylor & Francis, London.

Hamilton M (1993) 'Development of a rating scale for primary depressive illness', *Archives of General Psychiatry*, 50, p241.

Harding N & Palfrey C (1997) *The Social Construction of Dementia: Confused Professionals?* Jessica Kingsley Publishers, London.

Harper D (1994) 'The professional construction of paranoia and the discursive use of diagnostic criteria', *British Journal of Medical Psychology*, 67, pp131–43.

Hart KE (1995) *Stress Coping Strategies and Emotional Response to Stress Exposure: Different Methods of Scoring Coping Data Yield Divergent Results*, Paper presented at the convention of the Eastern Psychological Association, Boston, Massachusetts.

Harvey RJ (1998) *The Impact of Young Onset Dementia: A Study in Epidemiology, Clinical Features, Caregiving and Health Economics of Dementia in Younger People*, doctoral thesis, University of London.

Hobson JA (2009) 'REM sleep and dreaming: towards a theory of protoconsciousness', *Nature Reviews – Neuroscience*, 10, pp803–13.

Holden U & Stokes G (2002) The 'dementias', Stokes G & Goudie F (eds), *The Essential Dementia Care Handbook*, Speechmark, Bicester.

Holmes C, Cairns N, Lantos P, *et al* (1999) 'Validity of current clinical criteria for Alzheimer's disease, vascular dementia and dementia with Lewy bodies', *British Journal of Psychiatry*, 174, pp45–50.

Horowitz MJ (1997) *Stress Response Syndromes: PTSD, Grief, and Adjustment Disorders*, 3rd edn, Jason Aronson, Lanham, New Jersey.

IPC (Institute of Public Care) (2007) *Raising the Stakes: Promoting Extra Care Housing*, Project Report, Institute of Public Care.

Jacques A & Jackson GA (2000) *Understanding Dementia*, 3rd edn, Churchill Livingstone, Oxford.

Jacques I & Innes A (1998) 'Who cares about care assistant work?', *Journal of Dementia Care*, 6 (6), pp33–7.

James IA, Stephens M, Mackenzie L & Roe P (2006) 'Dealing with challenging behaviour through an analysis of need: the Colombo approach', Marshall M (ed.) *On the Move: Walking not Wandering*, Hawker Press.

Jex SM (2002) *Organizational Psychology: A Scientist-Practitioner Approach*, John Wiley & Sons, New York.

Johansson L, Guo X, Waern M, Ostling S, Gustafson D, Bengtsson C & Skoog I (2010) 'Midlife psychological stress and risk of dementia: a 35-year longitudinal population study' *Brain*, 133 (8), pp2217–24

Johnson J & Slater R (1993) *Ageing and Later Life*, Sage Publications, London.

Jones F & Bright J (2001) *Stress: Myth, Theory, and Research*, Prentice Hall, New York.

Jones GMM (2012) *Communications and Caregiving in Dementia: a Positive Vision* (course), Dementia UK, London.

Jones GMM & Miesen BML (eds) (1992–2006) *Care-giving in Dementia*, vols 1 to 4, Routledge, London.

Jones GMM, van der Eerden-Rebel W & Harding J (2006) 'Visuoperceptual-cognitive deficits in Alzheimer's disease: adapting a dementia unit', Miesen BML & Jones GMM (eds), *Care-giving in Dementia*, vol 4, Routledge, London, pp3–58.

Jones M (2000) *Gentlecare: Changing the Experience of Alzheimer's in a Positive Way*, Hartley and Marks Publishers, Vancouver.

Joseph A (2006) *Health Promotion by Design in Long Term Care Settings*, The Centre for Health Design.

Judd S, Marshall M & Phippen P (eds) (1998) *Design for Dementia*, Journal of Dementia Care, London.

Kharicha K, Levin E, Iliffe S & Davey B (2004) 'Social work, general practice and evidence based policy in the collaborative care of older people: current problems and future possibilities', *Health and Social Care in the Community*, 12, pp134–41.

Killick J & Allen K (2001) *Communication and the Care of People with Dementia*, Open University Press, Buckingham.

King's Fund Centre (1986) *Living Well into Old Age: Applying Principles of Good Practice to Services for People with Dementia*, King's Fund, London.

Kitwood T (1987) 'Dementia and its pathology: in brain, mind or society?' *Free Associations*, 1, pp81–93.

Kitwood TM (1990) *Concern for Others: A New Psychology of Conscience and Morality*, Taylor & Francis, London.

Kitwood T (1992) 'Quality assurance in dementia care', *Journal of Geriatric Medicine*, 22 (9), pp34–8.

Kitwood T (1994) 'The concept of personhood and its implications for the care of those who have dementia', Jones G & Miesen B (eds), *Caregiving in Dementia*, vol 2, Routledge, London, pp3–13.

Kitwood T (1996) 'Building up the mosaic of good practice', *Journal of Dementia Care*, 3, pp12–13.

Kitwood TM (1997) *Dementia Reconsidered: The Person Comes First*, Open University Press, Buckingham.

Kitwood T (1998) 'Towards a theory of dementia care: ethics and interaction', *Journal of Clinical Ethics*, 9 (1), pp23–34.

Kitwood TM & Benson S (1995) *The New Culture of Dementia Care*, Hawker Publications, London.

Kitwood T & Woods RT (1996) *Training and Development Strategy for Dementia Care in Residential Settings*, University of Bradford, Bradford.

Langer E & Rodin J (1976) 'The effects of choice and enhanced personal responsibility for the aged: a field experiment in an institutional setting', *Journal of Personality and Social Psychology*, 34, pp191–8.

Lazarus RS (1991) *Emotion and Adaptation*, Oxford University Press, New York.

Lazarus RS (1999) *Stress and Emotion: A New Synthesis*, Free Association Books, London.

MacLean PD (1990) *Triune Brain in Evolution: Role in Paleocerebral Functions*, Plenum Press, New York.

Mahan LK & Escott-Stump S (2000) *Krause's Food, Nutrition and Diet Therapy*, 10th edn, WB Saunders, Philadelphia.

Marshall M (2001) 'Care settings and the care environment', Cantley C (ed), *A Handbook of Dementia Care*, Open University Press, Buckingham.

Marshall M (2004) *Perspectives on Rehabilitation and Dementia*, Jessica Kingsley Publishers, London.

Martin P (1997) *The Sickening Mind: Brain, Behaviour, Immunity and Disease*, Flamingo Press, London.

McAndrew FT (1993) *Environmental Psychology*, Brooks/Cole, Pacific Grove, California.

McCormack B (2004) 'Person-centredness in gerontological nursing: an overview of the literature', *International Journal of Older People Nursing*, 13, pp31–8.

McKeith IG, Perry RH, Fairbairn AF, *et al* (1992) 'Operational criteria for senile dementia of Lewy body type (SDLT)', *Psychological Medicine*, 22, pp911–22.

McKhann G, Drachman D, Folstein M, *et al* (1984) 'Clinical diagnosis of Alzheimer's disease: report of the NINCDS-ADRDA Work Group under the auspices of Department of Health and Human Services Task Force on Alzheimer's Disease', *Neurology*, 34 (7), pp939–44.

Medina JJ (1996) 'The neurobiology of sleep', *Psychiatric Times*, 13 (5), p16.

Meddis R, Pearson AJD & Langford G (1973) 'An extreme case of healthy insomnia', *Electroencephalography and Clinical Neurophysiology*, 35 (2), pp213–14.

Mestal R (1998) 'Slaves to the rhythm', *New Scientist*, 48, pp32–7.

Miesen B (1999) *Dementia in Close-Up*, Palgrave Macmillan, London.

Moniz-Cook E *et al* (2000) 'Staff factors associated with perception of behaviour as "challenging" in residential and nursing homes', *Aging and Mental Health*, 4, pp48–55.

Morton I (1999) *Person-centred Approaches to Dementia Care*, Speechmark, Bicester.

Morton I (2000) 'Just what is person-centred dementia care?', *Journal of Dementia Care*, 8 (3), pp28–9.

Netten A (1993) *A Positive Environment? Physical and Social Influences on People with Senile Dementia in Residential Care*, Brookfield, Vermont and PSSRU, University of Kent at Canterbury.

Neuman B (1982) *The Neuman Systems Model: Application to Nursing Education and Practice*, Appleton-Century-Crofts, New York.

NICE/SCIE (2006) *Dementia: Supporting People with Dementia and their Carers in Health and Social Care*, National Institute for Health and Clinical Excellence & Social Care Institute for Excellence, UK, online, www.scie.org.uk/publications/misc/dementia/

NIMH (1999) *Men and Depression*, National Institute of Mental Health, Bethesda, Maryland.

Norden J (2007) *Understanding the Brain*, vols 1–3, The Teaching Company, Chantilly, Virginia.

Nystrom A & Segesten K (1994) 'On sources of powerlessness in nursing home life', *Journal of Advanced Nursing*, 19, pp124–33.

O'Donovan S (1997) *Simon's Nursing Assessment: For the Care of Older People with Dementia* [booklet: *Getting to Know You*], Winslow, Bicester, Oxon.

Ohta R & Ohta B (1988) 'Special units for Alzheimer's disease patients', *Gerontologist* 28, pp803–8.

Orrell M, Spector A, Thorgrimsen L & Woods B (2005) 'A pilot study examining the effectiveness of maintenance Cognitive Stimulation Therapy (MCST) for people with dementia', *International Journal of Geriatric Psychiatry*, 20, pp446–51.

Parkin AJ (1999) *Memory: A Guide for Professionals*, John Wiley & Sons, Chichester.

Penninx BW, Geerlings SW, Deeg DJ, *et al* (1999) 'Minor and major depression and the risk of death in older persons', *Archives of General Psychiatry*, 56 (10), pp889–95.

Peplau HE (1952) *Interpersonal Relations in Nursing*, GP Putnam's Sons, New York.

Perrin T (1996) *Problem Behaviour and the Care of Elderly People*, Winslow, Bicester.

Perrin T & May H (2000) *Wellbeing in Dementia: An Occupational Approach for Therapists and Carers*, Churchill Livingstone, Edinburgh.

Phillips SM, Tipton KD, Aarsland A, et al (1997) 'Mixed muscle protein synthesis and breakdown after resistance exercise in humans', *American Journal of Physiology*, 273, ppE99–E107.

Piaget J (1976) *The Origin of Intelligence in the Child*, Routledge and Keegan Paul, London.

Pigarev IN (1994) 'Neurons of visual cortex respond to visceral stimulation during slow wave sleep', *Neuroscience*, 62 (4), pp1237–43.

Pool J (2007) *The Pool Activity Level (PAL) Instrument for Occupational Profiling: A Practical Resource for Carers of People with Dementia*, 3rd edn, Jessica Kingsley Publishers, London.

Posner MI (1994) 'Attention: the mechanisms of consciousness', *Proceedings of the National Academy of Science*, 91, pp7398–403.

Power GA (2010) *Dementia Beyond Drugs*, Health Professionals Press, New York.

Prouty G (ed) (2008) *Emerging Developments in Pre-Therapy: a Pre-Therapy Reader*, PCCS Books, Ross-on-Wye.

Prouty G, Van Werde D & Portner M (2002) *Pre-Therapy: Reaching Contact Impaired Clients*, PCCS Books, Ross-on-Wye.

Riches I (director) (2012) *Overload* (film), Hearts and Minds series, UK.

Rogers C (1957) 'The necessary and sufficient conditions of therapeutic personality change', *Journal of Consulting Psychology*, 21 (2), pp25–103.

Rogers ME (1992) 'Nursing science and the space age', *Nursing Science Quarterly*, 5, pp27–34.

Rolak LA (ed) (2010) *Neurology Secrets*, 5th edn, Mosby Elsevier, Philadelphia.

Rossi EL (1993) *The Psychobiology of Mind-Body Therapy: New Concepts of Therapeutic Hypnosis*, WW Norton, New York.

Royal College of Nursing (2002) *Quality Dementia Care in Care Homes*, RCN Publishing Company, London.

Ryan T, Nolan M, Enderby P & Reid D (2004) '"Part of the family": sources of job satisfaction amongst a group of community-based dementia care workers', *Health and Social Care in the Community*, 12, pp111–18.

Schwarzer R & Taubert S (2002) 'Tenacious goal pursuits and striving toward personal growth: proactive coping', Fydenberg E (ed), *Beyond Coping: Meeting Goals, Visions and Challenges*, Oxford University Press, London, pp19–35.

Scottish Government (2007) *National Care Standards: Care Homes for Older People*, Scottish Government, Edinburgh.

Seligman MEP (1975) *Helplessness: On Depression, Development, and Death*, WH Freeman, San Francisco.

Seligman MEP & Maier SF (1967) 'Failure to escape traumatic shock', *Journal of Experimental Psychology*, 74, pp1–9.

Selye H (1956) *The Stress of Life*, McGraw-Hill, New York.

SfC/SfH (2011a) *Common Core Principles for Supporting People with Dementia: A Guide to Training the Social Care and Health Workforce*, Skills for Care/Skills for Health/Department of Health, Leeds & Bristol.

SfC/SfH (2011b) *Carers Matter: Everybody's Business*, Skills for Care/Skills for Health, Leeds & Bristol.

SfC/SfH/DH (2009) *Common Core Competences and Principles: A Guide for Health and Social Care Workers Working with Adults at the End of Life*, National End of Life Care Programme/Department of Health/Skills for Care/Skills for Health, UK.

Sheard D (2003) *Make a Difference in Dementia Care Training: Resources that are Effective, Meaningful and Fun*, Alzheimer's Society and Dementia Care Matters, London.

Sloane P & Mathew LJ (eds) (1991) *Dementia Units in Long Term Care*, Johns Hopkins University Press, Baltimore.

Smith J, Dellinger B, Guenther R, *et al* (2004) 'The elements of a caring environment', *Healthcare Design*, September.

Smith P (1997) 'A therapeutic approach to dementia', *European Journal of Social Science and Medicine*, 19, pp511–14.

Smith PTM (2000) 'Adaptive response: a model for dementia care', *European Journal of Psychotherapy*, University Press, Oxford.

Smith P (2006) 'Change management', Perrin T (ed), *The New Culture of Therapeutic Activity with Older People*, Speechmark, Bicester, pp54–70.

Smith P (2011) 'Using pre therapy to release long silent voices', *Journal of Dementia Care*, 19 (5), pp20–2.

Spector A, Thorgrimsen L, Woods B, *et al* (2003) 'Efficacy of an evidence-based cognitive stimulation therapy programme for people with dementia: Randomised Controlled Trial', *British Journal of Psychiatry*, 183, pp248–54.

Spector A, Thorgrimsen L, Woods B & Orrell M (2006) *Making a Difference: An Evidence-Based Group Programme to offer Cognitive Stimulation Therapy (CST) to People with Dementia*, Hawker Publications, London.

Sports Supplement Guide (1998) *Sports Supplement Guide*, Weider Publications, Woodland Hills, California.

Stokes G (1986) *Wandering*, Winslow Press, London.

Stokes G (1988) *And the Music Still Plays: Stories of People with Dementia*, Hawker Publications, London.

Stokes G (2000) *Challenging Behaviour in Dementia: A Person-Centred Approach*, Winslow Press, Bicester.

Stokes G (2005) *Challenging Behaviour in Dementia: A Person-Centred Approach*, Speechmark, Bicester.

Stokes G & Gouldie F (eds) (1990) *Working with Dementia*, Winslow Press, Bicester.

Stokes G & Gouldie F (eds) (2002) *The Essential Dementia Care Handbook*, Speechmark, Bicester.

Streim JE & Katz IR (1994) 'Federal regulations and the care of patients with dementia in the nursing home', *Medical Clinics of North America*, 78 (4), pp895–906.

Tenney L (1997) *The Immune System*, Woodland Health Series, Woodland Publishing, Utah.

Tilly J & Reed P (2008) 'Literature review: intervention research on caring for people with dementia in assisted living and nursing homes', *Alzheimer's Care Today*, 9 (1), pp24–32.

Von Bertalanffly L (1923) *The Art of Systems Thinking*, William Hill, London.

Welch WJ (1990) *The Mammalian Stress Response: Stress Proteins in Biology and Medicine*, Laboratory Press, Cold Spring Harbour, New York.

White R (1959) 'Motivation reconsidered: the concept of competence', *Psychological Review*, 66, pp297–333.

WHO (1992) *The ICD-10 Classification of Mental and Behavioural Disorders*, World Health Organization, Geneva.

Wolff HG (1953) *Stress and Disease*, Thomas, Springfield, Ill.

Wozniak MA, Mee AP & Itzhaki RF (2009) 'Herpes simplex virus type 1 DNA is located within Alzheimer's disease amyloid plaques', *Journal of Pathology*, 217 (1), pp131–8.

Index

Entries in **bold** denote figures and tables.